ISLAMIC
RESURGENCE
IN THE
ARAB WORLD

WRITTEN UNDER THE AUSPICES
OF THE
CENTER OF
INTERNATIONAL STUDIES,
PRINCETON UNIVERSITY
(a list of other Center publications
appears at the back of the book)

ISLAMIC RESURGENCE
IN THE
ARAB WORLD

edited by

ALI E. HILLAL DESSOUKI

PRAEGER

PRAEGER SPECIAL STUDIES • PRAEGER SCIENTIFIC

Library of Congress Cataloging in Publication Data

Main entry under title:

Islamic resurgence in the Arab world.

    Bibliography: p.
    Includes index.
    1. Islam and politics—Arab countries.
2. Arab countries—Politics and government—
1945-   . 3. Islam—20th century.
I. Dessouki, Ali E. Hillal.
BP63.A4A73   322'.1'0917671   81-12135
ISBN 0-03-059673-4   AACR2

Published in 1982 by Praeger Publishers
CBS Educational and Professional Publishing
a Division of CBS Inc.
521 Fifth Avenue, New York, New York 10175 U.S.A.

23456789   145   987654321

Printed in the United States of America

At the turn of each century there will arise in my nation
a man who will call for a religious revival.

Prophet Muhammad

PREFACE

This book is a contribution to a growing body of literature on the contemporary resurgence or revival of Islam. It is different, however, in a number of ways. First, its scope is confined to the Arab countries, rather than to larger entities such as the Middle East or the Islamic world. The objective is to provide a greater degree of similarity among the countries studied. Second, the book includes two kinds of contributions: theoretical explanatory articles that suggest different frameworks for the understanding of the Islamic resurgence in the Arab countries, and several case studies that enable the reader to examine the relevance and usefulness of these theoretical perspectives. Third, the book is written by a group of social scientists, and therefore, it aspires to be useful not only to students of Arab and Middle Eastern politics but also to social scientists interested in social movements and the dynamics of modernization.

Despite the increasing interest in the subject, our knowledge and appreciation of contemporary Islamic resurgence seems to suffer from a number of shortcomings. We tend too often to see Islamic resurgence in light of the political events in Iran and the hostage crisis. Moreover, we tend to lump together as Islamic resurgence a multitude of events that are, in fact, independent phenomena with different consequences and implications. There is also an irresistible temptation for some scholars to find a "master reason" or a "grand theory" to interpret these numerous events. Finally, there is a shortage of data on those Islamic groups that are today mushrooming in the Arab and Islamic worlds.

The chapters of this book deal with one or more of four interrelated questions.

1. What is meant by an Islamic resurgence and what are its contemporary manifestations as evidenced by governmental policies and dissident political groups?

2. What are the ideologies of the Islamic resurgence and what particular policy demands do Islamic groups advance?

3. What are the social bases of these groups and what social strata or classes do they appeal to most?

4. How do we explain the phenomenon of the Islamic resurgence and how is it related to the process of modernization in Arab society?

These questions are discussed from different perspectives by the contributors to this book. Their methodologies and ways of argumentation are similarly different. They all, however, emphasize the historicosocial context of the Islamic resurgence.

As to the transliteration of Arabic words, we have attempted to follow scholarly traditions without making the text overly difficult for the non-Middle Eastern expert. Common Arabic words or names have been rendered according to the spelling familiar to the Western reader: for instance, Nasser is preferred to Nāsir, Saud to Sa^{c}ud, Quran to Qur'ān, Faisal to Faysal, and sheikh to shaykh. Also, the names of those Arab authors who publish in English or French are given in the form the authors have chosen themselves.

The reader will notice that Jama^{c}at al-Ikhwān al-Muslimīn is translated differently by the authors as the Muslim Brothers or the Muslim Brethern. Both are correct and are present in the text.

The book was planned and completed during my sabbatical year as a Visiting Associate Professor at the Woodrow Wilson School of Public and International Affairs, Princeton University, 1980/81. My debts to two persons at Princeton are outstanding. Henry Bienen, director of the Research Program in Development Studies, was instrumental in arranging my sabbatical and provided a most conducive atmosphere for research and writing. Cyril Black, Director of the Center of International Studies, was supportive of the idea of the book and the Center, where I was a Visiting Fellow, provided valuable editorial assistance. My gratitude to both is of a kind that can hardly be expressed adequately in the form of an acknowledgment. In fact, this book is only one product of a very fruitful year I spent at Princeton.

Two meetings helped to stimulate and clarify my thinking on the subject of this book. The first was organized by the Hellenic Mediterranean Center for Arabic and Islamic Studies in September 1979 in Greece. To P. J. Vatikiotis, who chaired the seminar, I express my deepest thanks for a continuous dialogue on things Arab. The second was held at the State University of New York at Binghamton in March 1981, and I thank Richard H. Dekmejian and Don Peretz for giving me the opportunity to participate in what proved to be a very useful meeting.

In reading and editing this volume of 11 original essays, I received the assistance of a number of people. I would like, first, to express my appreciation to the distinguished group of scholars who contributed to the book. Michel Le Gall, graduate student in the Department of Near Eastern Studies at Princeton, was my research assistant and helped in all stages of the preparation of the manuscript. He also made the transliteration of all Arabic words and prepared a useful bibliography, which appears at the end of the book. Barbara Westergaard did an excellent job in editing the manuscript, and Dee Wilson, my secretary, typed it and was always available beyond the call of duty. To all I would like to express my thanks and gratitude.

CONTENTS

PART I

INTRODUCTION

1

THE ISLAMIC RESURGENCE: SOURCES, DYNAMICS, AND IMPLICATIONS

ALI E. HILLAL DESSOUKI

As more than 700 million Muslims celebrate the beginning of Islam's fifteenth century,* there is a growing Western interest in Islam and the contemporary Islamic resurgence. In 1980 alone, for instance, 27 conferences and symposia on different aspects of Islam were held in U.S. universities and research centers. [1] Islam has been, so to speak, rediscovered by those modernizers, Western and Muslim alike, who ruled it out as a potent force and believed that, with the passing of traditional society, it was destined to become increasingly irrelevant.

The interest is motivated by at least three factors. One is the increasing economic influence of oil-producing countries, which are mostly Islamic. Another is the concern with the security and the stability of the Persian/Arab Gulf countries, in particular Saudi Arabia. The strategic and social vulnerability of the Gulf area was exposed by the downfall of the shah's regime, the impact of the Islamic revolution in Iran on the region, the Soviet military presence in Afghanistan, and the seizure of the Grand Mosque of Mecca by a group of zealots in November 1979. The third, and possibly most important, factor is the new wave of Islamic resurgence in almost all countries where Muslims live. In the Arab world, the gradual decline since the late 1960s of revolutionary Arab nationalism as the dominant ideology and movement has created a hospitable environment for an Islamic alternative. By the late 1970s, Islamic resurgent movements constituted the major ideology of dissent in the Arab world regardless of the type of political system or its declared ideology. Whether in revolutionary Syria or pro-Western Egypt, in Islamic-oriented Saudi Arabia or secular Tunisia, the generalization holds true.

---

*It started in November 1979.

3

These Islamic movements and activities were variously called Islamic revivalism, revitalization, upsurge, reassertion, renewal, awakening, fundamentalism, neofundamentalism, and resurgence. Others referred to the return of Islam, militant Islam, and political Islam. The usefulness of these concepts as analytical categories is very much open to question.

In this book the term Islamic resurgence is employed to refer to an increasing political activism in the name of Islam by governments and opposition groups alike. It designates a politicized, activist form of Islam and the growing use of Islamic symbolism and legitimation at the level of political action. Islamic groups have assumed a more assertive posture and projected themselves in many Arab and Islamic countries as contenders for public allegiance and political loyalty. We are not dealing with calls for or attempts to provide a new interpretation of Quran but, rather, with social and political movements that are engaged in mobilization, organization, and possibly the seizure of political authority. Thus, Islamic resurgence refers to the increasing prominence and politicization of Islamic ideologies and symbols in Muslim societies and in the public life of Muslim individuals.

The thrust of my argument in this introductory chapter is that the Islamic resurgence represents diverse and complex phenomena that can only be properly understood within a sociohistorical context and as part of the process of social change taking place in the Arab countries. The analysis is primarily geared to the Arab situation, though a great deal of it is applicable to other Muslim countries.

METHODOLOGICAL CONSIDERATIONS

It is useful to start our analysis of the Islamic resurgence by outlining some basic limitations of research on these phenomena. Chief among these is the poverty of data, that is, the scarcity of hard information based on interviews or survey analyses of Islamic groups. We simply do not know much about these organizations or their leadership, membership, and social base. In many instances, the groups are engaged in clandestine activities, and our knowledge of them is derived solely from media coverage of the arrests and trials of their members. Most Arab governments control the media in one way or another and make sure that such coverage projects a negative image. Another limitation is that because these groups have emerged or reemerged so recently, many of them are still evolving. Their newness also means that we are too close to the phenomena and have not had time to form careful academic judgments. Because of these limitations, a word of caution is in order with regard to three tendencies apparent in the writings on the Islamic resurgence.

1. Sensationalism: There is first a tendency toward sensationalism. This is perhaps because the Islamic resurgence was brought to the attention of the Western public through journalists, and indeed, much of the available writing on the subject is more "academic" journalism than serious scholarship. As a result, certain images of "islam on the march,"[2] "the Muslims are coming," and "the Turks in the siege of Vienna" have been revived. These images can only lead to further misunderstanding of the Muslim situation.

2. Denial: Islam, the proponents of this view argue, has always been dominant and all-pervasive in the life of most Muslims. Islamic movements have been a constant feature of Muslim societies since the call of Jamāl al-Dīn al-Afghānī in the nineteenth century, and therefore, there is nothing in the contemporary phenomenon that warrants independent investigation. It simply repeats what we already know of previous revivalist or resurgent Islamic groups. Of course, Islamic movements have always shared, and are likely to continue to share, certain basic ideological tenets, such as the call for the application of sharīᶜa (Islamic law). To deduce from this, however, that all Islamic movements are fundamentally alike is not correct. Even movements that emerged at the same historical epoch, such as al-Mahdīya, al-Sanūsīya, and al-Wahhābīya, showed various dissimilarities.* Islamic movements differ, as is argued later and other chapters show, in terms of their social context, their understanding of Islam, their political alliances and actions, and their impact on society.

3. Retrogression: Islamic groups are portrayed sometimes as extremist, dogmatic, and a reaction against modernity. Implicit in the argument is the assumption that they represent a retrogressive development, an anachronism in a secular, scientific age. Indeed, nothing is inherently retrogressive or necessarily antimodern in Islamic resurgence. Various religions, including Islam, have experienced resurgent or revivalist movements at different times. Anthropological studies show more than 100 such movements among African religions in the twentieth century.[3] The 1980 U.S. presidential elections underlined the entry of religious factors into politics. Fundamentalist Christian groups insisted that abortion and the Equal Rights Amendment were moral and religious issues rather than social ones.†

---

*R. Stephen Humphreys's contribution to this volume compares the three movements and contrasts them with the present-day resurgence.

†In March 1981 a supreme court judge in Sacramento, California, ruled that the teaching of evolution did not violate the rights of Christian fundamentalists who believed in the biblical version of creation. However, in a concession to the fundamentalists, he ordered the State

The travels and activities of Pope John Paul II project the image of a Catholic church interested in public issues.

The three concerns—sensationalism, denial, and retrogression—are related to our perspective on Islam and Islamic resurgence. Our focus is not so much the theory of Islam as expounded in the Quran and Sunna but, rather, of Islam as it developed in history as a political force and a great civilization. Our interest in the Islamic resurgence lies more in the area of sociology of religion, and therefore the chapters deal in various ways with such questions as, Why does a ruling class feel the need to resort to Islamic ideology as a legitimizing device? Why do opposition Islamic movements emerge? What are the ideological and structural, internal and external, factors that create the milieu conducive to their emergence? Who are the potential, and actual, members of these groups and to what social classes or strata of society do they belong? Why do these movements have more appeal to certain classes and strata than to others? What do these groups understand of Islam, and which aspects of religion do they emphasize? and What impact do these Islamic resurgent groups have on social and political change? Thus, the emphasis is on the Islamic resurgence as related to a specific social context within which it emerges and operates.

This approach is predicated on two fundamental assertions of the Islamic historical experience: its specificity and its diversity. The Islamic resurgence, therefore, must be considered as being composed of historically specific and behaviorally diverse phenomena.

In theory, Islamic teachings have always emphasized the unity of the umma (the community of believers), and its message has definite universal overtones. In practice, however, the Islamic umma lost its political unity long ago. In a piecemeal fashion, the Islamic historical experience has moved away from several Islamic political and social, but not religious and spiritual, teachings; the caliphate became mulk (rule), the participatory principle of shūrā (consultation) turned into a hereditary monarchy, and sharīᶜa law was supplemented by qānūn (positive law). Islam has also had a remarkable ability to adapt to, and modify, various cultural traditions; undoubtedly, this has been a major factor in its expansion in areas far away and culturally different from its birthplace, particularly in India, Indonesia, Malaya, and sub-Saharan Africa. Thus, while Islam maintained a fun-

---

of California to forbid dogmatism in teaching the origins of life. The lawsuit contended that the schools taught evolution as a fact, not as a theory, and that this violated the religious rights of children who believed otherwise.

damental unity at the level of religious beliefs and civil-status issues, it allowed variations of the Islamic experience. The overarching unity expounded in religious texts is usually no precise indicator of social practices and popular understanding of Islam. Islam is better understood from this perspective as designating an "ideal type," which should be analyzed in relation to specific social structures. The basic assumption here is that the unity and universality of the ideal type are reflected in a multiplicity of actual historical experiences in specific social contexts. [4]

It follows that present-day Islamic resurgence is not just a revival of some past Islamic tradition or the result of Muslim yearning for a past golden age. Inherent in this latter view are two unsubstantiated assertions: (1) that there are eternal and unchanging behavioral features that Muslims share in all times and places and (2) that Muslims constitute an undifferentiated entity that transcends differences in education, class, social status, and cultural and national variations. Islamic resurgent movements are likely to be better understood in relation to a changing milieu. All these groups have a "selective" perception of Islamic history and emphasize certain aspects of Islam rather than others. Almost all of them, particularly those in the twentieth century, are not just revivalist, but rather, their ideologies involve reformulating and developing certain aspects of Islamic social teachings to enable them to deal with the new challenges of our times. One striking example is the development of a body of literature on Islamic banking. In the 1970s several Islamic banks and companies were established.* Another example is Ayātollāh Khomeinī's modification of Shī^{c}ite political thinking. No prominent Shī^{c}ite ^{c}alīm in the twentieth century, before Khomeinī, argued that ^{c}ulamā' could rule directly. Khomeinī condemned traditional Shī^{c}ite quietism and the practice of taqīya (dissimulation) while awaiting the return of the hidden imām and proposed, instead, political struggle to create the Islamic state. Finally, he democratized Shī^{c}ism by emphasizing mass participation as opposed to elitism. [5]

A major conclusion of this analysis is that widely varying groups are lumped together as manifestations of Islamic resurgence. Since Islamic experiences are not historically monolithic, neither are Islamic resurgence activities. The identification with Islam may tell us about symbolic and moral orientation, but it does not say much

---

*The first, the Dubai Islamic Bank, was established in 1975 by Kuwait, Saudi Arabia, and Dubai and operates in accordance with the precepts of Islamic law, which does not allow usury. These banks and companies operate in terms of profit sharing rather than a fixed-interest rate.

about social, economic, and political origins or programs. Thus, it is conceptually inadequate and factually problematic to aggregate the many diverse contemporary movements and ideas and come up with a general interpretation or a master cause for all of them. Rather, we need to disaggregate, classify, and make distinctions.* Such an approach is necessitated not only by the diverse nature of the phenomena but also by the scarcity of information about them.

An appropriate approach for the study of the contemporary Islamic resurgence has to be interdisciplinary, comparative, and integrative. It has first to be historical and relate the contemporary movements to previous ones. It must allow for diversity and contradictions among Islamic groups themselves and between them and secular or quasi-secular forces and regimes. Islamic movements have to be seen in relation to the specific process of social change taking place in their societies, in particular to issues of the changing position of classes and groups, political participation, identity crisis, the stability of regimes, and distributive justice.† Finally, the analysis cannot ignore the transnational nature of Islam and Islamic appeal and, therefore, must investigate the interaction of internal and external factors.

Based on these methodological considerations, there are two basic distinctions that must be drawn at the outset of any substantive discussion of Islamic resurgence. The first is made between the resort to Islam by governments or ruling classes and by opposition or dissident groups, which I call Islam from above and Islam from below. In the contemporary Arab world, Islam appears both as an apology for the status quo and as a regime-challenging ideology. On the one hand, there is an increasing tendency on the part of Arab and Islamic governments to employ religious symbolism and implement certain aspects of the sharī^{c}a. Examples from the Arab world include Egypt, Sudan, Mauritania, Somalia, and Libya. On the other hand, several opposition groups have emerged in the name of Islam in Egypt,

---

*In an essay entitled "The Return of Islam," Henry Bienen similarly argues that "to try to understand the political upheavals in North Africa, the Middle East, Southwest Asia and the Gulf through recourse to ideas about Islamic revival cannot take us very far and will mislead. There can be no substitute for specific and contextual analysis. . . . The desire to capture complicated events and forces through sweeping generalizations stems in part from an impatience with the particular and an inability to master it."

†Raymond Hinnebusch's contribution to this volume provides an excellent illustration of the interplay of sectarian, regional, and class factors in the making of Islamic resurgence in Syria.

Syria, Tunisia, Sudan, and Saudi Arabia. The policy demands of these groups differ from one country to another. Thus, while some of these groups in Egypt criticize Sadat's economic policies as favoring the rich, Islamic groups in Syria uphold the interests of the urban upper middle class against socialist, rural-oriented government policies. In Tunisia and Algeria, a prime concern of Islamic groups is teaching Arabic. Last, there are those in Saudi Arabia who think that the government has gone too far in the modernization process.

The second distinction is related to the context of the Islamic resurgence and to the kind of challenges faced by the Muslim community. The Islamic resurgence in societies in which Muslims constitute the majority is essentially different from the resurgence where Muslims are in the minority. The Islamic resurgence in the majority situation is likely to focus on the application of sharī^{c}a, albeit with a different understanding of it and of the social policies to be followed. Muslims in a minority situation are likely to advocate a greater degree of self-rule. Another important contextual factor is the nature of the challenge: whether it is directed against a non-Muslim government (as in the activities of the Muslim Brothers in Egypt against the British occupation in 1951-52 or of Mahdism in Sudan in the nineteenth century against the British and the Ottomans) or a Muslim government (as in most Arab countries now). A third contextual factor is the degree of external penetration and Westernization, which invites perceptions of "Islam in danger." These three factors—Muslims in the majority or minority, the nature of the challenge, and the perception of external threat—condition the type of Islamic resurgence, that is, its ideology, strategy, and tactics.

THE ISLAMIC RESURGENCE IN ACTION

Observers of the Arab and Muslim worlds have enough evidence to demonstrate the case for an Islamic resurgence that has assumed a definite political-activist posture. Since Islam is widely believed to be Dīn Wa Dawla (religion and a state), some view this activism as being in the nature of any Islamic movement. The dominant understanding of Islam underlines the pervasiveness of its teachings. Islam is presented as an all-encompassing system of beliefs and ideas in which the realms of ethics and politics are intimately related in a system of supreme all-embracing morality, something like Hegel's notion of sittlichkeit. This view, while correct according to the prevailing understanding of Islam, is not supported by Islamic history. From the beginning of the Ummayad Empire, rulers limited the actual sphere of sharī^{c}a. Muslim jurists found ways to justify the circumvention of certain injunctions, for instance, the cutting off of the hands of thieves. Religious and sociopolitical aspects of Islam have been neither in total harmony nor in clear opposition but, rather, in a dialectical relation of conflict and cooperation, or of uneasy synthesis, as Leonard Binder once suggested in The Ideological Revolution in the Middle East.

There is no historical evidence to support the assertion that all Muslim movements are necessarily activist. Quietism was a main current of Shī‘ite political history, and prior to the Western impact, a dominant form of religious expression in the Muslim world was inward-oriented Sūfī brotherhoods. Similarly, the history of modern Islam abounds with social and cultural associations and Sūfī orders that focused on the reform of the individual Muslim through preaching and worship. They did not engage in direct political action and believed that the reform of the individual would lead to the reform of the society. In twentieth-century Egypt, for instance, there have been approximately 135 associations and groups of this kind. [6] The Muslim Brothers Association distinguished itself in the 1940s with its use of violence and its more activist course, but political activism has not been a characteristic feature of all, or even most, religious groups in Egypt or in many Arab countries in this century.* Thus, contemporary Islamic activism is not to be understood exclusively as a function of the inherent unity between religion and politics in Islam but, equally important, as a function of the social context of these Islamic groups.

In the contemporary Arab and Muslim worlds, Islamic political activism manifests itself in one or more of five spheres.†

1. There is a call to reinstitute the Islamic law and abide by it instead of the Western-imported legal systems. The flogging of criminals in Abu Dhabi and penal amputations according to sharī‘a law in Libya and Mauritania are some of the more sensational manifestations. In 1978, Sudan set up a committee to look into the Islamicization of the constitution. [7] In the same year Mauritania decided that Islamic law would be applied in all domains and that existing legislation would be revised accordingly. The official reason for the change was

---

*The assertion runs against the general view of modern Islamic groups, which is derived primarily from the study of the Muslim Brothers and similar groups in the Arab countries. These groups attracted much academic attention because of their political significance. This should not, however, bias our analysis of Islamic movements in general.

†This section is not intended as a survey of Islamic resurgence in the Arab world. A general survey is to be found in Daniel Pipes's contribution to this volume.

to reestablish Mauritania's "original identity."[8] In Egypt sharī^{c}a law was included for the first time in the constitution of 1971 as a source of legislation, and in 1979 a referendum made it the source. Three years earlier the Parliament passed a law making it a crime for a Muslim to drink alcohol in public. The law forbade the sale of alcoholic beverages in public places other than those designated as touristic.

2. There is a change in the language of politics and the increasing use of religious symbolism. Arab politicians have always made sure that their ideas and programs are not perceived as un-Islamic or contrary to the principles of Islam. For instance, the main attack on Nasser's socialism in 1961-64 by Jordan, Saudi Arabia, and Yemen centered on its being "imported" and atheist. In the 1970s some leaders, such as those in Tunisia and Algeria, became more sensitive to the changing sentiment of their constituencies and began to pay more attention to Islamic symbols and legitimation. In other countries, such as Egypt, the leadership was partially instrumental in boosting Islamic groups as a counterbalance to its leftist opposition. Sadat of Egypt is frequently referred to as al-rā'is al-mu'min (the believing president), and he usually concludes his speeches with a religious quotation. The code name of the 1973 war, which was launched on the tenth of Ramadan, was Badr (a famous battle of the Prophet). Anathema became a central theme of Sadat's attacks on his political opponents.

Similar developments have taken place in other Arab countries. In 1975 North Yemen established the Office for Islamic Guidance to protect the country from "imported ideologies which oppose Islamic teachings and traditions."[9] In late 1978 Kuwait imposed restrictions on dancing shows in hotels and nightclubs. The official explanation was that some of these troupes used the name of art to present shows that "violate the Islamic structure of Kuwait."[10] Even Bourguiba, since 1956 the most secular Arab leader, has started to appease and co-opt rising Islamic sentiments. He increased religious instruction in the elementary curriculum and has occasionally delivered speeches on religious holidays from the pulpits of the famous Zaytūna and Qayrawān mosques. Last, in Libya Mu^{c}mmar al-Qadhdhāfī propagates interpretations of Islam that most Muslims would find difficult to accept. *

3. There is the resort to religious social symbols. Increasingly, many young men grow their beards in traditional Islamic manner, and a noticeable number of educated young women cover up in a way unknown for decades: they wear a dress that leaves only the face and

_____

*A critical discussion of Qadhdhāfī's views is in the chapter written by Ann Elizabeth Mayer.

hands uncovered. Two surveys conducted in Tunisia in 1967 and 1973 showed a marked increase in personal religious orientations. For instance, those who stated that they regularly practice religious observances increased from 18 percent to 61 percent, and those who believed that Muslims must observe the prohibition on alcohol increased from 46 percent to 73 percent. [11]

Of particular interest here is the increasing importance attached to Islamic education. In 1977 the first world conference on Islamic education was held in Saudi Arabia. Delegates from 40 countries approved a recommendation to adopt "an educational policy that is based on Islamic outlook and that derives its principles from Islamic sources." [12] The conference emphasized the importance of reconsidering the method of teaching physical sciences "to close the artificial gap between religion and science which was imported along with European methodology." [13] Tunisia and Algeria made changes in their school curriculums with the intent of increasing religious content.

4. There is the emergence of sociopolitical opposition groups in the name of Islam. Egypt again is an obvious example. Islamic opposition activities take four forms. One is the de facto rehabilitation of the Muslim Brothers Association; its monthly magazine al-Da^{C}wa (Call) circulates freely despite its harsh criticism of the government. Another is such underground militant groups as Jama^{C}at al-Takfīr wa'l-Hijra (Repentence and Holy Flight), Shabāb Muhammad (Muhammad's Youth), and Jund Allah (God's Soldiers).

A third form is the student groups called al-Jama^{C}a al-Islāmīya (Islamic Association), which exist in every university. By the late 1970s these associations had become the strongest and most cohesive political force on Egyptian campuses. They recruit primarily from the students, and they were responsible for most of the demonstrations against the shah of Iran's residence in Egypt or in favor of the application of sharī^{C}a. In May 1980 President Sadat banned all student religious societies and accused them of promoting religious fanaticism, extremism, and communal strife. He particularly warned against the use of mosques for political purposes. [14] The last form of Islamic protest in Egypt is the emergence of a few charismatic mosque preachers who attract thousands of Muslims to hear their Friday Khutba. Chief among them are Sheikh Muhammad al-Ghazālī, who was eventually removed from his post, and Sheikh Kishk. The latter's sermons are taped and sold commercially in large numbers. His appeal, which is based on intense emotionalism, is basically populist and sensational. [15]

In Algeria and Tunisia similar signs of Islamic unrest have appeared. In Tunisia Islamic activities invited government criticism of "those who were reviving fanaticism and obscurantism." [16] In December 1979 the government banned the Islamic monthly al-Mujtama^C

(Society) for three months. In a reconciliatory move, however, the government progressively restricted the hours of public drinking (of alcohol) in 1980 and served notice to several licensed bars in the capital. The authorities feel obliged to allow religious groups to propagate Islamic ideas and distribute its literature. In Algeria the government was worried by the growing Islamic-inspired clashes in several cities in 1980. In El-Oued prostitutes were paraded in the streets, and liquor stores were ransacked. Nonviolent demonstrations took place in Ouargla, Biskra, and Touggourt. [17] In response, the government restricted public drinking hours. A year earlier demonstrators in Algiers, the capital, and Oran demanded greater Arabization of education. [18]

In 1980 Islamic dissent appeared in other places. In January Palestinian demonstrators in Gaza burned liquor stores, movie theaters, and other entertainment centers. In May the Sudanese National Assembly elections returned 60 Muslim Brothers to the 300-member assembly.

Shīᶜite Arab Muslims have also become more activist in several countries. In Saudi Arabia, which has a Shīᶜite community of around 250,000 living in the important oil-producing eastern province, demonstrations erupted on the ᶜAshūrā feast day—which celebrates the martyrdom of al-Husayn ibn ᶜAlī—in November 1979. [19] In Iraq bloody riots took place in the holy cities of Najaf and Karbalā' in 1977. Responsibility for the attempt on the life of Tāriq ᶜAzīz, the most senior Christian in the government, in 1979 was claimed by the Mujāhidīn, a militant Shīᶜite group. The regime's reaction was harsh and swift; it arrested and executed Ayātollāh Bāqir al-Sadr, Iraq's senior Shīᶜite figure. [20] In September 1979 Ayātollāh Khomeinī's representative in Kuwait, Hojatollislām ᶜAbbās al-Muhrī, his son, and other associates were deported to Iran, though some of them were Kuwaiti citizens. In November a march of mainly Shīᶜite Kuwaitis on the U.S. embassy was dispersed with tear gas. [21] Finally, in Lebanon Imām Mūsā al-Sadr founded "the movement of the deprived" to raise the status of the Shīᶜites; the movement has a military branch, amal (hope). In 1980 the four Shīᶜite ministers in the cabinet resigned on the grounds that Shīᶜite demands were not met.

5. The fifth and last manifestation of the Islamic resurgence is international: the establishment of several Islamic organizations to encourage political and economic relations between Islamic states. Islamic solidarity is constantly emphasized in the groups' meetings. The international dimension of Islamic resurgence is dealt with again in a future section of this chapter.

TYPES OF ISLAMIC RESURGENCE

The thrust of my argument has been to demonstrate the diversity of contemporary Islamic resurgence—that it is not a monolithic phenomenon but, rather, socially and historically conditioned. These advocating the application of sharī^{c}a or the establishment of an Islamic social order have different, sometimes diametrically opposed, visions of economic, social, and foreign policies. Nothing perhaps illustrates the point more than the contrast between revolutionary Iran and Saudi Arabia; both claim having, or being in the process of establishing, an Islamic society. The differences between the two, however, are too obvious to require mention. Similarly, different rulers pursuing different policies, such as Sadat of Egypt, Hasan II of Morocco, Qadhdhāfī of Libya, and Numayrī of Sudan, pride themselves on working to make their societies more Islamic.

It appears that there are three types of Islamic resurgence in the Arab world: (1) there are regimes with a longstanding Islamic identity, such as those in Saudi Arabia and Morocco; (2) there are governments that use Islam as an apology to justify and legitimize their policies; and (3) there are Islamic protest groups, which advocate Islam as an alternative. Thus, depending on the specific situation, Islam can function as a stabilizing force serving to maintain the status quo or as an agent of change and revolution.

Regimes with Longstanding Islamic Identity:
Saudi Arabia and the Mecca Event

In Saudi Arabia Islam permeates all aspects of public life. The sharī^{c}a exercises more influence over the life of its inhabitants than anywhere else in the Islamic world. Nowhere, except in Saudi Arabia, can one find morality squads enforcing public observance of the daily prayers. The words of the shahāda (the Islamic proclamation of faith) are woven in Arabic script onto the Saudi Arabian flag. After all, Saudi Arabia is the birthplace of Islam. Its lands contain Mecca and Medina, the two holy cities of Islam, and the Prophet belonged to an Arabian tribe.* It is against this background that the seizure of the Grand Mosque of Mecca must be seen.

The mosque was seized by a group of armed insurgents shortly after 4:00 A.M. on November 20, 1979; the invaders occupied Islam's most holy shrine at the dawn prayers on the first day of the Muslim

---

*Farouk Sankari's contribution to this book analyzes the role of Islam in Saudi Arabia.

fifteenth century. The Saudi authorities immediately sealed off Mecca and imposed an information blackout. The first official reports referred to the invaders as misled religious heretics. Television reported the attack the same evening in four sentences. The attackers were described as renegades, and the government gave assurances that the holy mosque would be protected. [22] The government acquired a fatwa (Islamic legal opinion) from the ᶜulamā' allowing its forces to attack the mosque to root out the heretics; the fatwa described them as mufsidūn fī'l-ard (those who corrupt on earth) and allowed their killing. [23] The Saudi national guard attacked the mosque, and the rebels were slowly pushed back and eventually scattered throughout the basement of the mosque. During the fighting 60 military men and 75 of the rebels were killed, and 170 rebels were arrested. For the entirety of the two-week siege, the authorities let out little information, and therefore, the accounts of the event vary significantly.

Estimates of the number of insurgents range from 300 to more than 1,000. All agree that they were well trained and well equipped; they had supplies for up to three weeks and enough weapons to withstand attempts to retake the mosque for two weeks. The majority of them were Saudis, specifically from the Harb, Shammār, Qahtān, and ᶜUtayba tribes. They included also several Pakistanis, Palestinians, Egyptians, and Yemenis. The involvement of non-Saudis is shown by the fact that 22 of the 63 men executed were from other Islamic countries. Contrary to several reports, no Iranians or Shīᶜite Arabs were involved in the fighting. It was a fundamentalist Sunnī and primarily Arab group. Finally, it seems that the event was not an isolated incident. There were accounts of similar minor actions in Medina, and arrests were made in some Saudi cities.

What this group wanted is most unclear. The Saudi authorities' version emphasizes the deviant religious motivations of the attackers. They were described as renegades, a clique of deviants who misinterpreted Islam, or a group suffering from a "religious hallucination."[24] The leader of the group proclaimed himself a Mahdī (savior of the religion) and advocated a return to a more orthodox interpretation of Islam. He called for the end of most things that were modern, including a ban on television, movies, soccer, and women working in public places.

Other accounts of the events emphasize its political significance. During the two weeks of siege, the attackers announced several social and political demands. Thus, while religiously motivated, the action was intended as a political protest against the hegemony and policies of the Saudi ruling family. The position and demands of the attackers were reported as including the following:

1. The statement that the Saudi family had deviated from the teachings of Islam, one manifestation of this being the close links with the United States, the chief supporter of Israel;

2. The demand for an end to corruption, bribery, and the wasting of the nation's money;

3. The demand for the removal and trial of hypocrite sheikhs who were in fact puppets of the regime. [25]

It seems that the group was motivated by a mixture of religious and political factors. In a society whose political language is exclusively Islamic, it is only natural that political groups take a religious form. There are sectors of the population that view social changes taking place in Saudi Arabia as destroying the social and moral fabric of society. This concern is enhanced by the lavish life-style of certain members of the royal family. The impact of oil wealth creates an increasing gap between the excessively puritan Wahhābī ideas, upon which the state is theoretically predicated, and the changing ways of life of the ruling elite. It was no surprise, therefore, that later Crown Prince Fahd referred to the need for the royal family to provide an example; he stated that laws must be applied to all including the princes, and that a consultation council would be established. [26] Measures were taken to appease conservative sentiments, such as tightening up the prohibition on the consumption of alcohol or the mixing of men and women in public. [27]

The event at Mecca is a manifestation of the dilemma Saudi Arabia finds itself in; a political system based on tribal and religious legitimacy is attempting to control the consequences of accelerated economic and social change. The change involves detribalization and urbanization, an influx of foreign workers (half of the labor force), more education, and increased contacts with the outside world through travel and education abroad.

The Saudi ruling class faces a difficult choice. To the extent that it keeps the symbols of the traditional bases of legitimacy—tribe and religion—alive, the more it remains vulnerable to the challenge of Islamic orthodoxy. If, on the other hand, it moves to establish a new basis of legitimacy, it will be eroding its own position and privileges. Here lies the dilemma: the royal family cannot keep the traditional structure of social and political relations unchanged, nor is it ready to accept the eventual consequences of social change, particularly those related to political participation. A delicate balance was established in the 1960s by King Faisal and was made more effective in the 1970s by the oil wealth. But the divergence between a rapidly changing society and its political structure remains.

Islam as an Apology

Apology is an orientation that manifests itself in thought and practice. At the level of thought, it is as old as the early contacts between Europe and the Islamic world in the late eighteenth and early nineteenth centuries, and it has survived until now. Explaining Muslims' defeat and weakness, apologetic thinkers have been concerned with a passionate defense of Islamic teachings. For them, religion is the cure for all social ills. Islamic teachings have no need of Western ideas, because they are intrinsically valid and capable of providing the basis for a viable social order. Instead of attempting to analyze the problems facing their societies, this group of Arab intellectuals turned to the glorification of the past without trying to find out why this glory declined or how it could once again be restored.[28] An examination of their thought shows that their reasoning operates in the face of two challenges: the material advancement of Western civilization, on the one hand, and the impact of the ideas derived from this civilization upon Islamic teachings, on the other. When challenged by Western material civilization, these thinkers enumerate the achievements of a "secular" Islamic civilization in the fields of science, philosophy, mathematics, agriculture, and others, disregarding the fact that science and philosophy declined with the triumph of orthodoxy. At the same time, when reacting against the modern ideas based on science and technology of the nineteenth century, they uphold the tenets of an orthodoxy they identify with Islam.[29] Another form of apology is the tendency to Islamicize Western ideas and concepts. Thus, the two dominant ideological trends in the Arab world in the 1950s and 1960s, Arab nationalism and Arab socialism, were legitimized in the name of Islam. The tendency has been to make the exogenous appear as endogenous. The way of doing it is to find some reference, moot or indirect as it may be, to the Western concept in the Quran or the sayings of the Prophet, even if this entails rendering a new meaning to Arabic words. Employing this method, a great deal of the theories in such fields as agriculture, chemistry, and physics was found to have an origin in Islam.

At the level of practice, Islam functions as an ideology. It is used, in most cases consciously, by a ruling class to legitimize its position, justify policies, create consensus, generate mass support, and discredit opponents. In this endeavor the ruling class is usually supported, to varying degrees, by official ^culamā', by sheikhs and imāms who are actually employees of the state and who share the constraints and limitations of civil servants. It is interesting here to recall how Sadat's visit to Israel in October 1977 was both approved and attacked by various religious establishments. In Egypt, al-Azhar and the Coptic church supported the move. Later al-Azhar issued a communique approving, though not enthusiastically, the Camp David accords. In other Arab countries, the visit and the accord were condemned as contrary to Islamic principles.

A flagrant example of the political use of Islam was King Hasan II's statement after the attempt on his life in August 1972: "I will not hesitate in destroying the corrupt third of the people to achieve stability for the rest in accordance with the teachings of the Māliki doctrine."[30] Another interesting example was Nasser's public interpretation of the 1967 defeat. It was a qadar (predestined event), he told the people, and an imtihān (test) from God. Defeat was to be unquestioned, since it was God's will from which there was no escape.

Islam as an Alternative

In this type of resurgence, Islamic groups do not ally themselves with the government as in the previous type but, rather, project Islam as an alternative solution to the problems of society. These groups can be analyzed as a variant of Neil Smelser's norm-oriented social movements, which attempt "to restore, protect, modify or create norms in the name of a generalized belief."[31] Though broad variations exist between dissident Islamic groups, several general features of their ideology can be found.[32]

For these groups, Islam is a comprehensive and total way of life that provides answers to all questions of life and afterlife.* Islam is not just an alternative to the existing social order, but the only alternative capable of achieving Arab—and Muslim—renaissance, power, and dignity. The ideas of these groups tend to be general and holistic rather than programmatic. They usually make their appeal in terms of general moral principles, which renders them attractive and enables them to discredit their opponents. They radiate a sense of discipline, high moral standards, commitment, and confidence in a world of rapid social change, venality, and instability.† They are also radical

---

*Hasan al-Bannā described the Muslim Brothers in the following words: "Some people think of us as a group of preachers, concerned only to call people to do virtues and abstain from sins. Others believe it is a mystical trend. We are not any of those, we call to return for true Islam, which is a belief and application, a home and a nationality, a religion and state, a spirit and body, and a Quran and Sword" (see his message to the Fifth Conference of the Muslim Brothers [Cairo, 1938], p. 10).

†The slogan of the Muslim Brothers reflects this orientation: God is our highest end, the Prophet is our leader, the Quran our law, jihād our means, and death for the cause of God is our highest ambition.

in the sense of going to the roots of the problems and proposing fundamental solutions that involve the restructuring of individuals and society.

Their views tend to be simple and dichotomous and do not reflect a grasp of the complexities of modern society. One example is the view of international relations as a constant struggle between Islam and its enemies. The list of enemies includes almost everybody: the crusading Christian West, the atheist communists, and the Jews. A recurrent theme in their writings is the conspiracy against Islam. This feeling is likely a function of weakness, isolation, and a recognition of the gap between their ideas and actual developments in their societies. The simplicity of their thought is partially derived from their cultural classicism,* that is, their belief in the early period of Islam, the era of the Prophet and the rightly guided caliphs, as an image of what Muslim society should be. In particular, they fail to distinguish between aspects of that society that have universal—at least for Muslims—relevance (norms and values), and those that were historically specific (particular social or institutional arrangements). To that extent, their thought has a utopian component, a yearning for a perfect past that must be recaptured and revived.

Another important feature of their thought is its antimystical orientation. Contrary to the forms of Sūfī thought and practices that characterized the late medieval Islamic society, these groups aim at the reform of the society through the application of sharī^{C}a and, therefore, are more politicized and action oriented. For them the objective is to affect public policies, if not to seize political power and rule directly.

The forms of expression of this system of thought vary from the militant Jama^{C}at al-Takfīr wa'l-Hijra to the more conciliatory al-Da^{C}wa in Egypt. Since the idea of the first group is analyzed elsewhere in this volume,† I will confine myself to the latter. Al-Da^{C}wa was originally published on behalf of the Muslim Brothers Association from January 1951 until its suppression in 1956. It resumed publication 20

---

*The notion of cultural classicism was used by G. E. Von Grunebaum to refer to a situation in which (1) a past phase of cultural development is recognized as a perfect realization of human potentialities, (2) this realization is appropriated as a legitimate inheritance or possession, (3) the possibility is admitted that the present may be recast in terms of past perfection, and (4) the aspiration of the past is accepted as exemplary and binding on the present (see his Modern Islam Berkeley and Los Angeles: University of California Press, 1962], p. 72).

†In Saad Ibrahim's contribution based on interviews with members of the group.

years later in Jamād al-Thānī 1396 A. H. (July 1976). Some 80,000 copies of the first issue were distributed, and its present distribution is estimated at 150,000. The size of its circulation is partially attributable to its being an opposition journal as well as a religious one.

The journal defined its objectives as threefold: (1) explaining the teachings of Islam, (2) refuting the false accusations against the Muslim Brothers, and (3) advocating a return to Islam's ethics and politics. Since its reappearance, al-Da^cwa has dealt with a variety of social, religious, economic, and political issues. A favorite theme has been the attack on birth control and government efforts related to it. In the August 1977 issue, Sheikh al-Azhar wrote an essay entitled "Birth Control Is a Refuted Idea." According to him, it is a ridiculous idea that should not be encouraged, for God is capable of providing food to every human being on earth. The idea of Egypt's limited resources is also a myth. Egyptian deserts are vast and contain plentiful resources. The deserts can be cultivated, and some plants like olive trees endure lack of water for three years. What is needed is dedicated and daring people to conquer the desert and use its resources. Indeed, Egypt may suffer a manpower shortage in the future. Another writer in the November 1979 issue warned that birth control in the West led to the spread of immorality (because of abortion and because of unmarried couples having children) and the distortion of the age structure of the population (an increase in the percentage of old people). Almost every issue in 1980 and 1981 contained at least one reference to birth control. This emphasis is understandable, since during these two years, the Egyptian government launched a concerted mass-media campaign to bring to the Egyptians' attention the importance of family planning.

Another favorite theme is the law of personal status. In the July 1979 issue there is an essay in defense of polygamy and the right of men to divorce. The writer called upon the ^culamā to rise up and prevent the new conspiracy against Islam (referring to the deliberations about a new personal-status law, which was eventually issued by a presidential decree). In the following issue (August 1979) Sālih ^cAshmāwī, editor in chief of the journal, wrote an essay entitled "Prevent Adultery before Limiting Marriage." Again, he referred to the conspiracy against Islam and the attempts to weaken its role in society. He reminded his readers that Islamic law had already been replaced by Western imported ones in most areas. What was left from sharī^ca was the law of personal status and therefore it must remain untouched.

A third theme is naturally the application of sharī^ca. In the first issue (June 1976), the editor in chief wrote an essay entitled "In the Name of the Constitution We Call for an Islamic Law" and demanded that all legislation contrary to the sharī^ca be nullified. When political parties were allowed, one essay (March 1977) criticized the government for not approving an Islamic party. The journal condemned government laxity in applying the sharī^{c}a. Its writers recommended prohibiting the sale of alcoholic beverages or even the serving of them in hotels, taking measures to prevent public eating in Ramaḍān (the Muslim month of fasting from sunrise to sunset), and banning sex scenes in television shows and movies and atheist ideas in books and newspapers. The theme of conspiracy is present again in the editorials of al-Da^{c}wa: "Conspiracy against the Islamic Sharī^{c}a" (March 1979) and "Conspiracy: What Is Plotted against the Sharī^{c}a" (April 1979). In January 1978 ^{c}Umar al-Tilmisānī, the editor of al-Da^{c}wa, wrote an angry essay, "You Muslim Rulers . . . Do You Not Fear God?" in which he urged them to start implementing Islamic teachings for "God will not help people who do not help themselves." A year before (January 1977), he wrote "Oh You Arab Leaders. God's Way or Destruction?" When there was discussion of a constitutional amendment, he wrote in September 1979 that the Quran should become "the basis of our constitution."

The writers of al-Da^{c}wa were also active in commenting on foreign policy issues. The journal strongly supports Islamic solidarity. Muslims have no choice but to close ranks, since superpowers are determined to destroy Islam (January 1978). It consistently supported the Iranian revolution and criticized the shah's stay in Egypt. In 1981 almost every issue contained a feature on the Muslim struggle in Syria against the regime of Ḥāfiz al-Asad. It defends Muslim rights in India, the Philippines, and Uganda, and of course supports the struggle in Afghanistan.

In contrast to the other major opposition weekly al-Sha^{c}b (People), which is published by the Labor party and condemns Sadat's policy toward Israel in direct and sensational words, al-Da^{c}wa follows a more cautious path. Its writers obviously do not approve of the president's policy, but they express their views in conciliatory and rational terms. When Sadat visited Israel, al-Da^{c}wa neither supported nor condemned the move, but was not hopeful of its outcome (February 1978). The same caution was shown in the commentary on the Camp David accords (October 1978). However, the journal's orientation toward Israel and the Jews is unmistakably negative, and its writers do not hesitate to use the harshest words to express their views. In every issue one finds an essay or a comment on Jewish crimes in Palestine, the importance of Jerusalem in Islam, the dangers of establishing economic and cultural relations with Israel, and Israeli expansionist designs. Thus, while al-Da^{c}wa refrains from criticizing President Sadat directly, which al-Sha^{c}b regularly does, it leaves no doubt as to its views of his policies. This situation is a result of the journal's ambiguous legal position. The journal advocates the views of the Muslim Brothers Association, but the association itself remains illegal, which perhaps makes al-Da^cwa cautious in criticizing the president directly.

TOWARD AN INTERPRETATION

From the previous analysis it is clear that the Islamic resurgence is a complex multidimensional phenomenon that cannot be simply explained by a single factor. In general, two sets of explanatory factors—endogenous and exogenous—have been suggested. Proponents of endogenous factors make use of the sociology, social psychology, and political science literature on mass movements and social crises in their analyses. The Islamic resurgence is thus interpreted as a symptom of a society in a crisis. Advocates of exogenous factors refer to such variables as external activities by rich Arab countries, particularly Saudi Arabia and Libya, in support of Islamic groups or the impact of the Iranian revolution.

The tendency of most authors has been to emphasize one set of factors to the exclusion of the other. There is no reason to assume that the two are mutually exclusive. In fact, they interact with each other, and therefore, an integrative analysis must take both into consideration.

From the perspective of ideology and the history of ideas, Islamic resurgence provides further evidence of the failure of modern Arabic thought to reach a functioning and meaningful synthesis between Islam, the religion of the masses and a major source of their value system, and modernization. Neither Arab secular or semisecular ideologies (Arab nationalism, Arab socialism, and liberalism) nor Islamic modernism (Muhammad ^cAbduh and his school) have produced the much-needed synthesis. [33]

The analysis of Islamic resurgence must, however, go beyond the intellectual level to investigate its sociological sources and roots. Using the distinction suggested earlier between Islam from above and from below, it seems that the use of Islam by governments involves primarily the problem of legitimation, and that the use of Islam by dissident movements reflects the reaction of a social group, or groups, to a threat, real or perceived, to its interests or value systems. In both cases, Islamic resurgence is related to a social crisis. [34] R. H. Dekmejian perceptively outlines the attributes of the crisis as follows: a crisis of legitimacy of political elites and political systems, a paucity of social justice, an excessive reliance on coercion, military vulnerability, and the disruptive impact of modernization. [35]

From this perspective five substantive propositions seem relevant in interpreting Islamic resurgence.

Proposition 1: Ruling elites in Muslim countries may encourage Islamic groups as a legitimacy device, a diversionary tactic to divert public attention from other issues and to discredit their opponents, especially those of the Left. Generally, the more a political elite in a Muslim country lacks legitimacy, or is on the defensive, the more it will resort to Islamic symbolism and religious legitimation.

Proposition 2: At the level of the masses, Islam provides a frame of reference for their collective identity, a symbol of self-assertion, and a consciousness that is rooted in their own history and tradition as opposed to foreign penetration and cultural domination—thus the emphasis of Islamic writers on asāla (authenticity) as opposed to imported ideas.

Proposition 3: It follows that Islamic resurgence is in part a reaction, not to modernization per se, but to a particular type of modernization, that is, Westernization, which overlooks and sometimes despises national traditions and cultural symbols. It brings to the fore the importance of the cultural component of modernization and the necessity of mobilizing indigenous nonmaterial resources.

Proposition 4: In a situation of economic stress and sociopolitical alienation, the recently urbanized sector of the lower middle class is most attracted to the call of Islamic groups. These groups present a defense mechanism to protect this sector's social status from further deterioration and to maintain the integrity of its value system.

Proposition 5: The expansion of the recently urbanized provides the human raw material to Islamic groups. In the 1950s and 1960s the Arab world witnessed a massive internal migration to the cities, which resulted in increasing density in the cities. The consequences of this process are numerous and include the weakening of traditional sources of solidarity, identity problems, and a feeling of alienation.*

But the society-in-crisis analysis alone does not answer two important questions: Why is the change to Islam and not to some other radical persuasion? and Why did this change become so noticeable and acquire new dimensions in the 1970s?

---

*Ismail Serageldin's contribution develops this point further. Ibrahim's analysis may seem to contradict this proposition. He finds that those interviewed were achievers, were not uprooted, and came from "normal" families. But it would be erroneous to generalize his conclusions to the average members of Islamic groups or to the stratum of the population to whom the groups appeal most. His sample was confined to leaders and activists.

The increased emphasis on Islam is to be understood in the context of the dualism in Arab society and culture. One feature of social change in Arab countries is the coexistence of the old and the new. Thus, for instance, modern systems of education did not replace the traditional religious ones but coexisted with them. Most Arab men and women perceive no contradiction between being engaged in advanced science education or highly technical training while upholding traditional beliefs on the family, the status of women, or relations between the sexes.* Whether this dualism is characteristic of Arab and Middle Eastern development or a function of a particular phase of social change is beyond the scope of this analysis. The important point is that for most Arabs, including those who have a modern education, religion is important as a system of values and a component of national identity. For them, Islamic sentiments and loyalties have always existed. Thus, what we have witnessed in the 1970s is not the return of something that departed for a while, but the resurfacing of ideas that have always been there, albeit dormant and latent. Indeed, in the 1950s and 1960s neither Arab nationalism nor Arab socialism was presented as an alternative to Islam. On the contrary, both emphasized their links to it and were partially legitimized in religious terms. Nasser made sure that his brand of Arab socialism would not be confused with communism, one major difference being the belief in religion.

Islam also provides three significant political advantages. First, for Arabs Islam represents the familiar—their roots, their glorious past—which they have always been proud of and which no other nation can lay claim to. In a sense Islam is an Arab legacy: the Prophet was an Arab and the language of Islam is Arabic. The Quran became the norm of Arab literature and it can only be recited in Arabic. Second, Islam provides a definite organizational advantage. Islamic groups have the mosque as a ready-made meeting place and a forum for agitation. Recruitment usually takes place among devoted mosque goers. Third, Islam provides a distinctive language and vocabulary that separate its users from all other political groups.† Arab governments have used, indeed abused, most secular terms such as nationalism, socialism, democracy, and constitutionalism. When these governments fail in raising the standard of living of their population, they render their declared ideologies and clichés meaningless. Dissident Islamic groups offer an alternative

---

*Tawfic Farah's contribution to this volume includes the results of several survey studies in support of this assertion.

†The theme of Islam as an alternative political language is developed in Jean-Claude Vatin's chapter.

language of political discourse, a language that in most cases is easily understood by the masses and is not identified with the government.

Why did the movement gather momentum in the 1970s? One can argue that the "society in crisis" created the necessary but not the sufficient conditions for Islamic resurgence. We have to distinguish two sets of factors in interpreting the phenomenon: those responsible for establishing the milieu in which Islamic resurgence can develop and prosper (these may be called the structural conduciveness factors) and those acting as a trigger to the emergence, reappearance, or strengthening of Islamic groups (the precipitatory factors). The crisis variables did create structural conduciveness, but other supportive, precipitatory factors were needed to trigger the situation. These factors are to be found in the conditions of the Arab world in the late 1960s. These include two major developments: the increased incapacitation of "revolutionary" Arab regimes and the decline of their influence and prestige, and the new wealth acquired by the Arab oil-producing countries. The first development was due to Egypt's economic troubles, its inability to score a victory in the Yemen War (1962-67), the Egyptian-Syrian defeat of 1967, and the death of Nasser in 1970. On the other hand, wealth gave the oil-producing countries that happened to be Islamic oriented a new sense of confidence. This new confidence, also reinforced by the October war of 1973, must be appreciated against a history of Arab humiliation by Western powers. For a long period, Arab lands were occupied, and political and economic power was vested in the hands of foreigners. Islamic law was replaced by Western codes, and in the Maghreb states Arabic became a second-class language. The establishment of the state of Israel, the plight of the Palestinians, and Arab defeats in their military encounters with Israel, which enjoyed Western support, added to Arab feelings of frustration and humiliation.

To summarize our argument, an integrative interpretation of the Islamic resurgence must consider both internal and external factors. The social crisis created the environment for such a resurgence. The precipitatory factors provided the specific catalyst. The crisis factors explain the long-range reasons and fermentation that preceded the Islamic resurgence; the precipitatory ones underline the short-run and immediate factors related to its emergence.

THE ISLAMIC RESURGENCE
AND THE INTERNATIONAL SYSTEM

Another manifestation of the Islamic resurgence is the development in the 1970s of inter-Islamic organizations that have made it possible for Islamic states to become a subsystem in international politics. The call for pan-Islam, championed in the nineteenth century by Jamāl al-Dīn al-Afghānī, had a setback in the aftermath of World War I because of the defeat of the Ottoman Empire and the abolition of the Caliphate by Kemāl Atatürk. In the interwar era the call for pan-Islam—or rather, Islamic solidarity—took two forms of expression. The first was the convening of several Islamic conferences to discuss the revival of the Caliphate, such as those held in Mecca and Cairo in 1926. The other was the continued defense by Islamic thinkers, such as Rashīd Ridā and Hasan al-Bannā, of the necessity for Islamic solidarity.

After World War II, the idea was revived by the new Islamic state, Pakistan, which convened the Conference of the Islamic World in February 1949 with headquarters in Karachi. The delegates were nonofficials, and one of the objectives of the conference was to encourage cooperation between Islamic countries. Pakistan also called for an economic conference in November 1949, followed by another one in Tehran in 1950.[36] Nasser of Egypt also considered the political importance of Islamic solidarity. In his Philosophy of the Revolution, published in 1955, he defined the spheres of Egypt's foreign policy as Arab, African, and Islamic. He suggested that al-Hajj (pilgrimage) was a sort of annual Islamic world parliament that "should become an institution of great political power and significance."[37]

In the 1950s and 1960s, however, the call for Islamic solidarity was overshadowed by other political ideas and movements, such as Arab nationalism and the Afro-Asian and nonaligned movements. When King Faisal renewed the call for an Islamic conference in 1964, he was immediately condemned by Nasser, and the idea was described as conservative and serving Western imperialist interests. It was only in September 1969, after the 1967 defeat and the burning of al-Aqsā Mosque in Jerusalem, that the first Islamic summit conference was held in Rabat, Morocco, followed by a conference of Islamic foreign ministers in March 1970. The latter established a permanent secretariat, located in Saudi Arabia.

In 1981 the Islamic Conference organization included 43 states and more than 700 million people. The international influence of this group is derived from three sources: its obvious numerical power, the wealth of some of its members (oil wealth), and its members' participation in various international groups, such as the Organization of Petroleum Exporting Countries (OPEC), the Organization of African Unity, the League of Arab States, the Grouping of 77, and the Association of Southeast Asian Nations.[38]

The organization holds periodic meetings of heads of states, foreign ministers, and economy and finance ministers. It has estab-

lished several affiliated specialized associations, such as the Federation of Islamic Broadcasts, the Federation of Red Crescent Organizations, the Islamic Development Bank, the Islamic Afro-Asian Organizations, the Islamic Asian Conference, the Islamic Conference
for Science and Technology, the International Conference for Muslim
Youth, the International Association for Islamic Teachings, and the
Conference of Islamic Industrial States.

The declarations of the Islamic summit and foreign ministers'
meetings cover a variety of subjects; of particular importance have
been the issue of Palestine, support for the Palestine Liberation Organization (PLO), and the right of the Palestinians to self-determina-
tion. The declarations usually make a specific reference to al-Quds
(Jerusalem) as an Arab Muslim city and "as a unique symbol of the
confluence of Islam with the sacred divine religions."[39] Another recurrent theme is the call to promote solidarity among Islamic states.

The recommendations of the Third Islamic Summit Conference
held in Tā'if, Saudi Arabia, in January 1981 included a renewed demand for the liberation of Israeli-occupied Arab territories, including
East Jerusalem; a recommendation that the Arab economic boycott
of Israel be widened to involve all Islamic countries; a call for the
withdrawal of Soviet troops from Afghanistan; a call for an immediate
cease-fire in the Iraqi-Irani war and for the creation of an Islamic
mediation commission; and the announcement of a plan to form an Islamic court of justice and of the need to provide more economic aid
to poor Islamic states.[40]

Whether Islamic states will actually develop into an effective
international subsystem is yet to be seen. Their voting behavior in
the General Assembly of the United Nations shows a surprisingly high
degree of solidarity on a variety of issues, including international
security, arms control, nuclear proliferation, the Arab-Israeli conflict, racism, human rights, decolonization, and economic questions.[41]
It is not clear, however, whether this solidarity arises from their being Islamic or developing. There do not seem to be strong economic
ties between these countries: for instance, the volume of inter-Islamic trade is insignificant.

It is obvious that Arab states have successfully made the Palestine question a primary concern of the Islamic conference and that
non-Arab Islamic states have not hesitated to support the Arab cause
politically and diplomatically.* Thus, the future of Islamic solidarity
depends to a great extent on the willingness and readiness of rich
Arab states to share their wealth and help poor Islamic countries that

---

*When Egypt signed the Camp David accords, it was condemned
by the Islamic Conference and eventually dismissed from it.

have been hit hard by soaring oil prices. This expectation has likely lured many Muslim elites and encouraged them to share Arab positions. Its nonfulfillment, however, may limit the appeal for Islamic solidarity and encourage other policy options.

CONCLUSION

It is hoped that this book will increase our understanding of the Islamic resurgence and stimulate further research in areas in which our knowledge remains incomplete. In particular we need the following:

1. Case studies of dissident Islamic groups and organizations covering their ideology, social base, strategy, and tactics;
2. Studies of the impact of Islamic resurgence on the locus of political allegiance and of how Islamic activities relate to other political loyalties, such as pannationalism (Arab), particular or state-oriented nationalism (Egyptian, Iraqi), and substate loyalties (Kurdish, Berber);
3. Comparative studies of Islamic resurgent groups across time and place.

The future of Islamic movements is likely to differ from one Arab country to another. Their fate depends on the interaction of their activities and those of other groups and elites. Crucial to the conclusion of this interaction is the ability of Islamic groups to make their appeal to a broad coalition of social forces, similar to what took place in Iran before the revolution. This ability requires the emergence of a popular or nationally known leader, such as Hasan al-Bannā in Egypt in the 1940s or Khomeinī in Iran in the 1970s, which Islamic groups in most Arab countries lack. It also requires the development of a political program or objectives that various groups can relate to and identify with.

A limitation on the political ambitions of Islamic groups in Arab countries is the general character of their call. In many instances they advocate moral principles rather than provide programs or concrete solutions to social problems. Islamic groups have been called upon—and not always with the intention of embarrassing them—to clarify their positions on issues such as political freedom, particularly freedom of thought and freedom to establish political parties; their concept of citizenship and the equality of Muslims and non-Muslims in society; the status of women; and the type of political system. Another important factor affecting the future of Islamic groups is governmental policies toward them, ranging from co-optation to reconciliation to suppression. Their future will also be affected by the effectiveness of governmental programs in solving social problems and thereby increasing the regime's popularity and legitimacy.

It is to be recalled that the success of political movements does not depend on the superiority of their moral or ideological claims but on their platforms, programs, and policies, and their ability to establish political coalitions and broaden the scope of their appeal. There is nothing inevitable about the future of these Islamic groups. They can simply pass away, as happened before to a much more popular and powerful predecessor, the Muslim Brothers in 1955, or they may contribute to the evolution of the much-needed and long-awaited synthesis between Islam and modern times. Islamic groups are likely to remain a force to reckon with during the 1980s. Whatever path it may take, Islamic resurgence undoubtedly has again brought to the foreground the vitality of Islamic traditions, the importance of Islam in the life of most Arabs, and the continued crisis existing in the Arab world.

NOTES

1. Islam Centennial Fourteen Newsletter 11 (March 1981): 5-6.

2. Newsweek, December 5, 1977, pp. 58-59.

3. See the special issue of Social Research entitled Beyond Charisma: Religious Movements in Discourse, in particular, the contributions of Johannes Fabian, "The Anthropology of Religious Movements from Explanation to Interpretation," Social Research 46 (1979): 4-36; and James Fernandez, "On the Notion of Religious Movement," Social Research 46 (1979): 36-62.

4. See a case study in D. F. Eickelman, "Religious Tradition, Economic Domination and Political Legitimacy," Revue de l'Occident musulman et de la Méditerranée 29 (1980): 17-30.

5. Nikki R. Keddie, "Iran: Change in Islam; Islam and Change," International Journal of Middle East Studies 11 (1980): 527-42.

6. See a list in Zakariya S. Bayūmī, Al-Ikhwān al-Muslimīn wa al-Jama^{c}āt al-Islāmiya fi al-hayāt al-siyāsiya al-Misriya [The Muslim Brothers and Islamic associations in the Egyptian political life] (Cairo: Maktabat Wahbah, 1979), p. 67.

7. Andrew Lycett, "The Great Islamic Revival," in Arabia and the Gulf, no. 21 (May 28, 1979), pp. 8-9; and Arab Report and Record, April 16-30, 1975, p. 242.

8. Arab Report and Record, June 16-30, 1978, p. 444.

9. Ibid., August 1-15, 1975, p. 530.

10. Arabia and the Gulf, no. 46 (November 13, 1978), p. 5.

11. M. A. Tessler, "Political Change and the Islamic Revival in Tunisia," Maghreb Review 5 (1980): 14-15.

12. Arabia and the Gulf, no. 21 (May 22, 1978), p. 9.

13. Ibid.

14. Los Angeles Times, May 20, 1980.

15. Patrick Blum, "Islamic Revival Fuels Maghreb Discontent," Middle East Economic Digest 23 (November 1979): 5-7.

16. Ibid.

17. Middle East Newsletter 130 (January 28-February 10, 1980): 4.

18. Ibid., 128 (December 7, 1979-January 13, 1980): 10-11.

19. Ibid., pp. 7-8.

20. Ibid., 135 (April 21-May 4, 1980): 5-7.

21. Economist, December 13, 1980.

22. ᶜUkaz (daily Saudi newspaper), November 21, 1979; and Los Angeles Times, November 22, 1979.

23. ᶜUkaz, November 22 and 25, 1979.

24. Newsweek, March 3, 1980, pp. 34-38; and Arab World Weekly 540 (November 24, 1979): 1.

25. MERIP Reports 85 (February 1980): 16.

26. al-Hawādith (Beirut), January 11, 1980, pp. 17-21.

27. Middle East Newsletter 127 (December 31-16, 1979): 4.

28. W. C. Smith, Islam in Modern History (New York: Vintage Books, 1963), p. 124.

29. N. Berkes, The Development of Secularism in Turkey (Montreal: McGill University Press, 1964), pp. 263-64.

30. al-Ahrām, August 28, 1972.

31. Neil Smelser, Theory of Collective Behavior (New York: Free Press of Glencoe, 1963), p. 270.

32. Charles Adams, "Conservative Movements in the Arab World," Arab Journal 4 (1967): 57-62.

33. On this point, see Ali E. Hallil Dessouki, "Arab Intellectuals and Al-Nakba: The Search for Fundamentalism," Middle Eastern Studies 9 (1973): 445-46.

34. The theme of crisis situation was developed in R. H. Dekmejian, "The Anatomy of Islamic Revival," Middle East Journal 34 (1980): 1-12; Saad E. Ibrahim: "Anatomy of Egypt's Militant Islamic Groups," International Journal of Middle East Studies 12 (1980): 423-53; Nazih N. M. Ayubi, "The Political Revival of Islam: The Case of Egypt," International Journal of Middle East Studies 12 (1980): 481-99; Ali E. Hallil Dessouki, "The Resurgence of Islamic Organizations in Egypt: An Interpretation," in Islam and Power, ed. A. A. Cudsi and Ali E. Hillal Dessouki (London: Croom Helm, 1981); and P. J. Vatikiotis, "Islamic Resurgence: A Critical View," in Islam and Power, ed. A. A. Cudsi and Ali E. Hillal Dessouki (London: Croomhelm, 1981).

35. Dekmejian, "The Anatomy of Islamic Revival," pp. 5-10.

36. Rashīd al-Barāwī, al-Kutla al Islāmīya [The Islamic bloc] (Cairo: Maktabat al-nahda al-Misrīya, 1952), pp. 24-26.

37. Gamal Abdul Nasser, Egypt's Liberation: The Philosophy of the Revolution (Washington, D. C.: Public Affairs Press, 1955), p. 112.

38. Raphael Israeli, "The New Wave of Islam," International Journal 34 (1979): 381.

39. From the 1974 Lahore Summit Conference's declaration. See the Arab World Weekly 281 (March 2, 1974): 14-16.

40. New York Times, January 2, 1981.

41. See a statistical analysis of Islamic states' voting patterns in sess. no. 34 of the General Assembly, 1979, in Mohammad A. Sleim, "al-Tadammun al-Islāmī wa'l-nizām al-dawlī"[Islamic solidarity and the international system], al-Siyasa al-Dawliya [World politics] 62 (1980): 62-74.

PART II

THEORETICAL PERSPECTIVES

2

OIL WEALTH
AND
ISLAMIC RESURGENCE

DANIEL PIPES

That an Islamic resurgence has occurred cannot be taken for granted. With the rise of Ayātollāh Khomeinī in 1978/79, the role of Islam in public affairs attracted much international attention; while there seems to be general agreement that a growth of Islamic feeling has occurred in recent years, some experts on Islam dispute this notion. * These experts argue, with reason, that increased concern about oil supplies and Organization of Petroleum Exporting Countries' (OPEC) markets has caused the outside world to note with unprecedented interest the faith of Muslims. In their view, new attentiveness, not new activity among Muslims, marks the surge of Islam. To decide whether an Islamic resurgence does exist, one must begin by defining what it is; only then is it possible to establish whether one has recently occurred and, if so, to inquire into its causes.

DEFINITION OF ISLAMIC RESURGENCE

Islamic resurgence is understood to mean an increase in Islamic activism. Just as the spiritualism and theory of each religion are unique, so does its activism take special forms. How present-day

---

*For example, note the opening sentence of Mangol Bayat's article, "Islam in Pahlavi and Post-Pahlavi Iran: A Cultural Revolution?": "The 1978-79 Iranian revolution is too often perceived by the superficial observer, the uninformed media representative as well as the religiously inclined Iranian himself, as symbolizing the rise of Islam and the Muslims against its enemies from within and without."[1]

Muslims act on behalf of their faith differs fundamentally, for example, from what their Christian counterparts do. Christians demonstrate devotion and allegiance by attending services, making donations to the church, engaging in missionary work, and adhering to the ethic of love. In contrast, Muslim activism almost always involves working for the goals of the sharī^{C}a, the sacred law of Islam. * The sharī^{C}a, a legal structure without equivalent in Christianity, is therefore the key to understanding Islamic activism. †

Islam requires its adherents to follow the regulations of the sharī^{C}a in minute and exact detail. Developed between the seventh and tenth centuries, it is based both on Quranic commandments and on other sources (notably, the sayings and practice of the Prophet Muhammad, reasoning by analogy, and consensus of the Muslim scholars). A devout Muslim makes hardly a move without confronting precepts of the sharī^{C}a; they touch on most of his daily routine, including his eating habits and his familial and social relations. In the public domain, they cover taxation, justice, political authority, and warfare. Ideally, the sharī^{C}a should permeate the mind and actions of a Muslim. Among activist Muslims, it does just this.

The state has a major role in forwarding sharī^{C}a goals. Traditionally, Muslims have viewed their government primarily as a vehicle for implementing the sharī^{C}a; its legitimacy derived from enforcing the ways of Islam. In theory, the ruler must dispense punishments as prescribed in the law books, levy Quranic taxes, and respect the sovereign authority of the legal experts who interpret the sharī^{C}a. He also must protect Muslim subjects against non-Muslims; thus, in certain specific circumstances, Muslim rulers are dutybound to wage war, but they must never make war against fellow Muslims.

These requirements are too demanding; no Muslim community has ever maintained the public provisions of the sharī^{C}a to its own satisfaction. Islamic precepts covering private life are indeed substantially followed, but those covering public life have fared less well. Islam's public goals inspire and beckon, but they have never been fully attained. Much of Muslim political history should be viewed in the light of these unachieved goals. ‡

---

*Some modern Muslims, such as Mu^{C}ammar al-Qadhdhāfī of Libya, have their own ideas about the laws of Islam, which do not correspond to the sharī^{C}a.

† Sūfī movements sometimes show less interest in sharī^{C}a activism than do other Muslim movements.

‡ I use this idea of unachieved goals to explain the Muslims' development of military slavery in my Slave Soldiers and Islam (New Haven, Conn.: Yale University Press, 1981).

Rulers too little concerned with Islamic precepts must either be convinced to change their ways or be thrown out of office. By definition, non-Muslim rulers do not regard the sharī^{c}a as divine precept (even though they may adhere to some of its requirements for convenience' sake), and so they must be replaced by Muslims. This becomes more urgent when they rule Muslim subjects. The efforts of activist Muslims follow from this: either they put pressure on Muslim governments to apply the sharī^{c}a or they struggle against governments (Muslim or not) that refuse to heed it.

Movements in a Muslim-only context are called legalist (applying the law is their immediate concern); those directed against non-Muslims are called autonomist (for them, putting political power in Muslim hands is paramount). Dividing Muslim movements in this manner is somewhat artificial, as they all contain some elements of both legalism and autonomism; yet, the distinction is analytically useful, for in most movements one or the other of these has more importance. Legalism predominates where non-Muslims have no substantial role, autonomism where struggles against non-Muslims are not accompanied by efforts to apply the sharī^{c}a. Legalism attacks non-Islamic customs and attitudes, whether traditional or from the West; autonomism attacks non-Muslim power, whether held by pagan tribes or the British Empire. * Often the two elements exist simultaneously, sometimes in fairly equal proportion. For example, both are strong today in the Libyan government of Mu^{c}ammar al-Qadhdhāfī, among the Muslim Brethren of Eqypt, in the groups that attacked the Great Mosque in Mecca, in Khomeinī's revolution, and in Malayan dakwah movements.

Legalism and autonomism embody the permanent imperatives of Islam, inspiring all mainstream activist Muslims (fringe groups go off in unpredictable directions). † They impose a starkly dual view of the world on activist Muslims, reducing everything to Islam or its antithesis. Taxes, for example, are divided into those stipulated by the sharī^{c}a and those not (maks); meat between that ritually slaughtered and that not (mayta); territory by whether an area is ruled by Muslims (Dār al-Islām) or not (Dār al-Harb); non-Muslims into those under Muslim control (dhimmīs) or not (harbīs). Activists

---

*It does not attack non-Muslims as such, who are accepted if nonthreatening.

† Sometimes the activist groups go to extremes. Recent examples include Alhaji Muhammadu Marwa's group in Kano, al-Takfīr wa'l-Hijra in Egypt, and some of the Malaya's dakwah movements. Splinter Shī^{c}ī groups have a long history of moving beyond the pale of Islam (Assassins, Druzes, ^{c}Alawites, Ahl-i Haqq, Bahā'īs).

have simple goals: they battle for Islam and against non-Islam; the more extreme their views, the more simple they make this dichotomy.

During the past two centuries, European superiority in virtually all spheres of human endeavor convinced many Muslims to adopt Western ways. Impressed by the wealth and power of Europe, they hoped that emulating it would bring them some of its strength. Islam, hitherto the Muslims' sole political ideology, now faced a rival that advocated goals often contrary to those of the sharī^{C}a. Nationalism, with its emphasis on territorial allegiance, and secularism, which reduces religion to faith, pushed the sharī^{C}a aside in most Muslim countries. Virtually all independent Muslim states kept the Western institutions set up by the colonial regimes, and their leaders, like the colonial administrators before them, in good part, viewed Islamic traditions as not conducive to modernization.

Although Islamic faith never lost its hold, the sharī^{C}a way of life weakened drastically through 200 years of Westernization. Only a small portion of Muslim political elites held to the sharī^{C}a; the overwhelming majority wanted to reduce the role of Islam in the public arena. Then, around 1970, sharī^{C}a goals acquired new force.

ISLAMIC ACTIVISM IN THE 1970s

Legalist and autonomist movements did exist before 1970, but with only a fraction of their later force. During the 10 years preceding 1970, not a single major legalist movement arose; autonomist movements were only slightly more prevalent. In 1965 the editor of a book of conference papers about Islam in international politics concluded that "most of the principal speakers maintained that Islam is actually of quite limited significance in shaping the attitudes and behavior of Muslim states in international relations today."[2] Few would agree with this assertion anymore; herein lies the Islamic resurgence. Evidence for it comes from all parts of the Muslim world.[3]

Legalism

In Senegal, Sheikh Abdoulaye Niasse, a leader of the Tijānīya Sūfī order, organized the Islamic party.[4] Claiming 300,000 members, he called for an immediate return to the sharī^{C}a and a turn away from the West. The government of Mauritania began to apply the sharī^{C}a in 1978. Also in 1978, 87 Muslim members of Nigeria's Parliament, the Constituent Assembly, withdrew in protest against a ruling by the body against a sharī^{C}a Court of Appeal at the federal level, provoking a major political incident. Followers of Alhaji Muhammadu Marwa in Kano applied the sharī^{C}a with zeal; they came to international attention in early 1981 when thousands of them were killed in pitched battles against the army. In Morocco, Islamic sentiments have been growing during recent years. A branch of the Muslim Brethern has been flourishing; its most dramatic act has been the assassination of a socialist leader in 1975. Algeria's National Charter made Islam the religion of state and the basis for some laws in 1976.[5] The Society for the Preservation of the Quran in Tunisia has won great numbers of new members in the years since 1970 and now runs many cultural programs, leads public relations efforts, and puts pressure on the government to conform to the sharī^{C}a.

Soon after Mu^{C}ammar al-Qadhdhāfī came to power in Libya on September 1, 1969, he began to replace Italian laws with those of the Quran.[6] For all the attention that cutting the hands off criminals received, very few Islamic laws are actually in effect in Libya; in fact, less celebrated changes in Algeria, the Sudan, and Somalia have been more far-reaching.[7] In Egypt, many sharī^{C}a-oriented groups have grown significantly during the 1970s, especially the Muslim Brethren.[8] They put pressure on the government to reapply numerous sharī^{C}a regulations, especially those touching on personal status. In 1970 the Sudanese government of Ja^{C}far al-Numayrī bombed the headquarters of the Ansār, the Muslim party that traces its roots to the Mahdī of the late nineteenth century; some 5,000 to 12,000 Ansār were killed.[9] They and other Muslim groups attempted a coup six years later against Numayrī. In 1977 he acknowledged their strength by signing an agreement of national reconciliation, which led to al-Sādiq al-Mahdī, the Ansār leader and head of the Umma party, returning to the Sudan. The Muslim Brethren's leader, subsequently appointed attorney general, imposed Islamic regulations wherever possible.

Although Saudi Arabia's rulers pride themselves on their pure and consistent devotion to the sharī^{C}a, the persons who invaded the Great Mosque at Mecca in November 1979 thought otherwise. Among other demands, they called for full application of the sharī^{C}a, rejecting the emasculation it had suffered in recent decades. In April 1981 several events marked a sharp swing toward Islam in the United Arab Emirates: a bomb in Dubai's newest luxury hotel was exploded in protest against the lax sale of alcohol; the sexes were ordered completely separated in all UAE schools; and a sharī^{C}a court in Abu Dhabi ordered full Islamic punishments for two adulterers (death by stoning).[10] Activist Muslims made significant gains in the Kuwaiti elections of February 1981. Jordanian Muslim Brethren used the occasion of a sex scandal in high places to push their viewpoint and gain an unprecedented visibility. Muslim Brethren in Syria became the

central opposition to the Ba^{C}th government during the late 1970s, culminating in the near overthrow of the government in the summer of
1980. So badly did they scare the state that mere suspicion of membership in the Muslim Brethren was declared a capital crime.

Despite the near sanctity of Atatürk's secular legacy, the National Salvation party of Turkey prospered from the early 1970s with
a program of bringing Islam back into public life.[11] It won parliamentary representation and formed part of three government coalitions between 1974 and 1977. After the military took over in September 1980, it charged National Salavation party leaders with trying to
set up an Islamic state and prosecuted them.

Iran has had the century's most dramatic experience with legalism.[12] One moment, it had a Westernizing government in the
hands of a shah who hoped use Western techniques to make Iran an
industrial and military power. The next moment, a fanatic religious
leader replaced him, determined to reimpose the sharī^{C}a fully and
without delay. Iranians supported Khomeinī as a symbol of opposition
to the shah, not necessarily because they accepted his views. Yet
once Khomeinī took control in February 1979, his program met little
resistance. The drama of Iran's experience and the thoroughness of
Khomeinī's program have made Iran the key country for legalism.
How things turn out there will deeply affect movements elsewhere; if
Iran's Islamic venture fails, contemporary legalist movements around
the world will lose their most celebrated model and inspiration.

Through careful maneuvering, the Jama^{C}āt-ī Islāmī in Pakistan
has pushed through some of its favorite programs, such as changing
the constitution along Islamic lines; declaring the Ahmadīs, a splinter
group of Islam, non-Muslim; and making certain offenses punishable
according to sharī^{C}a regulations.[13] Pakistan is today one of the very
few countries, other than Saudi Arabia and Libya, that whips criminals and amputates their hands. It is also at the vanguard of efforts
to abolish interest; bank deposits invested in profit/loss-sharing
schemes earn no interest but get a portion of the bank's earnings or
deficits. The Pakistani state is the first in modern history to require
zakāh contributions (normally such charitable donations are voluntary)
and to collect them. The Council of Islamic Ideology coordinates
these activities.

After coming to power in 1978, Maumood Abdul Gayoom gave
public life in the Maldive Islands a new Islamic tone. A scholar of
Islam who studied in Cairo and taught in Nigeria, he has reversed
the secular policies of many decades; for example, he became the
first Maldive head of state in over eight centuries to lead the Islamic
prayers.[14]

When Ziaur Rahmān took over Bangladesh in 1975, he brought
an Islamic spirit to the government, and he talked of implementing

sharī^{c}a regulations. [15] In Malaya, large numbers of dakwah groups
are urging Muslims to live by the sharī^{c}a. Potentially the most powerful of these groups is the Muslim Youth Movement of Malaya
founded in 1971 by Anwar Ibrāhīm. Legalism in Indonesia has made
progress during recent years, and Suharto's government has taken
steps to accommodate it (for example, banning gambling in Jakarta). [16]
Still, the activists have not begun to challenge the state's determinedly
secularist constitution.

Autonomism

Beginning again in the west, Qadhdhāfī's first priority on taking
power in Libya in 1969 was to rid his country of its U.S. and British
bases; they left a few short months later. Qadhdhāfī vehemently opposes any non-Muslim interference with Muslim sovereignty. Under
his leadership, Libya has become a powerful international agent of
Islamic autonomism. Muslin Brothers in Egypt have long been fearful of domination by non-Muslims both domestic and foreign. In the
late 1970s they advocated laws that prompted fears among the Coptic
(Christian) community and resulted, in part, in the deterioration of
Muslim-Christian relations. The Muslim Brothers also strongly opposed peace with Israel and U.S. military presence in Egypt. [17]
Civil war in Chad began in 1966 when Muslims of the north rebelled against the central government dominated by Christians and
animists of the south. This conflict became more complicated in
1972 as Libyan intervention altered the political divisions, blurring
the Muslim/non-Muslim conflict. By early 1981, Qadhdhāfī, in alliance with one group of Muslims, had achieved some control over
the whole country. Idi Amin's policies resulted in a surge of Muslim
activities in Uganda. He appointed an increasing number of Muslim
officials and Islamic cultural and social activities were enhanced. [18]
Ethiopia faces a Muslim rebellion in the Ogaden desert, populated by
Somali who want the region to become part of Somalia. Somalia in
turn claims the Ogaden and aids the insurgents fighting the Ethiopian
armed forces there.
Saudi Arabia's close ties to the West were attacked by the Mecca
besiegers; they and other autonomists reject a key U.S. role in the
country's finances and defense. Israel witnessed a rise of Islamic
sentiment both among its Arab citizens, those who have remained
since 1948, and the Arab population of the West Bank and Gaza. In
February 1981 Israeli authorities broke up a group of Israeli Arabs
operating within an autonomist Muslim ideology.
Bosnian Muslims in Yugoslavia expressed such interest in the
activities represented by Ayātollāh Khomeinī that President Tito

visited their region and warned of "severe measures" against any efforts to attain Islamic political goals.[19] Albanian Muslims living in
the Kosovo Province of Yugoslavia staged violent demonstrations in
early April 1981 demanding autonomy and even unity with Albania.
Relations between Turks and Greeks on Cyprus degenerated so badly
in the early 1970s that the Turks rebelled and (with help from the Republic of Turkey's army) won their own autonomy in 1974. Similarly,
in Lebanon, persistent Christian political superiority contributed to
the outbreak of civil war. The National Front, predominantly a Muslim organization, rebelled against the controlling Christians, which led
to a bloody civil war during 1975-77 and which is not yet entirely over.
Islamic groups in Syria intensified their antiregime activities in 1980,
and a civil war almost erupted in Aleppo. One target of the attacks
of the Muslim group was Soviet military advisers.

Although autonomist strains in the Iranian revolution are often
overlooked, they were as important to Khomeinī's ascendancy as legalism.[20] Khomeinī contended that the shah had occupied the throne
since 1953 at the pleasure of the United States, that he was a U.S.
puppet who had in effect placed Iran under non-Muslim rule. Thus,
Khomeinī declared the shah to be a traitor to Islam, a claim that had
an important effect in galvanizing support for the revolution.

Reports about Muslim dissent in the Soviet Union are fragmen-
tary and inconclusive, but one finds indications of ferment even
there.[21] The 45 million Muslims under Soviet rule are the only large
Islamic population still part of a European state; eventually they will
awake to this fact. Reports about Islam's role in Iran have gotten
through, and, more important, hearing about Soviets killing Muslims
in Afghanistan spurred autonomist feelings.

Fighting in Afghanistan began as legalism in a struggle among
Afghans over the nature of their government. Since the Soviet intervention in December 1979, the conflict has increasingly pitted Muslim
autonomists against Soviets. Nearly all the Mujāhidīn groupings have
Islamic names. Since the war of 1971/72, Pakistan's dealings with
India have taken on a more Muslim tone. Within India, the Muslim
minority has grown more assertive and united;[22] especially since
1979 a string of riots has demonstrated the minority's unwillingness
to accede to Hindu interference. Most dramatically, in Kashmir, a
region claimed by both Pakistan and India, local Muslims in mid-
1980 for the first time publicly expressed their solidarity with Pakistan.

Burma has an embryonic Muslim autonomist organization in the
Royhingya Patriotic Front, disaffected Muslims pushed out of their
homeland. Thailand's Muslim minority in the far south has organized
several rebel groups, most notably the Pattani United Liberation Organization, which has been fighting the Buddhist-run central govern-

ment since 1975.[23] Likewise, Muslim groups on southern islands of
the Philippines, led by the Moro National Liberation Front, began
struggling in 1972 for autonomy, possibly independence.[24] Although
the Moros have won wide international Muslim support, they have extracted few concessions from the government of Ferdinand Marcos.

In Malaya, relations between the Muslim Malays and the non-
Muslims (mostly of Chinese origin, but including also Hindu Indians
and pagan tribesmen) have been tense since the communal rioting on
May 4, 1969.[25] In the subsequent decade many Muslim groups intent
on attaining unilateral Muslim control arose, but until now the United
Malay National Organization has continued to share political power
with Chinese and Indian parties.

Islamic feeling has also increased in countries far removed from
Islamic strongholds. Extreme legalism has developed among many of
the Turks living in West Germany (who for years have numbered more
than a million persons). German authorities are concerned about
violence among them; already one Turkish leftist, a teacher, has been
murdered.[26] A community of Muslim converts is growing quickly in
South Korea, as evidenced by the building of mosques and the Korea
Islamic College. In the United States, an extremely varied Muslim
population (made up predominantly of blacks and South Asians) has
organized itself politically in recent years.

CAUSES OF THE RESURGENCE

What has influenced Muslims to turn increasingly to Islam as a
political bond and a social ideal? Despite innumerable newspaper
articles on this topic and a fair amount of scholarly interest, few
analyses have encompassed the whole Islamic resurgence; most look
only at individual countries. Valuable as these are, they do little to
explain currents found in the entire Muslim world. Just as the causes
of such international developments as terrorism or inflation cannot
be located without an encompassing view of politics and economics,
so an explanation of the international Islamic resurgence requires a
broad perspective. It is not enough to look for common elements in
disparate countries and combine them into a pattern. If any single
explanation can deal with the growth of Muslim feelings during the
1970s in such varied countries as Nigeria, Libya, and the Philippines,
it must touch on the Muslim world as a whole. The Islamic resurgence is more than the sum of events in individual countries. What
are the larger currents of change that affect these countries collectively?

The most widely credited explanation emphasizes the failure of
Western ideology. R. Hrair Dekmejian argues this persuasively in

"The Anatomy of Islamic Revival."[27] Muslims abandoned Islamic political customs and goals during the nineteenth and twentieth centuries, when the West enjoyed predominant power. More recently, however, not only has the West lost much of its old power, but Western ways have failed to provide Muslims with the fundamental needs of public life: political stability, social and economic justice, and military success.

> By the late 1960s due to the confluence of these catalytic factors a multi-dimensional crisis situation was engulfing the Arab and Islamic countries, which continues to dominate their social and political life today. . . . To confront the crisis situation, élites and counter-élites have proposed and often implemented a variety of approaches ranging from communist totalitarianism, to socialist-etatist, mixed capitalist and theocratic systems. Thus, the Islamic alternative and its variants constitute but one of these approaches to crisis management.[28]

In their search for solutions, leaders in Muslim countries have tried a wide variety of alternatives; Islam is just one of these—yet one with growing appeal. It offers clear and confident answers to the problems Muslims face most acutely. Thus, "to an increasing number of alienated Muslims, Islam does appear to provide a practical political alternative as well as a secure spiritual niche and psychological anchor in a turbulent world."[29]

While Dekmejian's argument has evident truth, it does not explain why Muslims have turned to Islam at this time. Have Western ideologies failed them worse than previously? Such an argument appears untenable: many Muslims are experiencing a surge of political power and wealth without precedent in modern history. While some countries experienced severe strains in the 1970s (for example, Somalia, Lebanon, Turkey, Iran, and Afghanistan), others have settled down after years of tumult (for example, Nigeria, the Sudan, Syria, Iraq, and Indonesia). Systematic compilations of political and social unrest show no notable increase in disruption after 1970.[30]

Perhaps, then, the passage of time has aggravated matters? Colonial rule in most Muslim countries ended between the end of World War II and 1961. Independent now for some decades, perhaps they have grown more impatient with the shortcomings of Western ideologies? But Muslim encounters with colonialism have no chronological pattern; some never fell under European rule (for example, Turkey, Iran, and Afghanistan), while others remain ruled by non-Muslims (especially in the Soviet Union). These variations are simply too wide to find a rhythm.

Some tie the Islamic resurgence to the Arab-Israeli conflict, the most visible Muslim autonomist cause of the past generation. Raphael Israeli argues that the soul-searching that followed the collapse of Arab armies in the June 1967 war and the subsequent attempt to Islamize the conflict by bringing in other Muslim countries (especially Turkey and Iran) gave impetus to "a renascent sense of an international Islamic identity."[31] A fire at the al-Aqsā mosque in August 1969 furthered this sense and led to the convening of the Islamic Conference a month later; this organization gave Islam an international voice. Then Muslim confidence, already gaining, soared in late 1973; Arab military success in crossing the Suez Canal, the sudden quadrupling of oil sale revenues, and the oil embargo combined to give the Muslims a sense of power without precedent in modern times. This is the point to emphasize: the many ramifications of the OPEC boom that began in late 1970 and that steadily continues.

SAUDI ARABIAN AND LIBYAN ACTIVITIES

Increases in the price of oil affect everyone, but virtually only Muslims profit from them. True, smaller oil booms are taking place in Aberdeen, Alberta, and Alaska. True, most Muslims pay high prices for their oil. Muslims, however, virtually monopolize the export of oil. The Organization of Petroleum Exporting Countries has 13 members, all but 2 of which (Venezuela and Equador) are ruled by Muslims. Eight are Muslim states of North Africa (Algeria and Libya) and the Persian Gulf (Saudi Arabia, Kuwait, Qatar, the United Arab Emirates, Iraq, and Iran); Indonesia has a 90 percent Muslim population; Nigeria, about half Muslim, had a Muslim president in 1980; and though Gabon's Muslim population is minuscule, its president converted to Islam in 1973. In addition, numerous other Muslim states (Tunisia, Egypt, Syria, Oman, Bahrain, Malaya, and Brunei) gain significantly from oil exports.

The boom in oil exports has, more than anything else, caused the recent Islamic resurgence. The controlling of oil has brought new wealth and power, greatly enhancing the Muslim self-image. For so long, Muslims were poor and weak; today, a highly visible portion of the Muslim world enjoys an unprecedented affluence and influence. Further, these massive infusions of oil wealth have deeply disrupted normal life, causing Muslims to turn to the familiar—Islam. These general developments have been discussed elsewhere;* this

---

*Principally in "'This World is Political!!' The Islamic Revival of the Seventies," Orbis 24 (1980): 17-39. Briefly, the OPEC boom

discussion focuses on one dimension of the oil boom: how two countries, Saudi Arabia and Libya, help Islamic causes in the Arab states.

These two countries each have a long heritage of Islamic political action. The Wahhābī movement of Arabia began in 1745; the Sanūsī movement reached Libya in 1841. Both contained powerful legalist and autonomist elements; indeed, the Wahhābīs were probably the most fanatic and influential legalists in the history of Islam. Although these movements lost their fervor with time, Arabians and Libyans are long used to exerting an influence on foreign Muslims disproportionate to their small numbers and simple cultures. Wahhābīs expanded from their small area in Najd to control the huge area of present-day Saudi Arabia; they have tried to push their vision of Islam on all other areas of the Arabian Peninsula and in the past even reached militarily into the Fertile Crescent. Sanūsīs did not view Libya as their only home and made efforts to expand to its south and west. Although Qadhdhāfī overthrew the Sanūsīs in 1969, Libya still strongly bears the impress of their influence.

Saudi Arabia and Libya have complex relations. Their foreign policies, which operate in Arab, Islamic, and international spheres, occasionally coincide, but usually they conflict. In intra-Arab politics, the two countries invariably disagree; while the Saudis seek Arab tranquility as the best guarantee of their own stability, Qadhdhāfī prods and disrupts, not fearful for his regime but aggressively taking the fight elsewhere.

On the international level, they are also at odds. The Saudi government has been aligned for decades with the United States; it claims communism is antithetical to Islam and views the United States as its best defense. Despite his own reservations about communists, Qadhdhāfī has received nearly unbounded political and military support from them; by 1975 Libya was cooperating closely with the Soviet Union. Both of these countries are important in the current plans of the superpowers. Saudi Arabia exports several times more oil than

---

led to an increase of Islamic action for the following reasons: (1) It reconfirmed the validity of the Islamic message, put in doubt for many by the Muslims' poverty and weakness in modern times; (2) it gave Saudi Arabia and Libya the means to pursue Islamic policies internationally; (3) it caused massive dislocation in many oil-exporting countries, causing Muslims to turn to something familiar and solid— Islam (in Iran, these developments led to Ayātollāh Khomeinī's rise to power, a further powerful stimulus for Islamic action internationally); and (4) by bestowing new importance on Muslims, oil wealth made the world far more aware of activities in Islamic countries—If it were not for oil, who would have heard of the Mecca siege in late 1979?

any other country, it has immense reserves, and it straddles several of the world's most vital regions. Libya too has a key location, near Europe, the Middle East, and Africa, with ports on the Mediterranean; the Soviet Union will probably depend heavily on it for logistic support in conflicts in any of these areas.

The two countries also approach Islamic causes differently, yet here they often work in tandem. Temperamental and ideological differences remain, but their goals are compatible: both fervently support legalist and autonomist movements. The Saudis usually aid governments and apply pressure on them to favor Islam; Qadhdhāfī generally supports Islamic groups in the opposition. Between the Saudi anvil and the Libyan hammer, many Muslim communities have moved perceptibly toward Islam.

Virtually every Arab state has been the object of intensive Saudi or Libyan interest. The following surveys their activities, from west to east, in member countries of the Arab League.[32]

Mauritania's turn toward Islamic law began with the fall of Mochtar Ould Daddah. Explaining that "the defense of Saudi Arabia begins at the shores of the Atlantic,"[33] the Saudi leadership had supported his military efforts in the Western Sahara, where Mauritania and Morocco were battling Algeria. The Saudis were also involved in numerous nonmilitary projects in Mauritania. But early in 1978 Saudi suspicions about the use of their funds led them to reduce their aid; by June of that year, Ould Daddah, fearful of the growing discontent among his military officers who were owed back pay, was desperately awaiting its full resumption. The money did finally arrive in the middle of July, but too late; Ould Daddah had been overthrown on the tenth.

During the final month of his rule, Ould Daddah made the sharī^ca the basis of Mauritanian law and declared that the country would soon become an Islamic republic. These were final, desperate attempts to extract money from his two major donors, Saudi Arabia and Libya. A leading Mauritanian official visited Tripoli the day these measures were announced.[34] The Saudi press announced these Mauritanian intentions with favorable comment.[35] Subsequent Mauritanian rulers carried these intentions through, still hoping they would win Saudi and Libyan funds. Sharī^ca courts of the Mālikī rite were established in May 1980,[36] and Islamic punishments of death and the cutting off of thieves' hands soon followed.[37]

Socialist secularism weakened in Algeria after 1974. Islamic symbols came to the forefront: Friday replaced Sunday as the day of rest, and the campaign to replace French signs with Arabic ones became government policy. Libyan influence was reported to be a factor behind these changes.[38] Tunisian Muslim Brethren (properly, the Movement for the Renewal of Islam) are thought to receive funds from both Saudi Arabia and Libya;[39] according to another report, however, they anathematize Qadhdhāfī, calling him an "atheist, a miscreant, an agent of communism, a traitor to the Prophet."[40]

In the first four years after he came to power, Qadhdhāfī did his best to cooperate with Egypt, hoping eventually to unify the two countries. A high point of Libyan involvement came in June 1973 when Qadhdhāfī made a remarkable 18-day visit to Egypt advocating a "cultural revolution" along lines announced just two months earlier for Libya. Fundamental to it was a new legal code based on the Quran. Qadhdhāfī's relations with Anwar al-Sadat, always shaky, broke down after the October 1973 war, when Sadat negotiated with Israel to disengage Egyptian and Israeli forces in Sinai. As their relations further degenerated, Qadhdhāfī used every means available to strike at Sadat's regime; in particular, he worked through extremist Muslim groups in Egypt.

He first called for revolution in Egypt in December 1973 and first attempted a coup there in April 1974. Libyan funds for the Islamic Liberation party, Muhammad's Youth, the Army of God, the Society for Holy War, and other groups soon flowed in. In 1977/78, 42 members of the last named were tried on grounds of attempting to overthrow the Egyptian government.

The Muslim Brethren, whose original home is Egypt, had been outlawed by Jamāl ᶜAbd al-Nasser in 1954. They won de facto recognition again under Sadat; to remain acceptable, they had to toe a moderate line. Still, reports circulate that they receive money from Libya as well as from Saudi Arabia. Figures are hard to come by, but the latter apparently gave the Muslim Brethren $100,000 in early 1979, ostensibly for building mosques.[41] Qadhdhāfī used the Muslim Brethren as a weapon against Sadat's government even though he had called for their arrest within Libya, regarding them as enemies of the state no better than "Communists, Marxists, atheists, . . . advocates of capitalism and those spreading propaganda for Western countries."[42]

When activist Muslim leaders in the Sudan (al-Sādiq al-Mahdī of the Umma party, Hasan al-Turābī of the Islamic Charter Front, and al-Sharīf al-Hindī of the Khatmīya) grouped together in 1972 to form the National Front, they had Saudi Arabia's encouragement, perhaps also its funds. Qadhdhāfī's aid soon followed; before long, most of the National Front was based in Libya. These groups made a dramatic attempt at a coup d'etat on July 2, 1976, and came close to succeeding. Qadhdhāfī's backing was revealed by a Libyan military plane circling the skies above Khartoum, carrying the coup's leaders, who tried—without success—to direct their forces on the ground. So many participants in the coup had received training in Libya and carried Libyan arms that Numayrī called it "the Libyan invasion."[43]

This event apparently convinced both Numayrī and the National Front leaders that they should end their antagonism; with active Saudi encouragement, they signed their agreement of National Reconciliation in July 1977. For Numayrī to allow the National Front leaders a role in his government was so striking a change in policy that many observers thought he was motivated, at least in part, by a desire to please the Saudis. If Saudi leaders brought old enemies together, Qadhdhāfī encouraged them to stay apart. While Mahdī returned to the Sudan in September 1977, Hindī remained in Libya, causing a split in the National Front. Relations between Libya and the Sudan subsequently warmed to the point that Qadhdhāfī agreed in September 1978 to close all remaining National Front camps in his country. But then Numayrī supported Sadat's peace initiative toward Israel, angering Qadhdhāfī and delaying implementation of this agreement until May 1979. Two years later the problems continue, and Numayrī still fears an activist Islamic rebellion sponsored by the Libyans.

National Front activities, which have dominated Sudanese politics since 1976, have been manipulated by both Saudi Arabia and Libya. Perhaps more than anywhere else, domestic politics in the Sudan have been determined by these two countries. It is noteworthy that the Saudis aided both the government and its strongest Islamic opposition during most of the 1970s, assuring them a powerful voice in Sudanese affairs. (They have wielded a similar dual influence in other Arab states, too, notably Egypt, Jordan, and Syria.)

As Somalia and Ethiopia shifted great-power alignments, Saudi Arabia hastened to welcome Somalia back into the fold of Islamic-oriented, anti-Soviet states. In return for Saudi munificence, cushioning the Soviet cutoff, President Siyād Barre deemphasized Marxist socialism and made gestures in favor of Islam. "If you read the Quran properly and believe in it, then you have to be socialist," he has said.[44] Although it has not activated sharīᶜa regulations, the government treats things Islamic with new respect (in contrast to 1975 when 10 religious leaders were executed by firing squad). Somali efforts to take over the Ogaden also won Saudi support.

In Saudi Arabia itself, the single activist Islamic movement against the government apparently had Libyan backing. The two Libyans who took part in the Mecca mosque attack in November 1979 had connections to Qadhdhāfī's regime; much of the financing and gun-running for that escapade was reportedly arranged by Libya.[45] The Palestine Liberation Organization (PLO) is primarily a secular organization with leftist overtones, but its struggle against Israel embraces a basic component of the Muslim struggle against non-Muslim rule. Qadhdhāfī's strong antagonism toward Israel inspires him to support the most intransigent groups of the PLO. Palestinian radicalism distresses the Saudis, but they grant the PLO large sums in order to be left in peace. After 1967 most of the states bordering on Israel began to receive huge grants from the Arab oil producers, including Libya and Saudi Arabia.

Both countries aided the National Front in the Lebanese civil war between 1975 and 1977. Like the PLO, the National Front has no Islamic goals in its program, but in effect it fought for Muslim interests in Lebanon. Again Qadhdhāfī supported the group enthusiastically because of its radicalism; the Saudis did so despite this. Qadhdhāfī urged it to fight till victory; the Saudis arranged a peace settlement, which reduced the fighting.

Saudi aid to the Muslim Brethren of Syria helped propel them into a position from which they could threaten the regime of Hāfiz al-Asad. Although the Saudis provide his government with about $1 billion each year, they oppose many of his policies, especially his reliance on the Soviet Union. Funds to activist Muslims arrive through various means: the Muslim Brethren in Jordan (contributing to the tensions between Syria and Jordan, almost leading to war between the two countries in November 1980), Saudi-sponsored Islamic institutions (for example, the Muslim World League), and the Saudi ambassador in Beirut. This last in intriguing: the Organization of Muslim Officers was founded among members of the Syrian military serving in Lebanon who were displeased with their government's reliance on the Soviet Union; besides money, they apparently also receive false identity papers from the Saudi embassy. These they pass on to the Muslim Brethren within Syria. [46]

Perhaps foolishly, the Syrians antagonized Saudi leaders when the state-controlled press argued that the film Death of a Princess was much less anti-Islam than the Saudis claimed. [47] Saudi Arabia withdrew its ambassador from Damascus in protest and presumably increased its aid to the Muslim dissidents.

CONCLUSION

These Saudi and Libyan activities in Arab countries constitute only a small portion of the means by which the two countries exert international influence. Their pressure on the West with regard to the Arab-Israeli conflict has been widely noted, but their efforts on behalf of Islam go largely unremarked. Both countries have established extensive patronage networks that reach around the world and touch on many matters unrelated to Israel. Because Islam lies outside the usual concerns of journalists, political analysts, and government officials, these networks attract little attention—even now when one hears so much about Islam.

Just as the United States and the Soviet Union extend their influence through financial, cultural, and military means, so, too, do these Middle Eastern countries. Both great powers espouse a distinct world view (liberal capitalism, Marxist socialism); so, too, these states promote Islam. In country after country, they exert influence by adding their weight to activist Muslim movements. Though often working at cross-purposes, their effect is usually complementary.

Impressive as it appears today, however, Saudi and Libyan power is ephemeral. Neither country has a viable industrial base or the means to generate incomes internally; both depend entirely on wealth received from abroad. So long as the price and consumption of oil remain high, they will continue to enjoy wealth and power; but when energy needs change, the oil-based wealth that fuels so much of the Islamic resurgence will decline. Current waves of Islamic activism will die along with the OPEC boom. More than any other single factor, the oil market will determine how long the Islamic resurgence lasts.

NOTES

1. John L. Esposito, ed. , Islam and Development: Religion and Sociopolitical Change (Syracuse, N. Y. : Syracuse University Press, 1980), p. 87.

2. J. Harris Proctor, "Introduction," in Islam and International Relations, ed. J. Harris Proctor (London: Pall Mall, 1965), p. vii.

3. Cyriac K. Pullapilly, ed. , Islam in the Contemporary World (Notre Dame, Ind. : Cross Roads Press, 1980), includes articles on a dozen countries, but most of them are of poor quality; contributions by Ann Elizabeth Mayer and Nurcholish Madjid are exceptions. Esposito's Islam and Development covers seven countries. Michael Curtis, ed. , Religion and Politics in the Middle East (Boulder, Colo.: Westview, 1981), covers 10 Muslim countries and Israel.

4. Lucy C. Behrman, "Muslim Politics and Development in Senegal," Journal of Modern African Politics 15 (1977): 261-77.

5. Jamil M. Abun-Nasr, "Islam und die algerische National-identität," Die Welt des Islams 18 (1978): 178-94; and Konrad Dilger, "Die Stärkung des islamischen Rechts in Afrika," Die Welt des Islams 18 (1978): 155-62.

6. H. Breton, "Les fondaments de l'idéologie du colonel Mouammar El-Kadhafi," Maghreb-Machrek 62 (1974): 231-41.

7. Dilger, "Die Stärkung," p. 154.

8. Israel Altman, "Islamic Movements in Egypt," Jerusalem Quarterly 10 (1979): 87-105; Isabella Camera d'Afflitto, "At-Takfīr wa al-Higrah e l'intergralismo musulmano in Egitto," Oriente moderno 58 (1978): 145-53; Fadwa El Guindi, "Religious Revival and

Islamic Survival in Egypt," International Insight, May-June 1980, pp. 6-10; Emmanuel Sivan, "How Fares Islam?" Jerusalem Quarterly 13 (1979): 33-46; Saad Eddin Ibrahim, "Anatomy of Egypt's Militant Islamic Groups," International Journal of Middle East Studies 12 (1980): 423-53; and Nazih N. M. Ayubi, "The Political Revival of Islam: The Case of Egypt," International Journal of Middle East Studies 12 (1980): 481-99.

   9. Dilger, "Die Stärkung," pp. 162-77; John Voll, "Islam: Its Future in the Sudan," Muslim World 63 (1973): 280-95; and Gabriel R. Warburg, "Islam in Sudanese Politics," Jerusalem Quarterly 13 (1979): 47-61.

   10. Economist, April 25, 1981.

   11. Jacob M. Landau, "The National Salvation Party in Turkey," Asian and African Studies 11 (1976): 1-57.

   12. For a discussion of this experience, see Shahrough Skhavi, Religion and Politics in Contemporary Iran (Albany, N.Y.: SUNY Press, 1980).

   13. Detlev Khalid, "The Final Replacement of Parliamentary Democracy by the 'Islamic System' in Pakistan," Orient (Hamburg) 20 (1979): 16-38.

   14. Far Eastern Economic Review, December 1, 1978.

   15. Joseph T. O'Connell, "Dilemmas of Secularism in Bangladesh," Journal of Asian and African Studies 11 (1976): 64-81; David Pearl, "Bangladesh: Islamic Laws in a Secular State," South Asia Review 8 (1974-75): 31-41; and Henrich von Stietencron, "Zur Rolle der Religion in der pakistanischen Staatskrise 1970/71," Internationales Asienforum 4 (1972): 332-41.

   16. B. J. Boland, "Discussion on Islam in Indonesia Today," in Studies on Islam (Amsterdam: North Holland Press, 1974); Theodoric Dom, "Islam, Politik und Modernisierung in Indonesien," Internationales Asienforum 4 (1972): 97-109; and Sidney R. Jones, "'It Can't Happen Here': A Post-Khomeini Look at Indonesian Islam," Asian Survey 20 (1980): 311-23.

   17. Dilger, "Die Stärkung," p. 154.

   18. In 1981 Amin predicted, "Uganda will be lost to Islam" unless he returned to power, New York Times, February 8, 1981.

   19. Christian Science Monitor, December 28, 1979.

   20. Skhavi, Religion and Politics.

   21. Alexandre Bennigsen and Chantal Lemercier-Quelquejay, "Muslim Religious Conservatism and Dissent in the USSR," Religion in Communist Lands 6 (1978): 153-61.

   22. Theodore P. Wright, Jr., "Muslims and the 1977 Indian Elections: A Watershed?" Asian Survey 19 (1977): 1207-20.

   23. Astri Suhrke, "Loyalists and Separatists: The Muslims in Southern Thailand," Asian Survey 19 (1977): 237-50.

24. T. J. S. George, Revolt in Mindanao: The Rise of Islam in Philippine Politics (Kuala Lumpur: Oxford University Press, 1980); Peter G. Gowing, "Muslim Filipinos between Integration and Secession," South East Asia Journal of Theology 14 (1973): 64-77; and Lela Garner Noble, "The Moro National Liberation Front in the Philippines," Pacific Affairs 49 (1976-77): 405-24.

25. Gordon P. Means, "Public Policy toward Religion in Malaysia," Pacific Affairs 51 (1978-79): 384-405.

26. New York Times, March 23, 1980.

27. R. Hrair Dekmejian, "The Anatomy of Islamic Revival: Legitimacy Crisis, Ethnic Conflict and the Search for Islamic Alternatives," Middle East Journal 34 (1980): 1-12.

28. Ibid., p. 8.

29. Ibid., p. 9.

30. These "political event data plots" have been published only up to 1972. Charles Lewis Taylor and Michael C. Hudson, World Handbook of Political and Social Indicators, 2d ed. (New Haven and London: Yale University Press, 1972).

31. Raphael Israeli, "The New Wave of Islam," International Journal 34 (1979): 369-90; the quotation is from p. 370. A similar argument, presented from the opposite political viewpoint, may be found in Yvonne Haddad, "The Arab-Israeli Wars, Nasserism, and the Affirmation of Islamic Identity," in Islam and Development, ed. Esposito, pp. 107-21.

32. I have covered Saudi and Libyan activities in other regions in "Muslims of South East Asia," 8 Days, July 5, 1980; and "Arab influences in South Asia," International Insight, May-June 1981, pp. 7-10. See also a general review of Qadhdhāfī's foreign involvements in "No One Likes the Colonel," American Spectator, March 1980, pp. 18-22.

33. Jeune Afrique, September 20, 1980.

34. Le monde, June 20, 1978.

35. Majallat Rābitat al-cĀlam al-Islāmī, October-November 1978.

36. Impact International, May 23, 1980.

37. Jeune Afrique, November 5, 1980. For readers' comments, see the letters in the February 18, 1981, issue.

38. Ibid., May 10, 1978.

39. Le monde, September 15, 1977.

40. Jeune Afrique, March 28, 1979.

41. Afrique-Asie, March 15-18, 1979.

42. Africa Contemporary Record, 1973, p. 57.

43. Middle East Contemporary Survey, 1976-77, pp. 587, 597.

44. Arab Report, July 18, 1979.

45. Newsweek, December 24, 1979.

46. Jeune Afrique, April 23, 1980; and Atlanta Constitution, April 1980.

47. Economist, May 31, 1980.

3

INDIVIDUAL IDENTITY, GROUP DYNAMICS, AND ISLAMIC RESURGENCE

ISMAIL SERAGELDIN

The Arab world today is in the throes of a major, though subtle, upheaval. Everywhere, in every Arab country, a rekindling of interest in religion and religious affairs is noticeable. In some cases this takes the form of the resurgence of militant political Islamic fundamentalism.* In other cases, it takes the form of overt zealotry and adherence to patterns of ritual, dress, and behavior associated with medieval Muslim societies, even when many of these patterns of behavior contain little if anything that is inherently Islamic. Examples of this behavior would be the growing of beards (inspired by prophetic lore), the wearing of certain clothes among women,† and even the refusal of some of the more fervent young zealots to sleep on beds.

---

*The term <u>Islamic fundamentalism</u> is here employed to designate a body of beliefs (or a core ideology) prevalent among many Muslims in the Arab world today, which tends to oppose "Westernization," generally, and "the revisionism of the moderns" in Islamic theology. It tends to adhere to literal textual interpretations and favors following the rulings of the older scholars, al-salaf. This use of the word <u>fundamentalism</u>, therefore, should not be confused with the emphasis on fundamentals of Islam, which, in the author's judgment, do not in any way contradict the dictates of change.

†It is worth noting that the injunction requiring women to wear certain clothes appears in the Quran only in 24:31 and 33:59 and dictates nothing more than what a chaste woman in any society would do

---

The views and interpretations expressed in this chapter are those of the author alone and should not be attributed to the World Bank or any of its affiliated organizations.

Thus, the phenomenon of Islamic resurgence is widespread and deserves analysis. It is the thesis of this chapter that the observed phenomena are the result of a search for identity among large segments of society, primarily those that have been buffeted by the accelerating pace of social change; that this anomie is intrinsic to the pattern of social change that has been taking place in the Arab world;* and that group dynamics tend to reinforce both the alienation and the observed pattern of response.

Accordingly, this chapter describes a model of social change that is adequate to explain the observed phenomena, demonstrates how group dynamics tend to strengthen rather than weaken the patterns of individual and social behavior inherent in the model, and suggests some ways this model of social change could be altered so that its consequent social and individual patterns of behavior would be more harmonious for both individuals and groups in this rapidly changing society.

Some caveats, however, have to be stated at the outset. This chapter is an attempt to raise questions and, it is hoped, to give a few insights into a very complex problem. The analysis and discussion have been consciously confined to a sociocultural perspective. This is in no way meant to belittle the importance of economic, political, historical, or other relevant factors, but to limit the analysis to manageable proportions. Furthermore, the chapter is not intended to be a treatise and presents neither a detailed "tested" model nor a lengthy or cogent review of the pertinent literature. Rather, it is hoped that the broad-brush approach adopted here will help provide a unifying explanatory framework for the diverse component parts of the phenomenon.

(clothes should not be too tight, cleavage should be covered, and the like). The instructions to keep a veil or barrier between men and women (Quran 33:55) were specific to the wives of the Prophet, whose position in Muslim society has always been recognized as different (Quran 33:32). This question, however, has aroused strong feelings on both sides of the issue and has taken a disproportionately prominent role in contemporary discussions of Islam, tradition, and modernization. For a more conservative interpretation of the subject, the reader is referred to, inter alia, Muhammad Nasīr al-Dīn al-Albānī, Hijāb al-Mar'a al-Muslima [The veiling of the Muslim women] (Cairo: Dār Murgān li' l-Tibāᶜa, 1978); and Al-Sayyid Sabiq, Fiqh al-sunna [The jurisprudence of the Sunna] (Beirut: Dār al-kitāb al-ᶜarabī, 1971), 3: 475–97.

*Anomie is defined as a state in which normative standards of conduct and belief are weak or lacking and is commonly characterized by disorientation, anxiety, and isolation.

SOCIAL CHANGE

    The model outlined below is intended to describe the process
of social change and its cultural ramifications among Arab Muslims.
No claims are made for its applicability to other groups, nor is the
question of the relation between the Arab Muslims and non-Muslim
Arabs addressed. This limitation is important for it highlights the
cultural underpinning of this model of social change. In this respect
it differs markedly from both generalized models of social change[1]
and general theories of cultural evolution.[2] Nevertheless, it appears
adequate to explain the phenomenon of changing, evolving Islamic
consciousness among today's Arabs. The proposed three-tiered
model[3] is summarized in Figure 1.
    The figure shows three levels at which the Islamic conscious-
ness operates. The highest, theoretical ethics, refers to the accurate

FIGURE 1

Three Levels of Islamic Consciousness

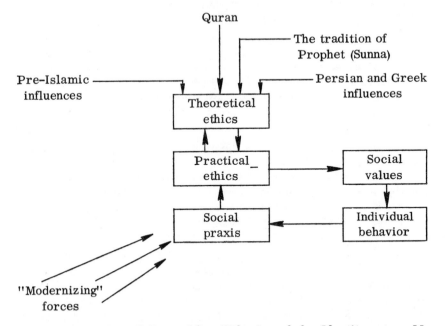

Source: Ismail Serageldin, "The Search for Identity among Muslim Youth: The Case of the UAR," in Non-Aligned Third World Annual 1970 (St. Louis, Mo.: Books International of DH-TE International, 1970), p. 246.

interpretation of Islamic teachings derived from the Quran, the tradition of the Prophet (Sunna), and the accumulated wisdom of previous scholars, in that order. This set of ethical values was therefore affected by Persian, Greek, and pre-Islamic Arab influences, but the Quran's influence remained paramount. This level, at which only the ^culamā' (religious scholars) and a few intellectuals operate, is not accurately perceived by the masses who embrace the Islamic world view. They see a distorted version of these ethics, mixing them with local lore, fetishism, obscurantism,* and local traditions that have survived from pre-Islamic days. This is the second level, called practical ethics, which defines the social values of the group. These values in turn determine individual behavior, which, when collectivized, is what can be termed social praxis, or loosely speaking, what people do in everyday life.

Social praxis, however, has a dialectic relationship to practical ethics, since a large part of practical ethics is derived from the existing social norms and beliefs; hence, they interact and the cycle is completed except for one more connection. The ^culamā' and the intellectuals operating at the highest level, theoretical ethics, tend to notice new developments at the lower levels if these persist long enough. Sometimes this notice is translated into action, developing the theoretical ethics further to deal with a new situation. †

---

*Perhaps no other religion has so vehemently opposed obscurantism as Islam. The appeal to reason and the urging of the faithful to study and learn are overwhelming. See, for example, ^cAbd al-^cAzīz Kāmil, Al-Islām wa'l-^cilm [Islam and science] (Cairo: Arab Socialist Union, n.d.), pp. 7-24.

†The most striking, and inspiring, examples of the adaptation of theoretical ethics to changing circumstances occurred in the reign of ^cUmar Ibn al-Khāttab, second caliph of Islam (634-44 A.D.), when the Muslim state grew into a far-flung empire with a wide mix of peoples. Milestone rulings included changing the rules governing property and the rights of conquest by refusing to distribute lands of the northern states among Muslims and refusing to pay alms to "those whose hearts have been (recently) reconciled" (a reference to non-Muslims who were generally sympathetic to Muslims and who had a right to alms from the Muslim state) even though it is stated in the Quran (9:60) and affirmed by the tradition of the Prophet. For an interesting discussion of the legal and philosophical questions involved, see M. Abū-Zahra, al-Takāfful al-^cijt imā^cī fī'l-Islām [Social solidarity in Islam] (Kuwait: Dār al-fikr al-^carabī, n.d.), pp. 36-37. More recent examples are the present-day efforts to establish Islamic banks, substituting equity financing for interest-bearing loans

The majority of the population is limited to the social praxis level of the schema. It is in that everyday life that they perceive the influence of the "modernizing forces."* The ethical constructs of the ᶜulamā' at the highest level have little bearing on their problems, while the distorted version seen in the practical ethics is incapable of holding their respect or of inspiring their actions and behavior.†

Many authors have commented on the two upper levels of the schema, frequently referring to them as "elite Islam" and "folk Islam."[4] Thus, in a review of the anthropological literature on Islam, el-Zein observes, "In spite of their differences, all positions approach Islam as an isolable and bounded domain of meaningful phenomena inherently distinct both from other cultural forms such as social relations or economic systems and from other religions. Within the domain of Islam, they also construct an internal dichotomy between local or folk Islam and the Islam of the elite, or ᶜulamā'. However, the criteria of distinction differ in order to serve each view of reality, history, and meaning."[5]

---

and exploring alternative means of risk sharing to avoid conflicts with usury rulings in the sharīᶜa.

*The debate about the equation of modernization and Westernization is not particularly relevant here. It is evident that in the case under consideration the two terms could be used synonymously. For a discussion of this question, the reader is referred to Cyril Black, The Dynamics of Modernization (New York: Harper & Row, 1966), p. 17; he presents a viewpoint that attempts not to equate modernization and Westernization: "If a definition is necessary, 'modernization' may be defined as the process by which historically evolved institutions are adapted to the rapidly changing functions that reflect the unprecedented increase in man's knowledge, permitting control over his environment that accompanied the scientific revolution." An opposite viewpoint is provided by S. N. Eisenstadt: "Historically, modernization is the process of change toward those types of social, economic and political systems that have developed in western Europe and North America." See Modernization: Protest and Change (Englewood Cliffs, N. J.: Prentice-Hall, 1966), p. 1.

†Gunnar Myrdal's statement regarding religion in South Asia complements this statement: "Religion usually acts as a tremendous force for social inertia. The writer knows of no instance in present-day South Asia where religion has induced social change. Least of all does it foster realization of the modernization ideals—though, of course, appeals to religious principles on the 'higher' level can be used for, as well as against those ideals." See Asian Drama: An Inquiry into the Poverty of Nations (New York: Random House, Pantheon, 1968), p. 103.

This three-tiered model will be a useful background for the ensuing discussion. Remember that though the ᶜulamā' and scholars operate only at the uppermost tier of theoretical ethics, the decision makers, bureaucrats, and planners, who have such a strong impact on the daily lives of people in the Arab societies of today, operate basically within the sphere of social praxis. Social values and behavior, however, are directly governed by the middle tier of practical ethics, where neither scholars nor planners and bureaucrats operate. Conceptually, this would not be a major problem if the modernizing influences (including the result of the work of the planners and bureaucrats) and the proclamations of the scholars were all pulling in the same direction. Change would be natural, endogenous to the system, and the system would be in harmony. This, however, is not the case. The modernizing forces are increasingly alien to the system. They increasingly pull the social praxis further away from the ethical superstructure and create a wrenching disorientation and anomie among the population.

From this brief description, two major questions emerge: Is this process a continuous one, and, if it is continuous, is it of an oscillating or linear nature? and How is the "strain" between the ethical superstructure and social praxis, which is inherent in the model, resolved?

Here one treads on fairly thin ice. Nevertheless, one can venture to say that change in any social system today has to be a continuous phenomenon.

That the process is one of cumulative additions that ultimately "break" the system's tolerance, thereby creating specific discontinuities, is one possibility. [6] A more likely model is that there is a general axis of cultural development that governs the process of change described here. The axis can be bent, but it cannot be broken. When either the elite of a society (in a top-down perspective) or the social praxis of the masses (in a bottom-up perspective) [7] strays too far from this axis of development, they generate opposition groups that, through pressure or confrontation, manage to pull the overall pattern of development back toward the axis, which may have been substantially bent in the process. This view of a continuous, oscillating pattern of development around a general development path is consistent with the observed cyclical nature of some movements and forms of cultural expression.

Clearly, the inherent stress in Figure 2 is due to (1) the fact that the modernizing forces act only at the social praxis level and (2) the weakness of the bottom-up channels. The inherent stresses and strains are partly resolved by the perceived oscillation, which represents shifts in public perception and mood, indicating cyclical responses of Muslim Arab societies in the face of the accelerating social

FIGURE 2

Some Possible Patterns of Development

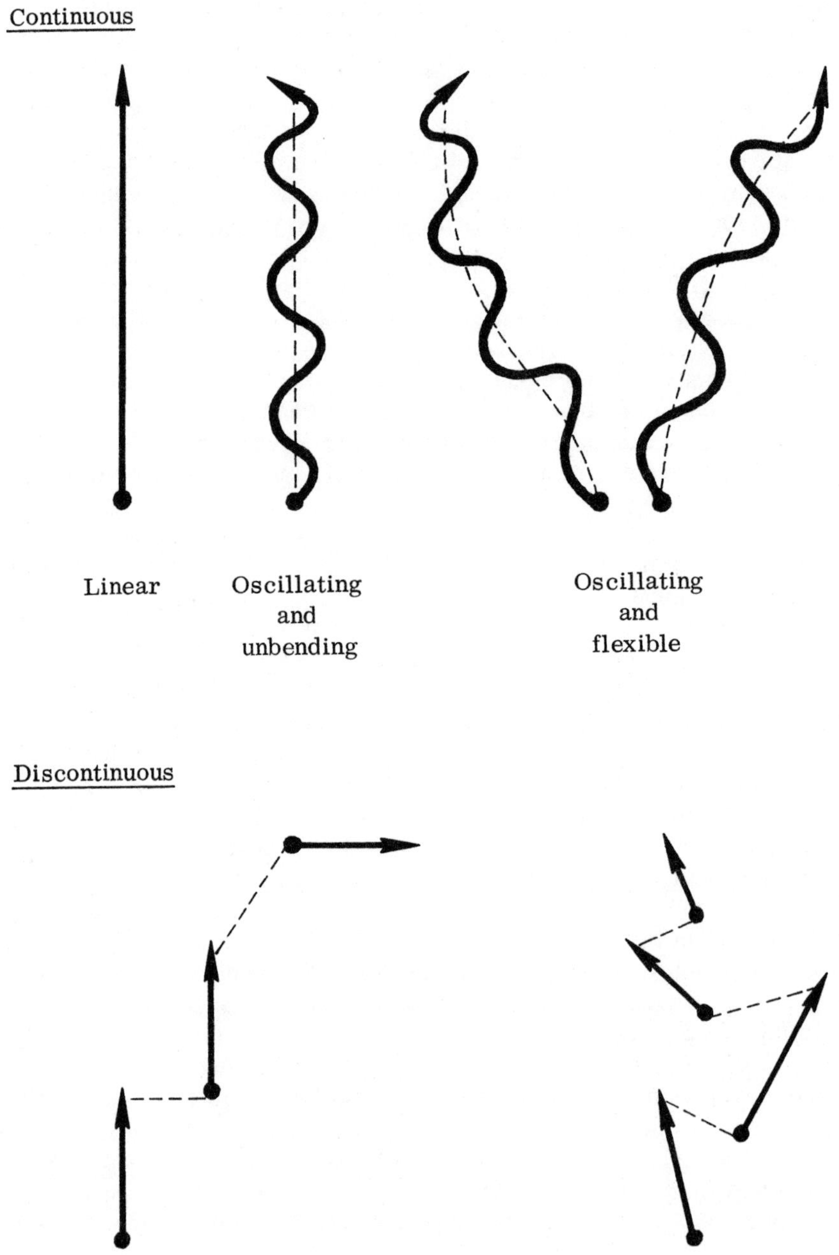

<u>Continuous</u>

Linear	Oscillating and unbending		Oscillating and flexible

<u>Discontinuous</u>

change that has been the hallmark of the post–World War II world. Oscillation alone, however, would be inadequate to account for the deep–rooted processes of adaptation that have taken place, such as the changes in patterns of family structure in response to increased participation of women in the labor force, increased mobility, international migration of young wage earners, and the like. These significant changes are the result of cumulative effects that shift or bend the presumed growth path away from a direct linear projection of past trends.

This perception of the growth path being somehow malleable is appealing insofar as it allows the interaction of diverse factions and views to have a clear resultant impact rather than assuming that oscillations all cancel out. It also allows particularly strong movements, whether self-generating or reactive, to have the ability to redirect the orientation of societal change. Both of these aspects seem to be more realistic interpretations of observed societal behavior in Muslim socities. The explanatory power of the schema is thereby enhanced. Its apparent instability (inherent stress) is containable and does not lead to explosion or breakdown except in extreme cases where all upward channels break down.

GROUP DYNAMICS

One of the prime tenets of Islam is that there exists a community of Muslims that has its distinct identity and function in the world order. * Individual Muslims are exhorted to maintain their membership in the group and adhere to the laws of God. † Islamic liturgy reinforces this communal spirit through group prayer and common experiential observances, which find their highest and most dramatic expression in the pilgrimage to Mecca. ‡ The tradition of the Prophet is replete

---

*"Thus have we made of you an Umma (nation) justly balanced, that ye might be witnesses over the nations" (Quran 2:143). Also, it was the first statement by the Prophet to the believers in the Constitution of Medina. See M. Hamidullah, Majmūᶜāt al-wathā'iq al-siyāsīya li 'l-ᶜahd al-nabawī wa'l-khilāfa [The collection of the political documents of the Period of the Prophet and Orthodox Caliphs] (Beirut: Dār al-irshād, 1969), pp. 39–47.

†"And hold fast, All together, by the Rope which God (stretches out for you) and be not divided among yourselves" (Quran 3:103).

‡Hajj is one of the five pillars of Islam and is a unique phenomenon: millions of believers, who are equated physically by their pilgrims' robes, are joined in prayer and ritual. Much has been written

with examples reaffirming this central theme of Islamic doctrine and exhortations to do so by word and deed.* Individual meditation is invariably subjugated to social interaction for the benefit of the Islamic community.†

If one addresses some of the other components of the cultural background of Middle Eastern Muslims, such as Arab cultural history of the peasant society of rural Egypt, one finds traits that tend to reaffirm individual identification with a group. Arab society emphasizes tribal and communal ties,‡ while rural societies, although identifying with a larger whole, have strong traditions of localized geographic identification. [8]

Reared in that background, a young Arab Muslim cannot easily accept an individualistic role in an atomistic societal setting. When confronted with situations that tend to push in that direction, such as urbanization, migration, sexual liberation, and the like, contemporary Muslim society tends to generate strong reactive movements that seek, though frequently fail, to stop such trends, if not reverse them, or at least to safeguard the faithful from perdition in the pursuit of these new models of social and individual behavior.

In such circumstances, it is not surprising to find that Muslims tend to seek psychological security in group membership. It is also not unexpected that when values are buffeted by change, the most common type of group to fulfill this function is religious in character, such as Sūfī orders# or other, more politically charged, forms of

---

on the value of this awesome experience. The reader is referred, inter alia, to S. Sābiq, Fiqh al-sunna [The jurisprudence of the Sunna] (Beirut: Dār al-kitāb al-ᶜarabī, 1971), 1: 625-29.

*Upon arriving in Yathrib (Medina) after the Hijra, the Prophet made brothers of the Meccans (Muhājirūn) and the Yathribites (Ansār) and emphasized the oneness of the Muslim community. This is also specifically reflected in the Prophet's "constitution of Medina."

†The Prophet is quoted as saying, "To go and help a fellow believer in a matter of need is preferable to spending a month in meditation in the mosque."

‡From pre-Islamic days to the classic age, the influence of ᶜasabīya was predominant in Arab interpersonal relations. In contemporary society, tribalism is still influential in parts of the Arab world, especially the peninsula. It finds its purest expression among nomadic and seminomadic groups, whose life-style is described in W. B. Fisher, The Middle East (London: Methuen, 1963), pp. 122-29. Revolutionary movements have made conscious attempts to destroy tribalism. These are reported on in F. Halliday, Arabia without Sultans (New York: Vintage, 1974).

#In a recent study of rural Egypt, the following observation was made: "Voluntary associations do not seem to have active existence

group religious expression. These politically oriented movements tend to become extremist in character, inevitably coming to forcible confrontations with the established order. [9]

As group identity becomes more important than individual identity, it follows that as societal tensions increase in periods of upheaval or rapid change, such groups tend to affirm their identity and to emphasize their uniqueness. This tends to sharpen differences between groups, as each stakes out its position on relevant concerns of its actual and potential membership. Elsewhere, Dessouki has spelled out the reasons leading to polarization and fundamentalism in the shaken Arab world of today. [10] He sees the resurgence of Islamic fundamentalist movements in Egypt as a natural reaction to the need for an easily understood message that provides a total view of the universe and supplies in a simplistic formula ready answers to all the problems facing society and individuals. [11] In terms of this analysis, the failure of practical ethics creates the vacuum that such a message seeks to fill. Hence, it can be said that the tendency toward polarization and absolutism in today's Muslim society reinforces the strain inherent in the model of social change presented here.

THE FUTURE

The preceding discussion leads to an unambiguous conclusion. The key to defusing the inherent stresses lies in ensuring that modernizing forces are introduced into the schema at the top (theoretical ethics), as well as at the bottom (social praxis), and in attacking the present rigidity of the middle level (practical ethics).

If these goals were realized, change would be less likely to lead to strain, and the amplitude of the oscillations would be greatly reduced, allowing for a smoother path of sociocultural development. To achieve this, a three-pronged agenda for action is proposed.

1. Intellectuals must be concerned with both temporal and spiritual problems. Religious culamā' and secular scholars and scientists must jointly work at providing a framework for thought that es-

---

in the villages. The main form of these groups is Sūfī orders, which exist in almost every village though on a small scale and with varying degrees of following. The newly born political parties (since 1977) have not created an impact on these villages yet." See A. Kamal, A. Dessouki, and I. de Sola Poole, "Communication System in Rural Egypt," Communication Needs for Rural Development Research Project, Report no. 11 (Cairo University/Massachusetts Institute of Technology, 1980), p. 62, mimeographed.

chews absolutist dogmas of atheistic or deistic persuasions. A courageous attack on the distortions of practical ethics must be accompanied by the provision for relevant alternatives that respond adequately to the psychological and sociocultural needs of a public faced with rapid change.

2. Practitioners who participate in making the day-to-day decisions that govern society's functions should be sensitized to the cumulative effect of their decisions and the need to keep the overall picture in mind at all times. This will necessitate a different type of training for the practitioners of tomorrow and a heightened awareness among those of today.

3. Communicators must see that communications are increased at all levels and in all directions; in particular, they should strengthen horizontal and bottom-up communications, not just enhance the leadership's ability to send its top-down messages to the broad base of the public at large.

The future will undoubtedly continue to be shaped by the interaction of competing views and conflicting perceptions of what was, is, and ought to be. Yet such dynamics are an integral part of the healthy process of adaptation and change that is the heart of any live social order. What Muslims can and should do is to internalize the process of change so that essential values and identity are not threatened by such adaptation. It is worthy of note that Islam, both as a social order and as a cultural system, lends itself admirably to this adaptive process. The faithful are urged to seek knowledge through reason and to innovate.* The Prophet has clearly indicated that in temporal matters, the Muslim community should find the most effective solutions,[12] provided these solutions do not counter the central tenets of God's injunctions. Such a mandate is surely broad enough to enable Muslims to face up to the challenges of the fifteenth century of Islam, while retaining the harmony and self-assurance that were the hallmarks of the Muslim identity at the time of its greatest sociocultural expression.

---

*The Islamic emphasis on knowledge cannot be overstated. The word ^{c}ilm and its derivatives appear 880 times in the Quran. The Prophet exhorted the believers to "seek knowledge even in China."

Reason (^{c}aql) is frequently mentioned as the attribute of the believers in the Quran. This is not to be confused with the act of faith, which transcends reason, as mentioned in verse 2:3 of the Quran.

Ijtihād has been the hallmark of Islam's greatest rulers. The Prophet strongly urged Mu^{c}adh Ibn Jabal to do so when he sent him to Yemen. ^{c}Umar Ibn al-Khāttab, arguably Islam's greatest ruler, was one of the greatest legislative innovators. See, inter alia, M. Haykal, al-Fāruq ^{c}Umar [Umar the Just] (Cairo: Maktabat al-nahda, 1964), 2: 273-302.

NOTES

1. For a superb, pithy review of at least four such theories, the reader is referred to John McLeish, The Theory of Social Change: Four Views Considered (London: Routledge and Kegan Paul, 1969). A recent and quite original viewpoint is given in Ralf Dahrendorf, Life Chances (Chicago: University of Chicago Press, 1980). This latter will probably prove to be a seminal work.

2. Examples of this viewpoint would be the works of Arnold Toynbee and Oswald Spengler. Lesser known examples would include the work of their nineteenth-century predecessor Nikolai Danilevsky, who wrote of civilizations as the real units of historical study (cited in J. G. de Beus, The Future of the West [London: Evre and Spotts-Woode, 1953], pp. 10-6).

3. This model was first developed some ten years ago. See Ismail Serageldin, "The Search for Identity among Muslim Youth: The Case of the UAR," Non-Aligned Third World Annual 1970 (St. Louis: Books International of DH-TE International, 1970), pp. 245-51. My thinking about such a model was triggered by M. Rodinson, "Muslim Ethics and Economic Development" (Paper presented at Harvard University Center for Middle Eastern Studies colloquium, Cambridge, Mass., February 1968).

4. For an excellent overview of the general literature on the subject, the reader is referred to Abdul-Hamid el-Zein, "Beyond Ideology and Theology: The Search for an Anthropology of Islam," Annual Review of Anthropology 6 (1977): 227-54. El-Zein reviews in detail the work of five authors (Geertz, Crapanzano, Gilsenan, Bujra, and Eickleman) whom he considers representative of the variation in viewpoints among authors writing from an anthropological perspective.

5. Ibid., p. 241. In fairness it should be stated that el-Zein personally does not espouse this approach. The dichotomy of folk Islam/elite Islam is infertile and fruitless. As I have tried to show, the apparent dichotomy can be analytically reduced to the logic governing it (p. 252). I believe, however, that the three-tiered model is useful.

6. For an example of this viewpoint, see E. A. Tiryakian, "A Model of Societal Change and Its Lead Indicators," in The Study of Total Society, ed. S. K. Klausner (New York: Praeger, 1967), pp. 69-97. It is interesting to note that in this paper, Tiryakian presents a conceptual dualism opposing a physical secular world to a spiritual one. His image combines the individual's religious experience and the institutionalized religious culture of the society.

7. This viewpoint of a bottom-up pattern of change and development is shared by a number of distinguished writers, for example, A. Kamal, A. Dessouki, and I. de Sola Poole, "Communication System

in Rural Egypt," Communication Needs for Rural Development Research Project, Report no. 11 (Cairo University/Massachusetts Institute of Technology, 1980), pp. 1-68, mimeographed, where the authors explicitly state on p. 2, "There are perhaps two implicit assumptions in this paper. One is that development is not a top-down process, but a decentralized bottom-up process."

8. See Robert Redfield, Peasant Society and Culture (Chicago: University of Chicago Press, 1956); Henry H. Ayrout, The Egyptian Peasant (Boston: Beacon Press, 1963); and H. Ammar, Growing Up in an Egyptian Village (London: Routledge and Kegan Paul, 1954).

9. For an interesting review of the history of the Ikhwān, the most important such movement in recent times, see R. P. Mitchell, The Society of the Muslim Brothers (New York: Oxford University Press, 1969). More recent and excellent work has been done by Saad E. Ibrahim on more contemporary movements such as al Takfīr wa'l-Hijra group in Egypt; see his chapter in this volume.

10. Ali E. Hillal Dessouki, "Arab Intellectuals and Al-Nakba," Middle Eastern Studies 9 (1973): 187-95.

11. See A. E. H. Dessouki, "The Resurgence of Islamic Organizations in Egypt: An Interpretation," in Islam and Power, ed. A. C. Cudsi and Ali E. Hillal Dessouki (London: Croom Helm, forthcoming).

12. See Ibrāhīm Madkūr, Ahādith Ijtimaᶜīya wa thaqāfīya [Social and cultural discourses] (Cairo: Dar al-shurūq, 1981), pp. 97-102.

4

THE COMTEMPORARY RESURGENCE IN THE CONTEXT OF MODERN ISLAM

R. STEPHEN HUMPHREYS

The events of recent years have demonstrated anew how readily the religion of Islam can be transformed into a political ideology of enormous scope and force. Such a situation is hardly unexampled, of course; it has occurred countless times in the course of Islam's 14 centuries. Still, it is hard to think that a movement of this kind has ever been simultaneously so intense and widespread as is the case today. Moreover, even experienced students of the Muslim world have been surprised by the appeal of Islamic ideology to the technocratic elites—that is, to precisely those professionals, scientists, bureaucrats, and military officers whom it had been supposed were committed to one or another secular vision of society and for whom religion seemed at most a matter of personal belief and morality. In such circumstances, a review of two questions, long discussed but still hardly resolved, seems urgently called for: Under what circumstances and by what process do the symbols and doctrines of Islam come to form an ideology? In what ways is the current resurgence comparable to the religiopolitical movements of the Islamic past, especially those occurring between the late eighteenth and early twentieth centuries?

IDEOLOGY AND ISLAM

Our discussion will depend on two broad and often very vague concepts—"ideology" and "Islam"—and so we must begin with an attempt to define these. Ideology is an elusive and abstract concept at best. Following the etymology of the term, we might start by saying that an ideology is a rational statement of ideas about politics and society. We might also claim that some ideology is implicit in any sociopolitical order whatever. That is, in any social and political system there must necessarily be a general set of rules to govern the relations of its members with one another; the distribution of wealth, status, and power; and the degree and character of each person's participation in the making and execution of decisions that affect the system as a whole. Rules of this kind are expressed first of all in patterns of everyday conduct; but they are also expressed in formal ways, through myth, ritual, and ceremony. So long as these rules are left merely implicit and are not spelled out as formal, abstract propositions, we cannot speak of ideology in the full sense of the word. Ideology in the full sense requires that a person ask certain kinds of questions about the cultural patterns in terms of which he thinks and acts. Why do we perform this ritual or tell that story? What does it mean to the life of our society? What aspects of our society does it symbolize? Typically, this kind of questioning arises only when the established sociopolitical order can no longer be taken for granted—when its members (some of them, anyhow) find that its ways fail to satisfy their needs and aspirations, or when some outsider appears on the scene to demand explanations or to offer alternatives.

In short, ideology is a form of thought and expression that usually arises in sociopolitical environments that are perceived to be changing. In such situations, spokesmen for the established order must begin to formulate the reasons things are as they are. Since their statements are intended to provoke action and sentiment in defense of this order, they must try to explain why it is right and legitimate that things should be as they are. In contrast, dissenters are compelled to explain how the current order of things is wrong and how it must be reformed or transformed so as to create a rightful society and polity. It thus appears that ideology only exists in a dialectical context, in situations in which opposing visions of a rightful order of things are in competition with one another. On the other hand, for such a competition to be possible, the ideologies that crop up in any given milieu must all be commensurate on some level of value and conceptualization; that is, each ideology must use language that makes it comparable to the available alternatives. Thus, in the contemporary Middle East, Islamic fundamentalism, Marxism, and liberalism, insofar as they try to appeal to the same social and cultural groups, all tend to use a remarkably similar logic and address similar issues.

Because ideologies come into being as part of a struggle for very high stakes—namely the right to define the governing principles of society and politics—the proponents of each tend to be driven into more and more absolute claims for the rightness of their vision. This fact suggests two important characteristics of ideology in general. First, any ideology is almost invariably linked to a general interpretation of the cosmos, that is, it embodies postulates about whether the world is essentially material, spiritual, or dual in nature; whether it is controlled by pure chance, impersonal law, or the active intervention of a personal deity or deities; and so on. Second, ideologies are utopian; each one claims that the achieving of its program will establish the best social order of which man is capable, an order whose rightness will be self-evident to all its members. The utopian goal is often portrayed as the reestablishment of a once-existing-but-now-lost golden age, but sometimes it is seen as the realization of aspirations only adumbrated in the past. Some ideologies are millenarian; they aim at ushering in a final and changeless era in man's historical experience. Others are contingent, for they can be realized only for a fleeting moment under very specific and unsustainable circumstances. *

From what has been said, we can derive a general definition of ideology along the following lines: an ideology is a critique of a given sociopolitical order that simultaneously describes that order and calls upon its members either to defend and preserve it or to overthrow and transform it. An ideology is at once a description of society and a program of political action.

Because every ideology arises within a specific cultural setting and is intended to address the problems of that setting, it is obvious that its proponents would make maximum use of the most powerful symbols available to that culture. These symbols are quite consciously chosen as symbols, to represent and recall a whole body of ideas that have already been worked out in general language. The mass of those addressed by an ideology may not be able to articulate very effectively the concepts underlying its chosen symbols, but certainly their leaders can. Ideology is often regarded as crude and emotional, but that is so (if at all) only on the level of overt action. For those who are intimately concerned with it, it may be extremely subtle, complex, and sophisticated.

Like ideology, Islam can also be understood in terms of language. But while ideology is language defined by its structure and function, Islam is language defined by its subject matter. In the most general sense, we might think of Islam as a discourse on the Quran and the life of Muhammad. From this perspective, a Muslim is a person who engages in a dialogue with the word of God as given

---

*At this point, it should be noted that among the multitude of ideologies generated within the framework of Islamic religious thought, one can find examples of every type just noted except the purely materialist. Some sense of the range of possibilities will become apparent when we discuss the religiopolitical movements of the early modern period.

in the Quran and with the teaching and example of the Prophet (the Sunna) in order to shape his conduct, values, and beliefs. Such a dialogue is never the same for any two persons, because each individual brings to it his own set of questions, his own conceptual framework and experience, his own needs and hopes. But it is also true that while one feels his questions, needs, and the like to be an individual matter, they are in fact formed to a great degree by his social, political, and cultural situation. Thus many persons at a given time and place are likely to be participating in essentially the same dialogue. Moreover, no one begins this dialogue with the Quran and Sunna ex nihilo, as if for the first time. On the contrary, every individual and every group since the time of Muhammad himself have confronted the Quran and the life of the Prophet in a cultural milieu that offers one or several traditional systems for interpreting and applying them. Such traditional systems may be accepted as authoritative; they may be rejected as spurious and distorted, but they cannot be ignored; they are at least implicitly present in every dialogue.

The problem for us, in dealing with any action or statement identified as Islamic, is to ask what kind of dialogue with the Quran and Sunna it represents. What problems is this statement or action intended to address? In what ways are the Quran and the life of the Prophet felt both to pose a problem and to provide a solution to it? Are the Quran and Sunna confronted directly in this dialogue or are they mediated, perhaps very indirectly, through some interpretive tradition? This kind of approach allows the comparison of highly disparate statements and acts, because it relates them to a common referent. At the same time, it permits each separate statement or act to be dealt with as a unique entity, as an object of study in itself.

The ongoing discourse of Islam can, of course, serve many functions—ritual, theological, ethical, legal, and so on. But as we have already noted, this discourse often takes place in the field of social and political action, and then it becomes ideological. Indeed, ideology has been a salient feature of Islamic discourse almost from the beginning—certainly from that moment when the Prophet led his tiny band of followers to Medina to establish a new community. It is not disrespectful, I hope, to say that the Quran itself is in part an ideological statement. The Quran demands first of all obedience to God and His Messenger, and such obedience requires the believer to strive to realize God's will for man in this world to the fullest possible extent. In calling for belief, piety, moral conduct, and charity, the divine will no doubt pertains to the thought and action of individuals. On the other hand, a careful reading of the text shows that in the Quranic framework a truly godly life can be lived only within the context of a godly community. Not only individuals but whole peoples are called to salvation, and communities, like individuals, suffer the awful consequences of disobedience. Clearly Muhammad's career, so intensely devoted to the construction of a new society and polity, exemplifies the Quranic concept of God's will and man's duty.

It is thus evident that insofar as the Muslim tries to obey the divine command and to model his life on that of Muhammad, he must on some level commit himself to the jihād fī sabīl Allāh (struggle in the path of God). Serious-minded Muslims at least have always accepted this proposition, but they have been of many minds as to what actions such a commitment should entail. On the minimum level, almost all would agree that it requires one to fight to defend Muslim lands from infidel attack or domination. Within the Dār al-Islām, there is similar assent that the jihād imperative calls for "commanding the good and forbidding the evil" (al-amr bi al-ma^crūf wa al-nahy ^can al-munkar); for teaching, admonishing, and reprimanding. Muslims with a Sūfī orientation have held that the greatest jihād is within the believer himself, whose first struggle must be to purify his heart of all vain affection and worldly desire.

But should the Muslim take arms to expurge tyranny and corruption within his own community? On this point, opinion has been bitterly divided since the first generation of Islam. In most periods, at least in well-established Muslim communities, the majority sentiment has been that if the government in power is nominally a Muslim one, it should be submitted to, however corrupt and tyrannical it may be. Armed revolt against such a government is justifiable only when submission to its policies constrains the individual to disobey the divine commands of worship and personal morality. * But on occasion, there have been those individuals, small groups, or whole societies who have felt that the tyranny and corruption of their times had reached an intolerable level, that to permit them to continue would put the whole body of Muslims in imminent danger of divine retribution. In such circumstances, open rebellion was the plain duty of every serious Muslim; since this rebellion was to be conducted in the name of God and for the sake of religion, it followed that the existing religious system was also assailed as corrupt, degenerate, and filled with reprehensible innovations. Sometimes such rebellions had quite limited goals; they would be aimed at the removal of some specific grievance (such as a new tax, or too privileged a role in the government for non-Muslims), which was conceived of in Islamic terms. But sometimes they were radical and comprehensive and proposed nothing less than the restoration of the early Community of Muhammad in Medina or the ushering in of the Messianic kingdom of the Last

---

*This view is reflected in the chapters on government and the imāmate, the classical collections of hadīth.

Days. These radical movements have always been led by a leader who was charismatic in the strict sense of the word; that is, someone who could claim to be divinely authorized for the task.

RELIGIOPOLITICAL MOVEMENTS
IN EARLY MODERN TIMES

Between the middle of the eighteenth century and the outbreak of World War I, the ideological tendency in Islam found expression on several occasions, but three movements seem especially paradigmatic. That is, they show the crucial characteristics of specifically Islamic political action with great force and clarity; they have been widely regarded throughout the Muslim world as expressing values and goals for which all should strive; and they have served on some level as models for other Islamic movements. The movements in question are the Wahhābīya in the late eighteenth- and, after a long hiatus, early twentieth-century Arabia; the Sanūsīya in Libya, from its origins in the 1840s down to its bloody suppression by the Italians in 1931; and the Sudanese Mahdīya, short-lived but spectacular, from 1881 to 1898. These three movements are very close in time to us, and if we can define certain of their ideological characteristics (sociopolitical program, conception of leadership, social and cultural milieu, use of Islamic doctrines and symbols), we should gain some important perspectives on the current wave of Islamic activism in the Arab lands.

One should stress at the outset that these three movements are far from replicas of one another, though they are often referred to as if they were. On the contrary, each represents a very distinct "reading" of the Quran and the example of the Prophet. In their origins and throughout much of their history, the Wahhābīya and Mahdīya were intensely militant. They both overtly aimed at the forcible overthrow of societies and governments that they regarded as scandalously corrupt and heretical, and both proposed to replace these with a society and polity that would replicate as closely as possible the early community in Medina. Indeed, the leaders of both movements stressed the exact parallels between their missions and that of the Prophet, and both tried to model their policies and state building on His, even down to quite petty details.

Yet, even between these apparently similar movements there are crucial differences. In the first place, Al-Mahdī Muhammad Ahmad (1944-85), as his title would imply, clearly regarded himself not only as divinely called to his task of purification but also as divinely inspired (through the medium of dreams about the Prophet) throughout it. In contrast, Muhammad Ibn ^CAbd al-Wahhāb (1703-92) never claimed anything of the kind; his status was at most that of a mujaddid, a renewer and restorer of the faith, and he was only doing what every seriously committed Muslim ought to do in the circumstances of his time. The Mahdī's movement was openly messianic and eschatological; it was to establish the universal reign of justice and equity before the final struggle of the false Messiah (al-Dajjāl) against God and the Day of Judgment. Under his successor, the Khalīfa ᶜAbd Allāhi (reigned 1885-98), these expectations were dampened and ultimately extinguished, but millenarianism was an essential part of the Mahdīya's origins. The Wahhābī utopia, on the other hand, was contingent in character: the restoration of the early community was to be based strictly on just government and rigorous adherence to the Hanbalī interpretation of the sharīᶜa, and these things could be achieved and sustained only so long as there was a conscious will to do so among the community's military and religious chiefs.

Further, the Mahdī had been reared and trained in a Sūfī environment. The language of his preaching and doctrine is strongly Sūfī in tone and color, and his movement in at least its early phases was clearly organized in the manner of a Sūfī confraternity. Muhammad Ibn ᶜAbd al-Wahhāb was a sworn enemy of Sūfism and every other kind of heretical innovation in the pure faith of the early community; his movement was a revolt against precisely this aspect of life in Arabia and the Fertile Crescent. Ibn ᶜAbd al-Wahhāb was no doubt inspired by Ibn Taymīya, but Ibn Taymīya, the polemicist against Sūfī and Shiᶜite innovation, not Ibn Taymīya, the advocate of ijtihād (independent legal judgment); he was a strict traditionalist, who adhered to the legal and theological doctrines of Ibn Qudāma (d. 1223) and the other great spokesmen of the Hanbalī school.

Beyond these differences in doctrine and conception of leadership, there are also important differences in the social and political settings of the two movements. The Sudanese Mahdīya arose in a socially and ecologically very diverse region that included grassland, immense deserts, a fertile though narrow river basin, swamp, and jungle. The peoples who inhabited these areas and their ways of life were similarly disparate. Thus, one of the most difficult problems facing the movement throughout its existence was that of reconciling the often conflicting material needs and cultural outlooks of its members. The Wahhābīs had, in this regard, a far less difficult problem, though one would not want to underestimate the differences between life in the steppe, the oases of eastern Arabia, and the religious centers of the Hijāz; nor should one overlook the political fragmentation of tribal life. Still, the degree of ethnic and cultural homogeneity in Arabia was a crucial factor in the capacity of the Wahhābīya to sustain itself long after the deaths of its founders and even to return in full strength after a forcible break of three-quarters of a century.

Finally, the contrasting political milieus in which the Mahdīya and the Wahhābīya arose require attention. The corrupt and heretical government against which the Mahdī rebelled was not merely a Muslim regime gone astray; it had for many years employed European officials and agents in growing numbers. It was increasingly run according to European criteria, and by 1881 it was in fact the creature of a European power. In short, the Mahdist rebellion occurred within an imperialist context. As it happens, the Mahdī and his followers do not seem to have been very aware of imperialism; their jihād was against the godless and corrupt Turks (that is, the Khedivial government of Egypt), but plainly much of what they objected to was the result of infidel influence. The Wahhābī revolt of the eighteenth century, on the other hand, took place entirely within an Islamic political and administrative order; the Ottoman government was (or soon came to be) the principal enemy, and the Europeans were not yet a factor. In the Wahhābī revival at the beginning of this century, of course, the British were very present indeed in the coastlands of eastern Arabia. However, the movement was in no sense a rebellion against a threatened imperialist domination, and the Saudi government since the mid-1920s has consistently followed a policy of accommodation, first with Great Britain and then with the United States, even while attempting to maintain a strict Wahhābī regime internally.

In many respects, the Sanūsīya contrasts strikingly with the other two movements. Muhammad Ibn ᶜAlī al-Sanūsī (the Grand Sanusi) began his movement as a missionary effort among the half-Islamized bedouin of Cyrenaica and the deserts to the south. Its vast expansion throughout the eastern Sahara was based not at all on military force but on the saintly baraka (divinely bestowed blessing) of its founder and on the crucial judicial and political roles his missionaries were able to carve out for themselves among the tribes of this region. What the Sanūsīya created was not a state of the Mahdist or Wahhābī type, but rather an intricate and fundamentally voluntary network of trade routes and pasture rights coordinated by the Sanūsī sheikhs. The movement became a militant one only in its third generation, when it confronted a grave and immediate imperialist threat. For the Sanūsīya, imperialism was not an aspect of jihād but the essential cause of it. Moreover, when its members were compelled to turn their attention to the jihād, their original raison d'être of religious purification and education had in effect to be set aside. The doctrine of Muhammad Ibn ᶜAlī was, in the Libyan context, puritan but not radical. He was a Maghribī of sharifian lineage, and he was thoroughly educated both in the traditional religious sciences and in conservative Sūfism. Already a member of several orders, his approach to the bedouin of Cyrenaica was to found yet another one. Like the Mahdīya, his movement was thus a tarīqa (a brotherhood), but one of very sober character. He and his disciples did not combat the veneration of saints among the bedouin, but neither did they do anything to encourage extravagant ritual or superstition. The sobriety of the Sanūsīya and the cultural, ethnic, and ecological milieu within which it operated recall the Wahhābī movement to some degree, but it is set apart by three things at least: its Sūfism, its original lack of militance, and—perhaps most crucially—its steadfast refusal to link its fortunes to any one chiefly family, as Ibn ^CAbd al-Wahhāb had done with the Āl Saud.

It is easy to see how all these movements could be attractive as symbols and models to contemporary Muslims. First, all three of them demonstrate that Islam is a religion of action, not merely of words. Moreover, all three of them originated in the pursuit of social and political goals through religious revival; the two aspects seem to go hand in hand. Two of them at least (the Mahdīya and Sanūsīya) symbolize resistance to imperialism and foreign domination, and even the Wahhābīs could be taken to represent aspirations for Arab independence. To the dispirited generation of the decades before World War I in the metropolitan centers of the Arab world— Cairo, Beirut, Damascus, Baghdad—the energy and sense of commitment of these movements must have been deeply impressive. And even now, after so many years and so much disillusionment, their names and memories still have a certain resonance in the political rhetoric of the Arab countries.

Even so, however, none of these movements can provide a really adequate model for contemporary organizers of Islamic political movements in Egypt, Syria, or even Jordan. The Wahhābīya, Sanūsīya, and Mahdīya all arose in marginal areas of the Muslim world—in areas long since converted to Islam but far from the metropolitan centers of learning and populated by nomadic pastoralists whose knowledge of and concern for the sharī^Ca-minded religion of the towns was minimal at best. On the other hand, however remote these groups felt the learned vision of Islam to be from their own lives, they all admitted its primacy and ultimate correctness. Among them, the value and meaning of the traditional symbols and doctrines of Islam were unchallenged by any other ideology of equal rank and legitimacy. When a religious leader arose among them to speak of instituting the sharī^Ca or restoring the early community, they knew (or could readily be taught) what concrete measures were meant and how these would apply to their own lives.

ISLAMIC IDEOLOGY IN A NEW MILIEU

It is precisely these social and cultural conditions that are not found in contemporary religiopolitical movements. These latter have

their roots and main source of support in the cities and towns, and
this means that they must try to appeal simultaneously to several
heterogeneous groups—to uprooted peasant immigrants, to traditional
townspeople who are trying to maintain something like the old values
and ways of life, to university students, and to Westernized elites.
They must try to reach people adhering to folk versions of Islam,
those who are in touch with the learned tradition of the Culamā', and
those attracted to secular Western value systems. For the Muslims
of the cities, Islam is no longer the sole available ethos and world
view; it must be consciously chosen and justified in the face of many
alternatives. In addition, the Muslims of the cities (even provincial
towns) are living in an environment in which the applicability of
sharīCa-based norms of conduct is not always apparent, while the un-
spoken and self-legitimating custom of tribal or village society is
eroded under a multitude of pressures. In the contemporary urban
setting, even family life is hard enough to maintain in the traditional
manner, and all other aspects of life (commerce, property relations,
politics, and the like) are carried on in frameworks that are largely
defined by European values and procedures.

In this milieu, one needs a statement of Islam that is effective
and convincing among the Westernized, while still commanding the
assent of the more traditional minded; it must be intelligible to persons of limited education and persuasive to those with secular university educations. The effort to achieve this difficult synthesis has
been a constant one throughout the past century, and, of course, it
still continues in many circles. In the Arab lands, the main effort
was doubtless that launched by Muhammad CAbduh and Rashīd Ridā in
Egypt at the turn of the century; and their movement, the so-called
Salafīya, was picked up in the 1930s by Ibn Bādīs and his colleagues
of the Association of Algerian Culamā'. After CAbduh's death in 1905,
the intellectual tone as well as the doctrinal substance of the movement became increasingly conservative, but it never lost sight of its
original mission: to rethink and restate Islamic doctrine in terms
that would be meaningful to educated twentieth-century Muslims, and
to base these statements directly on the ultimate sources of all Islamic thought, the Quran and the life of Muhammad.

On the level of political action, the Salafīya movement was distinctly quietist in its early phase; it made few demands on the established governments and even tolerated the imperialist presence with
rather good grace. Between the wars, however, the Salafīya reformists in both Egypt and Algeria took a far more active stance, and
their leading publicists were very must involved in the political and
social debates of the day. But even with this shift of emphasis, they
still regarded their proper role as one of teaching and advocacy rather
than direct political action. As to the growing tide of national libera-

tion movements, both in this period and after World War II, they were overwhelmingly articulated and led by secular intellectuals and politicians, though these latter certainly did not hesitate to exploit the mass appeal and cultural resonance of Islamic symbols. But for most of the nationalist leaders, Islamic slogans and terms had little real connection with the core concepts of their ideologies; they were simply useful devices for legitimizing these ideologies.

Had the political concerns of Islam been represented in this century only by the three militant movements, by the Salafīya, and by the traditionalist ^culamā', there is no reason to suppose that Islam would have remained a significant political force in the Arab lands after World War II. That such is not the case is due largely to the Muslim Brothers, who seemed to combine the militant activism of the Wahhābīya, the Sanūsīya, and the Mahdīya with the reformist Quran-centered thought of the Salafīya and the antiimperialism and mass politics of the secular nationalists. The Muslim Brothers brought two crucial innovations to Islamic political action after World War I: they were the first religiopolitical movement in the modern Arab world successfully to mobilize a predominantly urban following on a mass scale—a following of increasingly diverse background as the movement expanded in the mid-1940s; and they were the first such movement to be organized and led by a layman rather than a professional man of religion. It is thus no wonder that the Muslim Brothers have become the ancestor of and model for many current religiopolitical movements, even though the original organization was a truly powerful or decisive force in the political life of Egypt for hardly more than a decade before its suppression at the end of 1954.

To say that the Muslim Brothers combined many disparate strands of Islamic thought and action does little to explain their remarkable success. A reasonably adequate explanation, however, might be derived from the following statement: in a climate of rapid change and intense stress on all levels of life, the Muslim Brothers offered in highly effective language an ideology that appealed to a very broad and politically conscious social base. The problems of Egyptian life in the 1930s and 1940s hardly need discussion here, and we have already suggested that the principal clientele of the Muslim Brothers was located in the cities and towns. The question is what kind of message the brothers offered, and why this message was so readily received by a large segment of the urban population.

As to the message itself, it has perplexed if not infuriated many critics, both Western and Muslim, because of its emotionalism and vagueness. But this charge, of course, misconstrues its true character and purpose. Its propaganda was undeniably vague and general throughout the lifetime of the movement's founder Hasan al-Bannā; if one is trying to discern what its economic policy would be, what structure of government it aimed at, or how it proposed to deal with illiteracy, infant mortality, rural land pressures, and the like, there is hardly a substantive statement to be found. Specific demands are made only in regard to certain matters that seem purely symbolic, such as the institution of the Quranic penalties (the hudūd) for speci- fied moral and criminal offenses, the abolition of interest, the segre- gation of the sexes. Though these things do not add up to a real so- cial and economic program, they are precisely the visible symbols of the difference between the Islamic and "Frankish" ways of life; they stand for morality, sobriety, and integrity versus lust, obscenity, frivolity, corruption, and exploitation. Hasan al-Bannā's focus on these points made Islam (as popularly understood) the core of his ideology, and onto this core all other good things (like national inde- pendence, Arabism, economic progress, and social equality) were easily grafted. Their value and attractiveness were in fact enhanced by being stated in Islamic language. As to the specific programs through which these could be implemented, they were in part exem- plified in the various cooperative ventures of the Muslim Brothers; and for the rest one could trust that a government truly motivated by sound Islamic principles would be able to devise adequate programs by borrowing on an ad hoc basis, from whatever sources necessary, measures that could be squared with these principles. It is fair, to say, however, that the proposals of the Muslim Brothers became much more concrete in the few years of public activity that remained to them after the death of their founder, particularly perhaps in the efforts of Sayyid Qutb.

The language of Hasan al-Bannā and his associates deserves particular attention, because it reveals a key element of the move- ment's appeal. On the one hand, the Muslim Brothers adopted a characteristic phrase of modern Islamic apologetics: whereas tra- ditional writers would justify their teachings with statements like, "God says" (namely, in the Quran), "the Messenger of God said," "the learned concur," and the like, modern usage asserts simply that "Islam teaches." Islam is thus reified into a fixed and eternal body of ideal doctrine, not subject to human hypothesis or revision, which is readily available to anyone who cares to know about it. Those who use this phrase are not calling in the traditional manner on the au- thority of particular scholars or texts, but on the vague but powerful authority of an entire cultural tradition. They are addressing those whose fundamental identity is that of Muslim, but who feel that this identity is very immediately threatened by the presence of alternative ideologies and ways of life. On the other hand, the overwhelming majority of textual citations in the Muslim Brothers' literature are drawn from the Quran (and very secondarily the canonical collections of hadīth). This fact is doubtless to be connected with Hasan al-Bannā's sympathy in part for the ideals of the Salafīya, and it must also reflect the lay leadership of the Muslim Brothers, intensely committed men who were not systematically trained in classical scholarship. * Whatever the reasons for this Quranic preference, however, it was politically a stroke of genius. For the mass of Egyptians, the Quran was, and certainly still is, the only Islamic religious work that they really know and that is embedded in everyday life and thought. It has a tremendous impact and authority that no other book could possibly match.

In most respects, the current religiopolitical movements in the central Arab lands (in particular, Egypt, Syria, and Jordan) seem to be following the model of the original Muslim Brothers quite closely. Their propaganda retains the stress on Islam as a form of cultural identity, and their ideology continues to show a characteristic combination of high idealism and programmatic vagueness. Their political base is still found largely in the cities and towns, and their leadership—though there is considerable ^culamā' participation—seems to remain in the hands of laymen for the most part. But in addition to some fundamental similarities, there are at least two crucial differences as well, and these are vital to any proper understanding of the character and political effect of the current religiopolitical ferment.

First, the original Muslim Brothers benefited from the powerful charismatic leadership of Hasan al-Bannā from 1929 until his death in 1949. During the earlier phases of the organization's history, his energetic personality was clearly the glue that held the scattered chapters together. One must admit that even after an effective centralized, hierarchical structure was established in 1945, Hasan al-Bannā's leadership was still crucial—a fact sufficiently demonstrated by the bickering, dissension, and lack of coordination that set in after his death. This kind of charismatic leadership is simply not to be found today. No single figure has succeeded in establishing his dominance, his capacity to be the chief spokesman for the goals and aspirations represented by the religiopolitical movements, or even an ability to obtain a broad, nationwide following. This no doubt results in part from the police surveillance to which all these groups are subject; were a charismatic figure to emerge, he could not reasonably expect a very long public career. But plainly there must be other and more fundamental reasons.

The second major difference between the original Muslim Brothers and the current movements is the lack of centralized control

---

*One might compare their writings with those of Mawdūdī in Pakistan; although not an ^cālim, he was quite widely read in the classical jurists and was able to cite them extensively if somewhat haphazardly.

and coordination. There is no longer one dominant movement but a whole array of movements sharing broadly similar goals and often distressingly similar names. Obviously many of their members must be in contact with one another, but one cannot speak of any central planning or common policy. There is, of course, an organization in Egypt called the Muslim Brothers, and it is the direct lineal descendant of the original movement. Its leader, ᶜUmar al-Tilimsānī, was indeed a prominent figure in the latter. The main publication of this group, the weekly magazine al-Daᶜwa, is in addition one of the most widely distributed periodicals in Egypt and the Arab world as a whole. But in fact the most militant and activist religiopolitical groups in Egypt are only loosely connected on the organizational level with the Muslim Brothers. The internal structure of the Muslim Brotherhood in Syria is very difficult to discern, if indeed it is correct to think of it as a single, coherent organization at all. The Syrian movement almost certainly has significant links (but of what kind?) with the Muslim Brothers of Jordan. As to Egypt, however, although al-Daᶜwa keeps a close and sympathetic eye on Syrian affairs, it is dubious that there is an institutional connection. This sort of structural looseness has certain advantages: the current groups are much harder to control or suppress than the original Muslim Brothers proved to be, and because of their numbers and diversity they are probably better able to locate and exploit pockets of discontent. On the other hand, the lack of central direction tends to restrict them to a role of protest, disruption, or terrorism and prevents them from making an effective, coordinated bid for power.

The immediate programs of these groups vary. The Muslim Brothers in Syria have explicitly devoted themselves to the destruction of the government of Hāfiz al-Asad, which they accuse of gross corruption, brutal repression of dissent, collusion with Zionism and imperialism, and sectarianism. These are very diverse charges, obviously, but taken together they allow the Syrian-Muslim activists to build a considerable coalition of the discontented. On one level they appeal to groups involved in confessional rivalries. A population that is three-quarters Sunnī is bound to be affronted by a regime dominated by the Nusayrīs, not only despised heretics but coarse mountaineers. *

In addition, the Syrian Muslim Brothers aim at groups with grievances that are not primarily religious. Arab nationalist intel-

---

*Also called ᶜAlawites, this is an extremist Shiᶜite sect established in north Syria in the mid-tenth century. Its doctrine is akin to that of the Druzes. The name Nusayrī comes from the supposed founder of the sect Ibn Nusayr, a notable of Basra, who was active in the ninth century.

lectuals, Palestinians, and refugees from the Golan deeply resent the regime's failure to define a strategy for dealing with Israel. Government repression strikes intellectuals and university students with particular force, while corruption is felt especially by those (the petty bourgeoisie, presumably) who have to deal with the import-export brokers favored by the government.

The ideology of the Muslim Brothers in Syria is very rudimentary at this point, or at least it receives little attention in their propaganda, which is devoted overwhelmingly to attacks on the current regime. Even the Islamic language and symbolism in this material are rather sketchy, being largely confined to a few slogans and a generalized call for the institution of an Islamic law capable of establishing justice, equality, and progress. In short, Islam functions in their current literature chiefly as a badge of identity and a focus of cohesion. It is as if no serious progress toward defining even the governing values of political life, let alone institutional structures and a substantive socioeconomic program, can be made until the hated Nusayrī regime is extirpated. At that point, one is promised, all good things will follow; but for the moment all energies must be focused on the immediate goal. The parallels with Iran in the autumn and winter of 1978/79 will be apparent to many readers.

As to the Muslim Brothers in Egypt (that is the group of ᶜUmar al-Tilmisānī), they appear to oppose almost every major policy of the Sadat regime, but they do not call for its overthrow, at least not explicitly. However, the obvious intention and effect of their propaganda are to undercut the legitimacy of that regime. In contrast to the propaganda of the Syrian group, the publications of the Muslim Brothers in Egypt make a rather serious attempt to develop a set of social and political values and to proclaim a positive program. One must admit that on the level of values they are fairly successful; on that of program, they remain as general and vague as ever. At this point their program is mostly exhortation and assertion, namely that Islam (by which they mean the Quran and the hadīth) will enable the nation to restore morality, achieve economic growth combined with justice and equity, and withstand Zionist aggression.

This kind of generality may seem an index of political immaturity, but it is also possible to find it astute and insightful. On the deepest level, the Muslim Brothers and other like-minded organizations are addressing a very widespread fear that the inevitable (and of course much desired) social and economic transformation of Egypt will be brought about in an atmosphere of unprincipled amorality, that it will usher in a time when Egyptians are no longer Muslims in any meaningful sense of the word. As we can see from current trends in the United States, this fear of losing one's moral bearings in a value-free, egotistical society can be a very intense one in any setting. By addressing their countrymen on the level of fears about cultural identity and fundamental values, therefore, the Muslim Brothers can maintain a broad coalition of protest and discontent that would quickly break into pieces if they tried at this point to present concrete social and economic programs to their adherents and sympathizers.

NOTES

An essay of this kind does not require extensive notes; however, I think it both useful and appropriate to indicate the secondary literature that underlies my argument.

The conceptions of culture and religion used here own much to the ideas developed by Clifford Geertz in his The Interpretation of Cultures (New York: Basic, 1973). From one of the essays in this volume ("Ideology as a Cultural System," pp. 193-233, originally published 1964), I have gained some very useful perspectives on ideology, though my definition differs from his in important respects. Concerning ideological expressions of Islam, the same author's Islam Observed (New Haven, Conn.: Yale University Press, 1968) has many valuable suggestions.

My comments on the Quran can be followed out in Fazlur Rahman, Major Themes of the Qur'ān (Minneapolis and Chicago: Bibliotheca Islamica, 1980), especially chaps. 2, 3, 8. Some of my comments on the proper goals of political action in Islam and the role of charismatic leadership are more fully stated in my essay "The Political Values of Traditional Islam and Their Role in Twentieth-Century Egypt," Proceedings of the International Colloquium on Historical Interpretation and Self-Image in Egypt and Israel, Tel Aviv University, April 14-15, 1980 (forthcoming).

The classic account of the Sanūsīya is E. E. Evans-Pritchard, The Sanusi of Cyrenaica (Oxford: Clarendon Press, 1949). His analysis of the political role of the Sanūsī sheikhs in the Libyan tribal system should be compared with that of Ernest Gellner, Saints of the Atlas (Chicago: University of Chicago Press, 1969), regarding the Berber agurramen of Morocco.

For the Mahdīya, all the necessary references are given in the admirable account of P. M. Holt, The Mahdist State in the Sudan, 1881-1898, 2d ed. (Oxford: Clarendon Press, 1970). A very useful recent contribution for the study of Mahdist ideology is Haim Shaked, The Life of the Sudanese Mahdi: A Historical Study of Kitab Saᶜadat al-Mahdī bi-sīrat al-Imām al-Mahdī (New Brunswick, N.J.: Transaction, 1978).

On the first Wahhābī revolt, the most interesting account in many ways is still that of John Lewis Burckhardt, Notes on the Be-

douins and Wahabys, vol. 2 (London: Henry Colburn and Richard
Bentley, 1831). This can be supplemented by the following: D. S.
Margoliouth, "Wahhābiyya," Shorter Encyclopaedia of Islam (Leiden:
Brill, 1913-42), pp. 618-21; Henry Laoust, "Ibn ᶜAbd al-Wahhāb,"
Encyclopaedia of Islam, new ed. (Leiden: Brill, 1960-), 3: 677-79;
and George Rentz, "al-Ikhwān," Encyclopaedia of Islam, new ed.
(Leiden: Brill, 1960-), 3: 1064-68. (All articles by Rentz on Saudi
history, unfortunately badly scattered, are important.)

The Salafīya have been analyzed to the point of diminishing returns; see the truly admirable survey of Ali Merad, "Islāh," Encyclopaedia of Islam, new ed. (Leiden: Brill, 1960-), 4: 141-63, with full
bibliography. On the relations between Islamic reformism and Arabism between the wars, see Israel Gershoni, "Arabization of Islam:
The Egyptian Salafīya and the Rise of Arabism in Pre-Revolutionary
Egypt," Asian and African Studies 12 (1979): 22-57.

The Muslim Brothers and Hasan al-Bannā have also attracted
much attention. By far the best study of the original movement is
Richard P. Mitchell, The Society of the Muslim Brothers (London:
Oxford University Press, 1969). A useful anthology in English of the
founder's writings is Charles Wendell, trans., Five Tracts of Hasan
al-Bannā' (1906-1949): A Selection from the Majmuᶜāt Rasā'il al-
Imām al-Shahīd Hasan al-Bannā (Berkeley: University of California
Press, 1978), though the translator's introduction is unnecessarily
hostile in my opinion.

The use by secular nationalists of Islamic symbols has often
been noted; a good analysis of a key liberal figure is in Charles D.
Smith, "The 'Crisis of Orientation': The Shift of Egyptian Intellectuals to Islamic Subjects in the 1930s," International Journal of Middle East Studies 4 (1973): 382-410.

The current Islamic revival has already generated reams of
publications, but much of this is of little use. I would like to point
to a difficult but very interesting article by Michael Gilsenan,
"L'Islam dans l'Égypte contemporaine; religion d'état, religion popu-
laire," Annales: Économies, Sociétés, Civilisations 35 (1980): 598-
614. The unpublished work of Eric Davis on the religiopolitical
groups of contemporary Egypt is likewise very important.

Finally, I wish to thank the editor of this volume, Professor
Ali E. Hillal Dessouki, not only for his unfailing patience and good
humor but also for graciously lending me personal copies of al-Daᶜwa,
al-Iᶜtisām, and al-Nadhīr (a newsletter published by the Muslim
Brothers in Syria) without which I would have found it very difficult
to write the final section of this chapter.

5

PRUDENCE VERSUS LEGITIMACY: THE PERSISTENT THEME IN ISLAMIC POLITICAL THOUGHT

CHARLES E. BUTTERWORTH

By juxtaposing prudence and legitimacy as persistent themes within the history of Islamic political thought, I am attempting to cast doubt upon the opinion that the arguments set forth in the contemporary movement identified as Islamic resurgence are novel. To do so is not, however, to detract from the merit or the significance of those arguments. Rather I seek simply to prod those who investigate contemporary events to adopt a broader perspective, one that will lead to consideration of the influence reasoned thought has upon action. After all, the study of the history of political thought—whether it be Islamic or non-Islamic—is no more an exercise in cataloging anachronistic curiosities than one in enumerating current eccentricities.

Indeed, the study of the history of political thought, like political thought itself, is concerned with the fundamental issues of political life. And the very questions that presumably prompt us to examine political thought—questions about the ultimate soundness and the broader implications of various proposals or calls for alterations—should stir us to inquire about the foundations of those ideas and about whether they have been formulated with greater clarity in other contexts. With respect to the subject at hand, such an inquiry is all the more necessary because the principal spokesmen in what we term the Islamic resurgence movement frame their arguments precisely in terms of this history. It can be neglected, then, only at the risk of failing to understand their arguments.

For precisely this reason, it is worthwhile looking at the history of Islamic political thought in terms of the tension between prudence and legitimacy, that is to say, the tension between a philosophical understanding of politics and a strictly legalistic one. In the present instance, it must be remembered that no reference can be made to law, legality, or legitimacy without thinking of the Divine Law by which those who accept Muhammad's revelation strive to regulate their conduct. Thus, those who pursued the legalistic path stressed the need to understand and to implement the Divine Law as it was set forth in the Quran and the traditions of the Prophet, whereas those who praised prudence sought to understand politics as a craft or an art and how one skilled in it could rule well. For the former group, beliefs were as important as actions: for example, it was as necessary to hold certain beliefs about God, the Prophet, and the Divine Law as to direct one's life according to the prescriptions set forth in Islam. Moreover, because those who had first submitted to the Divine Law had lived together in political community under the guidance of the Prophet and because of numerous references in the Divine Law to regulate the life of the community of believers, this former group insisted that it was sufficient to look to those ordinances and examples to understand how to order subsequent political regimes. They further denied that anything could be gained by investigating the way thinkers not aware of the Islamic revelation had attempted to explain political life and its requirements. Thus, to speak of this group as proponents of legitimacy or as legalistic is simply to heed their own efforts to implement the Divine Law. When names like Abū Hāmid al-Ghazālī, Abū al-Ma ͨālī al-Juwaynī, and Ibn Taymīya are mentioned as representative of those whose thinking places them within this group, the point becomes perhaps clearer.

Those who favored understanding politics as an art or a craft took their bearings primarily from Greek philosophy. Thus, like Plato and Aristotle, they began by asking what political association was for and then inquired into the way political regimes might be ordered so as to fulfill their ends. As a result, their remarks were usually cast in terms of how the best regime would function, and they displayed a tenacious reluctance to move from that level of abstraction to one more directed toward the regimes of the day. Similarly, when reflecting upon the characteristics of a good ruler, this latter group tended to speak about general rather than particular qualities. They differ from the former group primarily because they started from the premise of the unity of knowledge and rejected the notion that true revelation could ever contradict correct human reasoning. Here, too, the general thrust of these remarks will perhaps be more readily apparent if Abū Nasr al-Fārābī, Ibn Sinā (Avicenna), and Ibn Rushd (Averroes) are cited as the more well-known figures within this latter group.

Their defense of the unity of knowledge was never presented as a challenge to the validity of the Divine Law, but rather as a rejection of the claim that the only truth that could interest the community of believers was that which came from Islamic sources. Taking seriously the various Quranic injunctions to reflect upon the heavens and the earth and to consider the order to which they attest, [1] these thinkers considered it appropriate to conduct their investigations by using the best available tools even if to do so obliged them to have recourse to books written by authors not aware of the Islamic revelation. They differ, moreover, from the proponents of legitimacy in that their primary concern was to understand what revelation as a phenomenon was and in that they were less anxious to defend the validity of this particular revelation or to show how it might be applied in specific instances. Yet in their writings they frequently indicated their awareness of living within communities that claimed to be guided by the Islamic revelation and addressed themselves, accordingly, to themes concerning the relationship between prophecy and rulership, how to preserve for subsequent generations the sound rules laid down by a good prophet, the qualifications to be sought in rulers whose duty is to preserve the regime established by such a prophet, and the goals these later rulers should seek to achieve in their regimes.[2] They also sought to understand prophecy and the character of a prophet as these related to the intellectual and moral virtues, especially to the virtue of practical wisdom. How, after all, does a prophet know what laws to set down for a people at a particular moment and for all time? They were not content with the retort that the prophet does not know, that he is only an inspired spokesman, because such a response simply points to the further problem of how such inspiration comes about and ultimately to the whole question of the character of divine knowledge.

Stated differently, seeking in no way to cast doubt upon the validity of the revelation as it was generally understood or upon the usual account of the Prophet's accomplishments, this group of thinkers inquired into the deeper significance of these phenomena. They did so in part because of the importance they attached to the metaphorical character of these accounts, that is, because they recognized that the Quran and the traditions needed to be interpreted in order to be fully grasped.[3] On the basis of such inquiries they tried to provide the outlines of a science of politics.

For these reasons, then, it is fitting to speak of this group as proponents of prudence or practical wisdom and to contrast them with the proponents of legitimacy. The juxtaposition makes sense insofar as it provides a ready characterization for what might be termed the two waves of the modern Islamic resurgence movement. Moreover, if those who speak of this movement as resurgent do so because they wish to liken it to surf pounding against a beach, it is perfectly in keeping with the image to designate its elements as waves, the only caveat being that if this imagery follows the real phenomenon in any way, one must be especially wary of the third wave.[4]

The following discussion is on the two groups of thinkers who have been most influential in drawing the attention of Muslims and

non-Muslims to the political viability of Islam. The first group or
wave, consisting of Jamāl al-Dīn al-Afghānī, Muhammad ^CAbduh,
and Muhammad Iqbāl, may be likened to the proponents of prudence
insofar as they urge their fellow Muslims to think broadly about Islam and to appreciate the unity of purpose it shares with science or
philosophy. Space does not permit a consideration of how correctly
they understood the teachings of either the ancients or the moderns,
nor is it essential to this account of their work. [5] Active in the latter
part of the nineteenth and early part of the twentieth century, they
were primarily responsible for kindling new interest in Islam among
Westerners and for encouraging fellow Muslims to profit from the
practical and scientific achievements of the West. Eventually their
teachings came to be opposed by other thinkers, thinkers who have
the same concerns as the ones earlier identified as being proponents
of legitimacy and who may be designated as constituting a second
group or wave. The more notable members of this group are, from
the perspective of Sunnī Islam, Abū al-A^Clā Mawdūdī, Hasan al-Bannā,
and Sayyid Qutb and, from the perspective of Shī^Cite Islam, ^CAlī
Sharī^Catī and Ayātollāh Khomeinī. It is, then, a group that came into
being only shortly before World War II, a group of individuals who insist on unconditional fealty to Islam and who consequently seek to undermine the validity of any learning that does not have its roots in the
Divine Law.

THE BEGINNING OF MODERN
ISLAMIC POLITICAL THOUGHT

When the name of Jamāl al-Dīn al-Asadabadī (1837-97)—that is,
Jamāl al-Dīn al-Afghānī or, depending on the circumstances, Jamāl
al-Dīn al-Husaynī—is mentioned, the name of his student and some-
time collaborator, Muhammad ^CAbduh (1849-1905), immediately
comes to mind. ^CAbduh acknowledges that from the moment of their
first meeting, he was overwhelmed with admiration for Jamāl al-
Dīn's broad knowledge of Western culture and deep comprehension of
the Islamic tradition. Accordingly, he frequented Jamāl al-Dīn's
company as much as possible during the latter's first sojourn in Cairo
from 1868 until his expulsion in 1870 and then again when Jamāl al-
Dīn, expelled this time from Istanbul, returned to Cairo in 1879 for
a stay of four or five years. After being expelled again from Egypt
and passing some time in Hyderabad, Jamāl al-Dīn was reunited with
^CAbduh in Paris, at which time they began to collaborate on the famous,
but short-lived, political journal al-^CUrwa al-Wuthqā (the Most Solid
Link). For the several months during which the journal was published, the two found themselves to be in such basic agreement that

they saw no reason to speak as individuals; all articles appeared under the names of both. Even in 1886, two years after the journal had ceased to be published, Muhammad ᶜAbduh was quite content to write a highly eulogistic biography of Jamāl al-Dīn as a preface to his Arabic translation of the latter's The Truth about the Neicheri Sect and to do so without disassociating himself in any manner from Jamāl al-Dīn's positions. There were, nonetheless, fundamental theoretical differences between them, but each apparently considered agreement on practical goals and methods so important because of the exigencies of the day as to make it imperative to emphasize publicly only their areas of agreement.

Jamāl al-Dīn's writings, though multitudinous, are primarily occasional pieces. They consist above all of speeches or short articles drawn up to respond to a particular practical question of the day.[6] Thus, even though his thoughts are coherent enough that we can look at them as pointing to a broader teaching, it can be ferreted out only by reading these speeches and articles without regard to their chronology and sometimes without concern for the immediate cause that prompted them.

The basic premise of Jamāl al-Dīn's teaching is that science is useful to human beings in numerous ways. Science alone gives man greater control over the universe and allows him to improve his material life. It thus stands to reason that human beings should strive to master the sciences. However, to master them thoroughly, it is important to recognize the hierarchy existing among the sciences, to discern how some sciences prepare the way for others. Such discernment can be acquired only by studying philosophy, for it is philosophy that understands this hierarchy and is able to order the sciences in accordance with the hierarchy existing among them. To counter the notion that philosophy and science are harmful to religion, Jamāl al-Dīn reminds his readers of the many benefits most of us enjoy owing to the material advances made possible by science and the cultural awareness resulting from philosophical study. In neither instance do science and philosophy threaten religion. After all, it is evident that the Creator desires the material and intellectual well-being of mankind and therefore that only ignorant Muslims would seek to keep others away from science or philosophy in order to further the goals of religion.[7]

Because of the influence exercised over the Muslim people generally by its religious teachers (those whom Jamāl al-Dīn denotes as the ignorant or traditional-minded), he considers it appropriate to exhort most Muslims to break away from blind adherence to tradition and to think anew about philosophy as well as about human thought in general. He tries to overcome the initial reluctance people might have about such a move by stressing that the history of philosophy demonstrates how man has gradually become more adept at understanding himself and his place in the universe. Thus, for a Muslim to pursue philosophy is simply to fulfill Quranic injunctions to reflect upon the Creator and the significance of His creation. This is not to deny, however, the presence of dangers within such a pursuit. Too many people have become utterly confused about, or even strayed away from, the teachings of religion because of their philosophic investigations for him to be able to pass over these dangers in silence. Nor does Jamāl al-Dīn hesitate to point to the great harm that has arisen because of the careless manner in which traditional Muslim thinkers have read philosophy and science. In his eyes, then, the way to avoid these pitfalls is to abandon former prejudices and to strive to bring the advances of science as well as the riches of philosophic culture to bear on the needs of the people. [8]

Jamāl al-Dīn's conviction that the primary advantage of studying philosophy or science is the relief of man's estate obliges him to think in terms of advancement or progress and thus to judge ideas as better or worse according to how much they permit man to overcome his natural environment. Nonetheless, he is sufficiently schooled in the history of philosophy, especially medieval Islamic philosophy, to recognize the improbability of achieving the Enlightenment dream of a thoroughly educated citizen body and thus be wary of the mid-nineteenth century positivist attempts to denounce all religious belief. Consequently, he endorses the fledgling efforts of his fellow Muslims to educate themselves in the ways of the West and agrees that they do need a learned guide who can help them overcome the stifling bonds of tradition, but vehemently rejects the proposition that Sayyid Ahmad Khān (1817-98) qualifies for this role. His criticisms of Sayyid Ahmad Khān center around the latter's failure to appreciate the political relevance of religious belief. Jamāl al-Dīn's examination of Sayyid Ahmad Khān's commentary on the Quran reveals that Khān somehow neglects to consider the importance of religion or of religious ethics, cheapens the idea of prophecy by stretching that category to include contemporary statesmen or reformers, and seems to have no notion of how religion can and has fostered the acceptance of scientific teachings among its adherents. Because this commentary has been extolled as a modern interpretation by someone thoroughly educated in Western thought and consequently as a work that will surely improve the lot of Muslims everywhere, Jamāl al-Dīn concludes that Sayyid Ahmad Khān seeks to accomplish his goal by destroying their beliefs and thereby preparing them to accept the religion as well as the political domination of Western imperialists. [9] In other words, Jamāl al-Dīn thinks that a people cannot do without religious belief if they are to guide their actions correctly and that, properly understood, religious belief should lead them to pursue science in order to solve more complex problems as well as to advance materially.

This penchant for defending religion is equally obvious in Jamāl al-Dīn's famous essay entitled The Truth about the Neicheri Sect. Couching his arguments in thoroughly traditionalist terms, he contends that the Neicheris (that is, naturalists) are materialists at heart and must be combated because of the threat they pose to religion. Because their teachings tend to denigrate religion, reduce man to the level of beasts, deny the existence of an afterlife, and weaken the human sense of shame, they must be vigorously combated. At the same time, the basic beliefs of religion—man being the noblest of God's creatures, his community being the noblest, and his life on earth being for the sake of a better life beyond—must be defended. Here, then, Jamāl al-Dīn is the consummate friend of religion and of traditional social order.

However, he changes his stance remarkably in his famous exchange with Ernest Renan, conceding the folly of thinking that religion and science could ever be reconciled and acquiescing in Renan's assertion that whenever religion has the upper hand it will try to stifle thought. Similarly, he agrees with Renan's suggestion that the majority of the citizens aid religion in this task, because they find scientific thought too difficult. [10]

At no point does Jamāl al-Dīn draw upon the lesson he learned from his study of medieval Islamic philosophy: namely, that philosophy and religion are not ultimately in conflict because both bear witness to the same truth and that there is an appearance of conflict only because religion expresses in poetic and rhetorical speech the same ideas that philosophy presents more directly. Instead he presents this argument as something of a counterpoise to his attack upon the Neicheris.

There the purported conflict is resolved in favor of religion; here it is resolved in favor of philosophy. But in both instances, his arguments are based on an inadequate presentation of the relationship between philosophy and religion. The inadequacy of the perspective is all the more striking given the fact that he has proved in other writings how much more thoroughly he understands the relationship between philosophy and religion. If any sense can be made of such an apparent contradiction, it must be that Jamāl al-Dīn wants to strike a balance between the claims of religion and those of philosophy or science. More concerned about immediate action than his medieval mentors, he wishes to open religion to the advantages of philosophic and scientific learning without endangering the moral teaching so masterfully presented by religion as well as to remind the adherents of philosophy and science that, as members of a political community whose highest aspirations are derived from revelation, they must reconsider the origins of their learning. Unfortunately, he never carries this critique to its logical conclusion, which would be to reexamine his own understanding of philosophy and science in order to determine whether they must be grounded on materialist premises. To do so he would have been obliged to rethink the history of philosophy and to pay as much attention to the nonmaterialist arguments of thinkers like Plato and Aristotle as he does to the materialist arguments of Democritus and Epicurus.

Jamāl al-Dīn does not engage in such a program because he is more interested in action than in contemplation, and it is this same concern for action that prompts him to plead for limited political change even while holding out the hope that a better political regime may one day be achieved. Though he readily acknowledges the merits of republican government, even going so far as to claim that it, like limited or constitutional government, makes its citizens more deserving of being called men, he does not believe that his fellow Muslims are now capable of governing themselves in a republican fashion. He arrives at this judgment because of his conviction that they have lost all capacity for making independent moral judgments (a result of having been under the rule of despots for so long), have become too accustomed to superstitions, and have for too long opposed the true sciences about man's nature and about government. Consequently, he tries to persuade them to remain under despotic rule, but to modify it so as to render it compassionate and wise. [11]

To move people in this direction, one must be careful not to ask for too much at any particular moment. The cherished beliefs of today must be protected, however much they may eventually be transformed, and great efforts made to enlist the assistance of those officially charged with inculcating these beliefs. This is why those who, like Sayyid Ahmad Khān, wish to move too quickly and thus threaten all attempts at reform must be refuted by fair means or foul. At the same time, those foreigners, like the French in general and Ernest Renan in particular, whose goodwill may one day be useful to developing nations are to be cultivated. Once the reform movement gains impetus and it becomes possible to move against the English, whose continued presence will nullify any attempt to bring about republican government, it will be essential to have Western allies who can testify to the intellectual soundness of the movement or its leaders and assure other Western powers that this is in no fashion the work of fanatics. To read Jamāl al-Dīn in this fashion is to understand his thought correctly. Yet, while such a reading resolves the apparent inconsistencies or contradictions in some of his arguments, it does not provide an answer to the other problem it raises, namely, whether given the tactical character of his conservative attack upon Ahmad Khān and his liberal alliance with Renan he is ultimately a greater friend of religion or of philosophy. That Jamāl al-Dīn forces us to ponder this question is a fine indication of the extent to which he does represent the proponents of prudence, for it is the single question that runs through all of their works.

Muhammad ^CAbduh certainly agrees with this line of reasoning. In fact, as mentioned earlier, he is in virtually complete agreement with Jamāl al-Dīn and differs only with respect to the way he presents his teaching. He produced not a series of occasional writings, but several thoughtful and closely reasoned treatises. Of these, his Risālat al-Tawhīd (Treatise on Unity) sets forth the basic themes of his political thought most succinctly. ^CAbduh's basic premise is that Islam is a religion of reason. Thus someone who has reflected about Islam can explain its goals and its character in readily comprehensible speech. Such reflection shows why human beings need to live in society and how the Islamic revelation has provided for this need.

^CAbduh reminds us of the assistance God has provided by sending prophets who have shown men how to live together in a political community.[12] Apart from teaching mankind about the existence of God as all-powerful and all-knowing and leading human beings to perform God's work without harming others or causing evil as well as setting times of worship so that they might pause in their daily activities to remember God, prophets train men to live together in love, control their desires, redirect their passions, and regulate their actions. They perform all of these tasks in order to help men live better social lives, but they constantly remind human beings that his life is only a short preparation for a more pleasant life in the hereafter. In other words, God helps man live well now so that he might merit a better life for eternity.[13]

This emphasis on the dual character of the Islamic revelation is at the center of ^CAbduh's political thinking and is a theme to which he frequently returns. Nor is it foreign to the thought of Jamāl al-Dīn, especially on those occasions when he addresses himself to his fellow Muslims about their pressing problems. It is a theme that has great significance for the further development of Islamic political thought. In al-^CUrwa al-Wuthqā, for example, Jamāl al-Dīn and Muhammad ^CAbduh argue that Muslims need no social bond (^Casabīya) other than their religion, because this religion provides for reciprocal relationships among human beings and gives guidance about the way power should be used. From this they infer that as long as the Divine Law is the source of legislation, a Muslim can live in any country. Conversely, provided that the ruler is guided by the Divine Law, it does not matter who rules. It follows, therefore, that if Muslims can only rid themselves of foreign rulers and bring themselves back under the tutelage of the Divine Law, they will soon improve their estate.[14]

In another article, Jamāl al-Dīn and ^CAbduh pose as physicians in order to analyze the illnesses afflicting Muslim nations. They begin their analysis with the obvious analogy that the physician who treats nations, like the physician who treats individuals, must examine the particulars of the illness, but they then go on to claim that the physician of nations must also know something about divine inspiration. Such awareness is necessary because only through knowledge of how divine inspiration affects Muslim nations can a cure be prescribed. Their confidence that health lies in this direction allows them to eschew all of the more homely remedies that less skillful physicians might suggest: publishing newspapers so that ideas might be disseminated, expanding the national territory, and educating the whole populace. They reject such remedies in favor of returning the nation to the principles of religion that it had in the beginning and do so on the grounds that a religion with rules that call for love, purification of hearts, and regulation of human affairs is the only force that can make a nation truly well.[15] Implicit in this argument, as well as in the larger theme on which it is based, is the notion that moral virtues or ethics are essential to the proper functioning of political society. Both Jamāl al-Dīn and Muhammad ᶜAbduh think human beings cannot discover the principles of ethics without the aid of religion.[16]

This emphasis upon moral virtue as the foundation for sound political life and the conviction that people cannot arrive at a proper understanding of moral virtue by dint of their own natural lights link Muhammad Iqbāl (1876-1938) to his two illustrious predecessors. Another link to them is the concern he expresses about the economic and political weakness as well as the apparent backwardness of the Muslim nations. However, his recourse to poetry, on the one hand, and to academic treatises, on the other, in order to express his thoughts distinguishes him from them. Another distinguishing feature is his constant attempt to bring the East and the West together, to explain the East to the West, and to show the East what it has to gain from a greater awareness of Western thought, especially in its contemporary scientific mode. Finally, whereas Jamāl al-Dīn and ᶜAbduh regret that Islamic regimes have not always been faithful to principles of republican government and conclude that their contemporary fellow Muslims have been so ill-served by the regimes they have thus far lived under as to be unfit to assume the tasks of self-government, Iqbāl makes light of such prudence. He is so taken with the merits of republican rule as to insist that the end forever envisaged by Islam is that of egalitarian democracy and thus urges bringing about such a regime as soon as possible.

In verse as well as in prose, Iqbāl's basic query centers on the marked change in the material condition of the Muslim peoples. As he ponders why they no longer enjoy the glory that was formerly theirs, he finds himself obliged to conclude that they no longer deserve it. They have lost their former conviction and have become utterly confused about how to defend their faith in the modern world, so confused that nothing short of a rebirth will meet their needs. Differently stated, their doubts have arisen from their own contact with modern technology and material power. Consequently, Iqbāl thinks that any attempt to give them new grounds for faith must start from a consideration of modern thought itself. Since religious faith is especially concerned with the soul, Iqbāl seeks for such grounds in modern psychology as well as in the physical science that lies behind it. He also urges a reform of the educational system so as to develop force of character and independence of thought. By means of this judicious borrowing from the West, then, Iqbāl seeks to heal the physical and mental wounds of his fellow Muslims, to enable them to occupy once again their prestigious role among the nations of the world. He strives to bring them back to such a position of greatness because he thinks that Islam alone can answer the needs of mankind. [17]

In other words, despite great respect for modern Western learning, Iqbāl discerns fundamental shortcomings within it. Primary among these is the tendency to neglect the spiritual realm or to subject it to the material realm. Thus, even though he usually prefers to discuss revelation in psychological terms, he refuses to accept the logical conclusions of such discourse and insists instead upon judging revelation by evaluating its historical results. Similarly, even though he claims not to know what the end of religious devotion might be, he insists adamantly upon its intimate connection with the development of the ego and therefore labors mightily to show that, however much we might learn about how to manipulate the physical world from the writings of Western philosophers and scientists, we must turn to Eastern philosophers and mystics to learn about the ego or soul. Another problem with Western thought for Iqbāl is its failure to pay sufficient attention to the infinite character of the universe and to the evolutionary capacities inherent therein. Precisely because classical Greek thought completely ignored this problem, he cannot take seriously the claims that it exerted a major influence on the development of Muslim thought. Because Neitzsche's attack upon Greek thought leads to the doctrine of eternal recurrence—which for Iqbāl is repetition rather than evolution—he rejects Neitzsche as well as those who follow his lead. He more readily endorses a Comtean positivism along with its emphasis on spirit, equality, freedom, and republicanism, all qualities he claims to find in Islam. [18]

THE MOVEMENT FROM PRUDENCE TO LEGITIMACY

Whereas Jamāl al-Dīn places primary emphasis upon the usefulness of religion for bringing citizens to perform the civic duties they would otherwise tend to neglect and speaks only rarely about its

importance for preparing them to merit the life to come, Muhammad
CAbduh pays equal attention to both aspects. Iqbāl moves a step beyond CAbduh insofar as he places primary emphasis upon the importance of religion for the development of the ego or soul and thinks
only subsequently of political order. Yet all three agree that the study
of philosophy and science, whether Western or Eastern, contributes
to the understanding of the Islamic revelation. With the advent of
Abū al-AClā Mawdūdī (1903-80), the terms of the discussion are completely altered. For Mawdūdī, the revelation can be understood on
its own terms, and to have recourse to other sources—especially non-
Muslim ones—would be both harmful and morally wrong. Similarly,
since the only valid concern for a Muslim can be the extent to which
his actions and beliefs accord with the prescriptions of the Divine
Law, politics comes to be understood as an exercise in implementing
the Divine Law. Considerations of prudence are replaced by questions of what the Law says or how its prescriptions might apply in an
otherwise novel situation.

Mawdūdī's basic premise is that Islam can provide a sufficient
response to any problem that arises with respect to economics or
politics and even to problems related to the drafting of constitutions.
Taking the Muslim creed that there is no divinity but God at face
value, he reasons that insofar as a Muslim literally surrenders himself to God he can recognize no other being or entity as sovereign.
Two other principles follow from such total submission, namely,
acknowledging that none but God can be a lawgiver and that the goal
of all human government must be to implement the Divine Law.
Mawdūdī's endorsement of such principles also stands behind his
steadfast rejection of Western statecraft, especially secular Western
democracy. Such regimes insist upon the sovereignty of the people,
whereas Mawdūdī is willing only to grant the people executive or administrative authority. For him, the agreement (ijmāc) of the community with respect to the prescriptions of the Divine Law constitutes
a kind of general will, and he therefore claims that a truly Islamic
regime would most appropriately be designated a theodemocracy.

This understanding of where sovereignty resides in an Islamic
regime leads him to argue that even the caliphate cannot be the seat
of sovereignty, that the caliph can never be more than a "vice-regent"
of God. Moreover, taking literally the Quranic verse, "God has
promised to make those of you who believe and perform good deeds
vice-regents on earth just as he made vice-regents of those who preceded" (XXIV:55), Mawdūdī argues that all Muslims can become
caliphs and insists that this notion is the incontrovertible basis for
democracy in Islam. The consequences he draws from such reasoning are that in the truly Islamic regime there will be no class distinctions and no handicaps attaching to social status or occupation, that

there will be, in short, complete equality of opportunity for all believers. In addition, since all believers are to be considered caliphs,
no one individual dare raise himself up as an absolute ruler. Finally,
this caliphal status of all believers means that no individual can be
denied the right to express his or her opinion, because no single individual or group of individuals can reasonably claim to speak for
all.[19]

As idealistic as this account might appear, Mawdūdī should not
consequently be accused of completely ignoring the way human beings
usually act. Indeed, he recognizes that the Quranic provisions for a
political community among the believers have ends that are consonant
with our own awareness of human frailties. The Islamic state, like
other political entities, exists, then, to prevent people from exploiting one another, to safeguard the freedom of individuals, and to protect the community from foreign invasion. It differs from other
states insofar as it also seeks to evolve and develop the system of
social justice set forth in the Quran, thereby eradicating evil and
promoting virtue among the members of the community so that they
may earn the right to eternal happiness. Mawdūdī also recognizes
that any political order that pursues such comprehensive goals comes
dangerously close to regimes generally decried as totalitarian but
argues that the emphasis on the individual's well-being and the basic
goodness of the goals preserve the Islamic state from deserving such
an epithet.

Even his account of the structure of such a state is cast in
terms that suggest his own awareness of and respect for the institutions now deemed fundamental for the safeguarding of individual freedom. The chief executive officer or leader is to be selected by the
believers on the basis of his personal piety and his proved good conduct and is to be guided in his decisions by an advisory council composed of those whose character is above suspicion. Though Mawdūdī
betrays a certain ambivalence about whether the members of the advisory council are to be appointed by the chief executive or selected
by popular vote, he is adamant about forbidding any electoral campaigning. Finally, he insists on the need to keep the judiciary separate from and independent of the executive, a separation he traces
back through the history of Islamic rule. In sum, Mawdūdī's prescriptions rest on a very literal understanding of Muhammad's message
and on a privileged interpretation of what he as well as the first four
caliphs did or sought to do.[20] Confident that nothing new has occurred
since those halcyon days to render the principles or practices obso-
lete, Mawdūdī strives simply to show what an Islamic state should be
and why it is necessarily different from, and certainly superior to,
any non-Islamic state.

The solicitous concern Mawdūdī shows for Western sensibilities
and his occasional display of wry wit as he addresses himself to pre-

sumably Western objections are totally missing from the writings of
Hasan al-Bannā (1906-49). This former schoolteacher, who founded
the society of the Muslim Brothers in 1929 and served as its supreme
commander until his assassination, is interested only in speaking to
those fellow Muslims susceptible to heeding his call. His style is
consequently somewhat abrupt and generally free from sustained argumentation. Nonetheless, his conversational tone as well as his
tendency to pose questions, which he then answers immediately, do
impart a certain charm to his otherwise sparse enumeration of principles.

Hasan al-Bannā's writings center around attempts to explain
what he terms da^{c}wa (the call) of the Muslim Brothers and the beliefs
that members of the society share. The call is divine and worldwide,
which means that its sole purpose is to teach reverence for God, the
creator, to all of mankind throughout the world. Thus even though it
originates in Egypt, the homeland of the society, and can be immediately received by Arabs insofar as it is uttered in Arabic and is based
on sources familiar to them, it should reach eventually throughout the
East and then on to the rest of the world. Such a call is needed now
because human knowledge, in spite of its many material advances, is
not capable of solving the problems faced by people throughout the
world and because the Islamic and other non-Western peoples have
suffered far too long from Europe's attempts to extend its political
sway. Moreover, the careless atheism, unbounded pleasure-seeking,
narrow dedication to self or social class, and relentless profiteering
endorsed by European mores have now become so uncontrolled as to
threaten European society as well.

Consequently, Hasan al-Bannā's call is for a spiritual awakening based on the principles of Islam that will affect the individual, the
household, and the nation. Although the Muslim Brothers dare not
relax their efforts until they have succeeded in rebuilding a truly Muslim state, they must not fail to develop their own moral character or,
so to speak, put their own house in order. The mark of an individual's spiritual awakening is that one learns to distinguish the noble
from the base and right from wrong, that one engages in daily acts of
worship and takes the basic beliefs of the Islamic revelation as one's
own, and that one strives to acquire the moral virtues prescribed by
Islam. Similarly, when the Muslim male has provided for the Islamic
upbringing of his children and is confident that he treats his wife with
all the respect due her as a fellow Muslim, he can claim to have
brought spiritual awakening to his household.[21]

Providing for spiritual awakening within the nation is a more
complex matter, and Hasan al-Bannā distinguishes between two sets
of goals in this regard. The primary task is to liberate the Islamic
fatherland from all foreign rule. The right to national liberation

strikes Hasan al-Bannā as so fundamentally natural that he thinks only
an unjust criminal or a victorious despot would gainsay it. Once liberation is achieved, a free Islamic state must be constituted according
to the rules of Islam. These rules are, he claims, set forth in the
Quran and consist of the succinct prohibition of any distinctions between individuals and the equally succinct exhortation that duties always be linked with rights; or they can be enumerated at greater
length as consisting of a set of 11 rules, which range from counsel to
provide for the recognition of God to the reminder that the unity of the
community must be ensured by removing all of the causes of factionalism as well as their manifestations. [22] Among the secondary goals
are achieving a better economic distribution by ridding the nation of
foreign monopolies, ensuring better health care for the citizens, providing general education to all of the citizens, bringing about a de-
crease in crime, and building a decent army.

Unfortunately, commendable as these goals are, Hasan al-Bannā's only suggestion about how they might be attained is to enumerate
three general means—deep faith, careful organization, and work—and
to encourage the Muslim Brothers to think about how these means
might be elaborated. [23] The reason for his reticence about these
practical steps is that the time for practical politics has not yet arrived. Though he perceives clearly the goals to be achieved and repeatedly insists that they accord with the Divine Law, he is still engaged in calling out to brother Muslims. His first task is to interest
others in his cause and encourage them to continue this work, in spite
of the obstacles others will certainly place before them, until the
time to constitute a truly Islamic state.

Perhaps the best indication of the different stages through which
he believes the struggle must pass is to be found in a curious juxtaposition of characteristics of Islam that he gives as part of a statement to the "true brothers" or the "warriors" (mujāhidūn) about the
ten basic elements in the oath of the society. To explain what he
means by the first of these basic elements, understanding, Hasan al-
Bannā states that he would like them to consider Islam within the
bounds of 20 very abbreviated principles, which he then goes on to
enumerate. In the first of these principles he makes a general statement about Islam, "Islam is a comprehensive system which deals with
all aspects of life," and proceeds to illustrate that statement by juxtaposing, at five intervals, two pairs of descriptions that may appropriately be said of Islam. The parallels he seems intent on drawing
come forth more clearly when the characteristics are presented in
something like a table, the lead-in phrase being: "Islam is a comprehensive system which deals with all aspects of life, for it is

state and fatherland	or	government and community
creation and power	or	mercy and justice
culture and law	or	knowledge and carrying-out
matter and revolution	or	acquisition and wealth
struggle and call	or	army and thought

just as it is true belief and worship. "[24] The first pairs of characteristics ("state and fatherland," "creation and power," and so on) are illustrative of the way Islam appears now, prior to the founding of the Islamic state, whereas the second pairs ("government and community," "mercy and justice," and so on) describe how it will function once that goal has been achieved. Islam is present now just as it will be then, but its transformed character is a sign of the many improvements to come at that time.

Sayyid Qutb (1906-66), a schoolteacher and government official who became a prominent leader of the Muslim Brothers, has a style somewhat reminiscent of Mawdūdī's, and, like Mawdūdī, he addresses himself to the kinds of issues that are eventually as interesting to a non-Muslim as to a Muslim audience. His teaching centers around the basic principle that Islam provides a necessary and a sufficient solution to the problems that overwhelm mankind, but especially Muslim peoples, today. A resolution of these problems by recourse to Islam is now necessary because Marxism and capitalism have failed. Economic crises in Europe and the persistent efforts made by the Soviet Union to import wheat and grain are signs of the extent to which each of these economic systems has failed materially. Nor can anyone help but notice how confused people living under those systems are about values, that is, about how to live—a confusion that attests to the spiritual failure of Marxism and capitalism. Moreover, given the fundamental principles of each system, this latter instance of failure is inevitable. Marxism, after all, is based on a denial of the importance of the spirit and thus exaggerates the importance of the material. Similarly, due to the liberal insistence on the separation of church and state, there is nothing within the capitalist system to counter the excessive importance it attaches to material gain. Qutb claims that Islam provides a sufficient solution to these problems because it alone unites spirit and matter or heaven and earth, thereby responding to all the needs of mankind. [25]

To show how Islam responds to these needs, he explores at some length its teaching about social justice. However, because he, like Hasan al-Bannā, conceives of Islam as a comprehensive system, he prefaces his discussion of social justice with an account of what he calls its universal concept. Islam's concept must be so designated because it explains everything: divinity, existence, life, and man. Yet, since it can be derived only from its own true sources—the Quran

and the Sunna, the life of the Prophet, and His practical ways of acting
—it has nothing at all to do with Greek philosophy and is in no way
informed by that movement or by its adherents. For Qutb, this independent character of the Islamic universal concept is so self-evident that he simply asserts it and, on the basis of such an assertion,
dismisses the philosophical efforts of al-Fārābī, Avicenna, and
Averroes as irrelevant. Nor does he deem it worthwhile to expatiate
on the characteristics of the concept in the course of his exposition
of social justice. Instead, he refers the reader to two other treatises
in which the concept has been discussed at greater length and explains
that the elements of the concept, as it relates to social justice, are
that God created the universe as a unified whole; that God's provision
or care for this universe embraces its spiritual as well as its material or economic aspects; and that God's concern for all things within
the universe explains why there is no emphasis within the Islamic
teaching about social justice on any one single question (such as the
equal distribution of wealth) to the exclusion of other questions. [26]

Qutb's further discussion of the Islamic concept of social justice is equally abstract, for he limits his discussion to what he believes to be the three foundations of social justice as set forth in
Islam. The first of these is that Islam provides man with absolute
emotional freedom from all limitations. For example, the poor tax
liberates the less fortunate from economic need without being so bur-
densome as to weigh upon the industrious. Moreover, by its rigorous
emphasis upon the principle that a Muslim is the servant of God alone
and that there can never be any intermediaries between God and man,
Islam frees people from all forms of subjugation. Similarly, the
emphatic teaching that a Muslim should trust in none but God delivers
the faithful from undue concern about misdirected social values and
especially from false pride. Second, by its insistence on the same-
ness of all human beings and denial that any individual has a superior
or even a divine birthright, Islam provides for human equality. Qutb
also avers that Islam insists upon equality between the sexes and allows it to be infringed upon only to the extent required by the physical
differences, customs, and differing responsibilities, such as those related to breast-feeding infants versus earning the family income. Finally, Islam teaches mutual social responsibility. Thus, concern for
others can limit individual freedom, as can the exigencies of family
life. The individual's normal right to dispose of his property as he
sees fit may also be restricted for the sake of the community. Thus,
to borrow from one of the hadīth cited by Qutb, people can no more be
allowed to do whatever they wish with their property than some of
the owners of a ship can be permitted to tear up the planking of its
lower decks on the pretense that they are simply disposing of what is
their own as they see fit. A slight extension of this principle explains

why theft, murder, and general immorality must be prohibited. At the same time, such reasoning calls to mind the other side of the mutual social-responsibility question, namely, the community's responsibility for the welfare of its weaker members. Just as it must watch over the infirm and the elderly, who might be victims of robbery, or the innocent youth, who can be led astray by witnessing the immoral conduct of others, so, too, it must consider the physical needs of the sick, of widows, and of orphans—in short, of all those who are unable to provide for themselves through no fault of their own.[27]

The means by which social justice is achieved in Islam are twofold. One is by the exhortations to perform certain acts and the prohibitions against others, as these are set forth in the Quran. The other is by the steps taken within society to implement the Divine Law. Were it needed, an additional proof of the practical merit of an Islamic society could be found in the harmonious interaction of these two means. Thus, the poor tax serves as a perfect complement to the numerous Quranic injunctions about charity, and prohibitions against the serving or sale of alcohol fits in with the denunciations of drunkenness to be found in the Quran.[28]

As with his discussion of social justice, with his discussion of political rule, Qutb prefers to speak in general or abstract terms. He is more desirous of showing the equitable character of Islamic political rule than of exploring the particular institutions that might come into being in an Islamic state or in Islamic government per se. In fact, nowhere in the entire chapter entitled "Siyāsat al-Hukm fī 'l-Islām" (Political Rule in Islam) are the terms dawla (state) or hukūma (government) mentioned. Even in the course of his attack upon Muhammad Haikal's attempts to show the parallels between Islamic regimes and Western regimes, he uses the term nizām (system or order). He insists that the Islamic regime borrows nothing from the West and is totally sui generis because of its two principles or foundations, namely, its insistence upon the oneness or unity of man with respect to race, nature, and origin and its unique claim to be the al-nizām al-ᶜālamī al-ᶜāmm (general world system), that is, to be for all people or to provide the legislation needed by all people.

Now Islamic political rule, according to Qutb, is grounded in the Muslim's confession that there is no god but God, that is, that God is one and that the rulership in the life of the individual is centered on God's unity. As long as that confession of, or testimony to, God's being is held, rulers will be just and the ruled obedient. Moreover, the force of the testimony (the acknowledgment by the rulers and the ruled that God alone has real power) is such as to permit shūrā (consultation) between the rulers and the ruled. Were it needed, additional justification for such consultation is to be found in the Quran as well as in the practice of the Prophet.

Consequently, no Muslim government can claim that its authority comes from heaven. A Muslim ruler rules only by dint of the ikhtiyār (choice) of the community of believers, and his authority derives from his fidelity to the Divine Law. In other words, he has authority only as long as he remains faithful to that Divine Law. It follows, then, that apart from his justifiable claims on the obedience of the subjects and his right to ask for their advice or for their help in enforcing the Divine Law, a Muslim ruler has no rights other than those of the common subject. He has no special privileges and certainly no right to oppress others. Yet, because as ruler he is ultimately responsible for his custody of the believers, he is allowed great discretion in his custodial activity. To those who are fearful that given such leeway the ruler may oppress the believers, Quṭb can only reply that in the final analysis Islamic political rule rests on the damīr (inner heart or conscience), that is, on the belief that God is present at every moment.[29]

Like Mawdūdī and Hasan al-Bannā, Sayyid Quṭb acknowledges that his whole argument ultimately points to a call for a renewal of Islamic life. He deems such a call warranted because, despite claims to the contrary, contemporary Islamic society is not truly Islamic. Still, the successful instauration of Islamic regimes in Pakistan and Indonesia encourages Quṭb and permits him to believe that an Islamic renewal is indeed possible. For it to succeed, he thinks that it will first be necessary to bring about a renaissance or rebirth of religious belief and then to structure legislation so that all facets of public life are ordered in accordance with the Islamic framework. At this juncture, Quṭb reintroduces what he terms the "universal Islamic concept" and shows how it will be used to model education. Though he admits the necessity of accepting the results of Western technology and of science generally, he sees no reason to allow philosophy, literature, history, or law to be taught according to the Western or European fashion, as they are now. Instead, denying that there is any such thing as simply human culture in any but the pure sciences, Quṭb insists that in an Islamic society, such subjects must be taught according to the Islamic concept. For example, whereas history is now taught according to the premises that spiritual factors have little or no effect on what happens and that Europe has greatly influenced events while Islam has done so only slightly, that must be changed. Once those premises are rejected, history can be taught from an Islamic point of view with Europe receiving no more than its just share of credit, and Muslim students can learn what non-European authors have to say about the events of most immediate concern to them. Apart from his conviction that the Western understanding of things is simply wrong, Quṭb can be so sanguine about this suggestion because "history is not events, but the interpretation of these

events and the discovery of the obvious and hidden links which bring
them all together."[30] So if history and all other learning repose on
nothing but interpretations, Qutb wants to be sure that his own interpretation is accorded its place. The corollary is that as the revision
of education proceeds apace, legislation that provides for the public
interest and ensures the means to secure it must be introduced (the
public interest here, too, defined from the Islamic point of view).

The frustrating unwillingness to attend to particulars that marks
Qutb's argument is equally present in the writing of ᶜAli Sharīᶜatī
(1933-77). Sent by the Iranian government to Paris in order to complete his higher studies in sociology and become a university professor, Sharīᶜatī's political activities in France so angered Iranian authorities that upon his return he ended up spending more time in
prison or in compulsory retirement than in teaching. Having finally
obtained permission to leave Iran for the United States, he died in
England under most suspicious circumstances. Though his teaching
is not as explicitly political as that of Mawdūdī, Hasan al-Bannā, or
Sayyid Qutb, it does have clear political implications and is highly
critical of both Iranian and Western society.

Sharīᶜatī is particularly incensed about the lack of attention paid
to Islam in Iranian society, and, reasoning that his fellow citizens have
come to neglect Islam out of the erroneous belief that Western science
and philosophy respond more directly to their particular problems,
he tries to show how one can derive a theory of philosophy as well as
an understanding of history or sociology from Islam. His arguments
to prove that an Islamic sociology would explain what makes a society
change provide a ready illustration both of why he may have incurred
the displeasure of those in power and of the extent to which he joins
forces with Sayyid Qutb and others in insisting upon a simply Islamic
point of view. Rejecting the school of thought that seeks to explain
societal change on the grounds that things happen only according to
chance, that which explains societal change in terms of determinism,
and that which explains it as the consequence of a great man or strong
personality, Sharīᶜatī turns to the Quran and discovers the importance
attributed there to al-nās (the people). Then, reflecting somewhat
on the significance of the Prophet and on other aspects of the Islamic
teaching, he concludes that personality, tradition, and accident, plus
the people constitute the primary factors in social change.[31] In the
end, this account differs very little from some of the doctrines rejected in the beginning, but Sharīᶜatī is not troubled by such inconsistencies as long as they do not deter him from his attempt to show
that Islam provides an account of social and historical phenomena
that is better and more complete than Western accounts as well as
more suited to Muslim peoples.

Philosophy, especially as it appears in the philosophy of history, is the other area in which Sharīᶜatī argues for Islam's superior-

ity, and the basic premise of the argument here is that Islam alone
provides an adequate account of man's dual nature or being. He returns again and again to the Quranic account of man's creation, that
is, that God shaped man from clay and then infused the clay with the
breath of life. Because of the way it points to the physical, material,
or base elements of man's being as well as to his spiritual or noble
character and thus to his potential for a higher or more divine kind
of existence, this account is highly significant to Sharī^{c}atī. Then,
combining his understanding of the verses constituting this account
with a highly original retelling of the Cain and Abel story, Sharī^{c}atī
explains how men can eventually arrive at their true end and become
God's vice-regents upon earth. However, unlike Mawdūdī, Sharī^{c}atī
dwells not upon the political manifestations of this vice-regency but
upon its spiritual aspects. In part, he does so because he seems to
think that a political solution to human ills depends upon better human
beings or that moral reform must precede political reform.[32]

He is particularly taken by the clay-spirit dualism and by the
tension between Cain and Abel, because he thinks that they attest to
the fundamentally dialectical character of human life, a dialectic that
will inevitably lead to a revolution culminating in a perfect human society, that is, a society so ordered that justice, equity, and truth
triumph. However, apart from telling us that such a triumph requires
changes in the present structures of society and alluding to some of
the problems with the present structures through his analysis of the
Cain and Abel story, he never explains the features or the institutions
of that perfect future society.

Sharī^{c}atī enriches the basic facts of the Cain and Abel story as
set forth in Genesis and alluded to in the Quran by traditions that explain that the enmity between the two brothers arose in the following
way: Abel and Cain each had a twin sister, and Adam betrothed each
brother to the twin of the other; but when Cain objected, claiming that
his own twin was more beautiful and that he preferred to have her as
a bride, Adam proposed that each brother should offer a sacrifice and
that the contested sister should go to the one whose sacrifice was accepted. Cain's sacrifice of withered corn was rejected, whereas
Abel's offering of a fine, young, red-haired camel was accepted.
Angered by this outcome, Cain killed Abel.

The additional elements in the tale permit Sharī^{c}atī to speak
more pointedly about the character of the two brothers and to reflect
upon the social significance of their different occupations. As a
herdsman, Abel represents a primitive, egalitarian form of society
that knows no private ownership, and in his character he testifies to
the docility, good-naturedness, obedience, and guilelessness that
mark members of such societies. Cain's pursuit of husbandry, however, represents the society in which individual or even monopoly

ownership has come to the fore, and his character betrays the harsh-
ness, avidity, cunning, and selfishness that Sharī^catī associates with
societies based on private ownership. Cain's killing of Abel signifies,
then, the destruction of primitive socialism by individual ownership
or at least the domination of Cain's way over Abel's. As Sharī^catī
understands the symbolism, however, Abel has never really been destroyed: he as well as the system he represents continue on, and the
struggle with Cain or the system he represents persists until the end
of time, when the true umma (community) will come into being. In
other words, all the problems that have beset human beings in past
ages, or which continue to plague them today, are only so many manifestations of the struggle between the character of Cain and the character of Abel, between the kind of society Cain's husbandry stands for
and the one Abel's herding represents, or between the clay-like feature of man's being and his spirit-like feature. The struggle will end
only when Abel finally triumphs over Cain, that is, when all men become as pure and as good as Abel. It is not clear just how Abel's
primitive socialist society will function within this final community,
nor does Sharī^catī deem that a question worth dwelling upon as long
as it is clear that equity, justice, ownership by the people, human
equality, and brotherhood will then be firmly established. [33]

As intriguing as Sharī^catī's account of the tale is, his nearly exclusive reliance on an admittedly narrow version of it to explain the
whole of human civilization is disconcerting. At the very least we
would like to have learned of the deficiencies in the Genesis version
that prompted the changes he favors. Without such an explanation,
Sharī^catī's claim of novel insight is hardly compelling. To embrace
the new, especially when it is so foreign, we must be made to understand the need for rejecting the old. These doubts are prompted all
the more as we discern the numerous instances in which his arguments are based on faulty knowledge. Frequently, for example, he
makes sweeping generalizations that are simply erroneous or cites
phrases of Western philosophers without paying due attention to the
context from which they are derived. [34]

Though less poetic than Sharī^catī, Ayātollāh Khomeinī (1900–)
is by no means less polemical. As the first two words of his most
famous book and the title of the series of lectures upon which it is
based (wilāyat al-faqīh) suggest,* Khomeinī is primarily concerned
with the governance of the jurist. For him, government can never be
Islamic unless it is grounded in the Divine Law, and the only acceptable ruler as long as the Imām remains in occlusion is a jurist who

---

*Generally translated as Islamic government, but a literal trans-
lation of the title is Government by an Expert of Islamic Law.

knows the Divine Law and is just.[35] To buttress his argument, he
draws upon the collections of traditions compiled by various jurists.

Were it not for the confusion generated among the people by the
enemies of Islam, the character of governance by the jurist and the
need for it would be self-evident. However, because this confusion
is so widespread, Khomeinī deems it necessary to explain that Islam
is concerned with government, that there is now a need for Islamic
government, what the general outlines of that kind of government are,
and how one might bring it about. A clear proof that Islam is and
always has been concerned with governance are the provisions made
by the Prophet for a khalīfa (successor). That is, his provisions for
a successor are clear indications that he wanted there to be someone
in the community after his death who could administer the Divine Law
that had been revealed to him. Since the Divine Law is still valid, the
need for someone to administer or execute it has in no way been eliminated. Moreover, the comprehensiveness of the Divine Law shows
how necessary it is to have someone who can devote all of his attention to its administration. The need for such a government presses
now because Muslims have for too long been subject to the rule of
foreign interlopers who know nothing of the Divine Law or to fellow
Muslims who neglect it in order to rush after foreign laws and customs that are not really suited for such a community. Thus, to help
the Muslim peoples return to God's rules, and thereby abolish injustice,
it is necessary to put those rules into effect.[36]

Khomeinī rejects the advice of those who, like Jamāl al-Dīn or
ᶜAbduh, would argue in favor of a republican government. He insists
instead on the idea that Islamic government is constitutional insofar
as it is based on the Quran and the Sunna. Consequently, such a form
of government has no need of a legislative body. In its place stands
a planning council to coordinate the activities of the various ministries
and executive agencies and to advise the ruler. Although Khomeinī is
persuaded that ultimate authority for the administration of the laws
should reside in the hands of one man, he insists on the qualifications
of the ruler (knowledge of the Divine Law and personal justice) and on
the principle that no privileges attach to this position. To ensure that
the Divine Law is implemented correctly and to permit the people re-
dress for grievances against one another or against government officials, Khomeinī foresees the necessity of an independent judiciary.
Given the principle that the sole task of Islamic governance is implementing the Divine Law, it should be considered as nothing more than
a means to an end. As such, no one should seek office for its own
sake. Thus, like Mawdūdī, Khomeinī bans political campaigns.

The preciseness of his suggestions for bringing about an Islamic
government contrasts sharply with his elusive or vague explanations
of its character and institutions. Addressing himself to young students

of the Divine Law, he calls for numerous and varied propaganda campaigns directed toward the goal of informing the people about how those now in power permit foreigners to distort or discredit the Islamic faith, while themselves failing to live according to its prescriptions. At the same time, the people must be taught about the fundamentals of the faith and apprised of the merits as well as of the possibility of Islamic government. Moreover, because the existing Christian, Jewish, and Bahā'ī religious centers have goals opposed to these and sometimes even engage in missionary activity, they must be forced to close. Finally, an attempt must be made to reach those who attend colleges and universities in order to inform them of the harmful character of the Western ideas they are so innocently taking over.

In addition to this indirect propagandistic activity to be carried out on a more or less individual level, meetings should be held to bring more people together and to sensitize them to the political implications of Islam. Every occasion to reach out and explain the faith should be seized: Friday prayers, pilgrimage periods, feast days, and especially times of special mourning, such as that of ^cAshūrā. Nor can currently recognized religious authorities be neglected. They must be persuaded to help rid the nation of the foreign forces and the false opinions that weaken Islam and be encouraged to teach others about Islamic government.

Yet, Khomeinī recognizes that such activity does not bear immediate fruit and therefore counsels patience. This advice is meant, however, to encourage those who accept his argument and to stimulate them to continue spreading these teachings, not to still their activity in any way. As he sets forth these various suggestions about persuading the people, encouraging religious teachers to emphasize the political character of Islam, and rejecting the religious authorities and jurists who have sided with those in authority, it becomes evident that his propaganda and reforming activities reach out to the people at their most sensitive points. He concludes by exhorting his followers to boycott government agencies and to refuse to cooperate with government officials or to perform any act that might help them, while at the same time erecting parallel agencies to perform the same services.[37] Clearly, then, once this is accomplished, Khomeinī and his followers will be able to point to a fledgling Islamic government in action.

CONCLUSION

In the preceding pages, attention has been focused almost exclusively on the writings of these various thinkers. References to his-

torical events or to aspects of their biographies have been very
sparse. The emphasis has been almost entirely on the explanation of
what they are saying, what their arguments seem to imply, and the
general soundness of those very arguments. Little to no attempt has
been made to judge the soundness of what they are saying by looking
at what they have achieved or by looking at how successes and failures
have led them to modify their original arguments. Although there
admittedly may be a place for such a method of criticism, it has not
been employed here because it is of no value for inquiry into the logical and practical soundness of the arguments or ideas themselves.
Until we have clear and distinct knowledge concerning what a particular author has said and why he has said it, that is, for what reasons
or ends, we cannot begin to answer those questions. We cannot hope
to evaluate the practical merits of their arguments until we understand them in this comprehensive sense.

An integral part of understanding what an author is saying involves identifying his audience. The authors described as fitting into
the first wave primarily address themselves to educated individuals,
to those familiar with the culture of the West as well as with their
own. The actions they call for are for the sake of distant goals, and
they clearly distinguish these more remote goals from the proximate
ones of a practical nature that must be achieved before any attempt
can even begin to be made toward the others. Islam is important for
them, and it must be praised as well as defended. But it must also be
recognized as a religious revelation and, thus, constantly scrutinized
from the perspective of reason.

With the exception of Abū al-Aᶜlā Mawdūdī and Ali Sharīᶜatī,
the audience and the tone of discourse change for those described as
fitting into the second wave. Mawdūdī sides with Jamāl al-Dīn, ᶜAbduh, and Iqbāl insofar as he speaks primarily to the educated Muslim,
and he takes a leaf from Jamāl al-Dīn and Iqbāl, as it were, by speaking as well to the concerns of Westerners. Though insistent upon the
necessity of erecting an Islamic state as soon as possible, Mawdūdī
discerns the need to reassure those Westerners who might fear such
a state. Hasan al-Bannā is by no means so concerned about placating
fearful Westerners, nor does he desire to persuade more than a few
educated fellow citizens. He is primarily interested in finding people
of modest situation who have a deep faith and who are willing to devote
themselves fully to improving the lot of Muslim peoples. Sayyid Qutb
falls between Mawdūdī and Hasan al-Bannā, the former insofar as
many of his arguments in Social Justice in Islam are addressed to
Egyptians sufficiently learned as to be familiar with Taha Husayn or
Muhammad Haikal and that he is willing to explain his ideas to the
West as he does with the English translation of this book, and the
latter insofar as those arguments reinforce the most simplistic or
basic kind of religious faith.

More than any of those other thinkers, except perhaps Jamāl al-Dīn, Ali Sharī^catī and Ayātollāh Khomeinī address themselves to the young. However, whereas Sharī^catī speaks to the students who have all but turned away from their religious convictions and tries to lead them back to an interest in Islam by critiquing the Western authors and movements of which they have some awareness, Khomeinī focuses his attention on those who have already devoted themselves to the study of the Divine Law. As a consequence, he buttresses his arguments with references to traditional sources and is content to castigate the West in broad, general terms. However, as a result of the success of Mawdūdī's efforts to interest Muslims in state building, Hasan al-Bannā's and Sayyid Qutb's efforts to strengthen Muslim solidarity, and Ayātollāh Khomeinī's exhortations to destroy the unjust regime of the shah, plus a great increase in literacy through-throughout the Middle East, these teachings have now filtered down to the general populace. As this has occurred, increasing emphasis has been placed on those aspects of their arguments that favor popular rule, with frequent attempts being made to recast the arguments of Jamāl al-Dīn and ^cAbduh so as to portray them as forerunners of Islamic democracy.

There are, nonetheless, basic differences between these two waves or two groups of thinkers that cannot be neglected. First, each group approaches Islam differently. Whereas Jamāl al-Dīn, ^cAbduh, and Iqbāl treat it as something that needs to be understood intellectually as well as appreciated emotionally and consequently expend considerable effort to show how it fits in with what we know by means of the human sciences, Mawdūdī and those subsequent to him consider such arguments worthless. For them, there is no need to defend Islam in such terms, for it is self-sufficient. They conduct themselves, as it were, like theologians or defenders of the faith rather than like philosophers or scholars seeking to understand the relationship between faith and reason. At the same time, they are proud to reject Western learning and to proclaim that they have no need of Western tutelage in any respect. Their arguments in favor of clearly defined moral goals and their confidence that government can and should address itself to all aspects of human existence contrast sharply and, at first glance, even favorably with our present confusion in the West over what, if anything, is morally good and with our reluctance to let government infringe upon any aspect of human existence that can be labeled private. Yet, when one pauses to reflect upon whether we would be willing to become citizens of such a political regime, the merit of the traditional safeguards of human liberty becomes much more evident. Though a regime based on safeguarding human liberty will be able to educate its citizens in moral virtue only with great difficulty, it will not run the risk of depriving

its citizens unjustly of property, limb, or life because of requiring
all to conduct themselves in a manner to which only a few can aspire
or because inadequate attention has been given to procedural safeguards. Differently stated, a regime as good as that desired by the
proponents of Islamic government is too good for most human beings.
Like the city sketched out in a speech by Socrates in the Republic, it
is of more use when it is regarded as an unattainable standard against
which one measures actual regimes than as a blueprint for a regime
one is to bring into being.

Moreover, when one looks at these discussions of Islamic government as practical proposals, one cannot help but subscribe to W.
Cantwell Smith's judgment, as set forth in his fine review of Qutb's
Social Justice in Islam, that most of these suggestions are too un-
sophisticated to be of any value in solving the complex issues now
facing the world. Principles are, of course, important. But they
are only the beginning. How, for example, could we hope to implement the otherwise excellent principle of ijmā^C (agreement)? Must
all policy decisions be deferred until the citizens can express themselves via a referendum?

In part, these difficulties arise because none of the authors distinguishes adequately between hukūma (government) and dawla (state).
Each presents a plea for Islamic government, that is, for a political
order that models itself upon the principles set forth in the Divine
Law, but none explains the practical functionings of an Islamic state,
that is, a regime that strives to apply the Divine Law in foreign and
domestic politics. To call for Islamic government is useful when
one wants to rally Muslims around a common goal. However, to go
beyond that stage and form the institutions by which the Divine Law
can be justly implemented requires far more attention to practical
details. This is the task to which the third wave of thinkers must address themselves.

NOTES

1. Compare the Quran 3:191, 7:185, 59:2, 88:17–18; also Ibn
Rushd, Kitāb fasl al-maqāl, ed. George F. Hourani (Leiden: Brill,
1959), pp. 1:10–3:1 (Mueller pagination).

2. See, for example, Abū Nasr al-Fārābī, Kitāb arā' ahl al-
madīnah al-fadīlah, ed. Nasirī Nādir (Beirut: al-Matba^{C}ah al-
Kathūlīkiya, 1959); and idem, Kitāb al-milla, ed. Muhsin Mahdi (Beirut: Dār al-Mashriq, 1968).

3. al-Fārābī, Kitāb al-milla, para. 6.

4. Compare Plato, Republic, trans. Paul Shorey (Cambridge,
Mass.: Harvard University Press, 1963), pp. 500–16.

5. For a general account of some of the problems with their understanding of tradition, see Muhsin Mahdi, Die geistigen und sozialen Wandlungen im Nahen Osten (Freiburg: Rombach, 1961), pp. 24-34. What Gilbert Delanoue does with respect to earlier thinkers in his Moralistes et politiques musulmans dans l'Egypte du XIXème Siècle (1798-1882) (Lille: Services de Réproduction des Thèses, 1980) represents perfectly the kind of analysis that needs to be done for the thinkers considered all too briefly here.

6. A. Albert Kudsi-Zadeh, Sayyid Jamal al-Din al-Afghani: An Annotated Bibliography (Leiden: Brill, 1970), pp. 3-18.

7. See "Lecture on Teaching and Learning," in An Islamic Response to Imperialism: Political and Religious Writings of Sayyid Jamāl al-Dīn "al-Afghānī," trans. Nikki R. Keddie (Berkeley and Los Angeles: University of California Press, 1968), pp. 101-2, 103, 104, 105, 107.

8. "The Benefits of Philosophy," in An Islamic Response, trans. Keddie, pp. 109, 110-12, 112-14, 115-20, 121-22.

9. "Commentary on the Commentator," in An Islamic Response, trans. Keddie, pp. 123-25, 125-29.

10. See "The Truth about the Neicheri Sect," in An Islamic Response, trans. Keddie, pp. 141-44, 147-48. See also Ernest Renan, "L'Islamisme et la science," in Le journal des débats, March 30, 1883. Arabists will be interested to note that to prove the extent to which high medieval Islamic culture is in fact Greco-Sassanian, Renan points to the uncontested fact that the Arabic word for philosopher (faylasūf) is derived from the Greek philósophos, but in so doing transliterates the Arabic as filsouf, a transliteration he repeats throughout the article. See also "Answer of Jamāl al-Dīn to Renan," in An Islamic Response, trans. Keddie, pp. 182-83, 184-86, 187. Renan's own comments on this response, published in Le journal des débats on the day following Jamāl al-Dīn's remarks, reveal that he had already made the acquaintance of Jamāl al-Dīn (whom he calls an "enlightened Asiatic" and likens to Avicenna or Averroes) two or three weeks before his lecture. In these comments, Renan rejects Jamāl al-Dīn's attempt to defend the Arabic character of Islamic civilization by pointing out that even though Albertus Magnus, Roger Bacon, and Spinoza wrote in Latin, it would be incorrect to speak of them as Latin or as influenced by Latin culture. Such an argument fails to pay sufficient attention to Jamāl al-Dīn's emphasis on the way Arabic culture permeated all aspects of the life of Muslim peoples. However, that is a minor point of disagreement. Renan wishes above all to point to what he takes to be Jamāl al-Dīn's basic agreement with his principles.

> Above all else, let us establish freedom and respect
> for men as the supreme rule. The duty of civil society
> is not to destroy religions, but rather to treat them
> benevolently as free manifestations of human nature
> without protecting and especially not defending them
> against the faithful who wish to break with them.

See Oeuvres complètes de Ernest Renan, ed. Henriette Psichari, vol. 1 (Paris: Calmann-Lévy, 1947), pp. 960–65.

11. L. M. Kenney, "Al-Afghānī on Types of Despotic Government," Journal of the American Oriental Society 86 (1966): 20, 21, 25–27. Kenney's article is a very competent annotated translation of Jamāl al-Dīn, "al-Hukūmah al-istibdādīyah," Misr, vol. 2, no. 33 (February 15, 1879).

12. This is the basic argument set forth in the chapter entitled "Man's Need of the Prophetic Mission," in ᶜAbduh's Risālat al-tawhīd. The treatise has been translated into English by Ishaqq Musaᶜad and Kenneth Cragg, The Theology of Unity (London: Allen and Unwin, 1966), pp. 85–86, 86–88, 89–91, 91–93.

13. Ibid. , pp. 101–3.

14. See Jamāl al-Dīn al-Afghānī and Muhammad ᶜAbduh, "Islamic Nationality and Religion," in al-ᶜUrwa al-wuthqā (Cairo: Dār al-arabī, 1957), pp. 10, 11–12.

15. See Jamāl al-Dīn al-Afghānī and Muhammad ᶜAbduh, "The Nation's Past, Its Present, and the Treating of Its Ills," in al-ᶜUrwa al-wuthqā, pp. 13–15, 16, 20–21.

16. The preceding analysis considers simply irrelevant Kedourie's contention that Jamāl al-Dīn and ᶜAbduh were not as pious as their followers have made them out to be. It is a position that can only make sense if one holds to a rigorously traditional view of Islam, a view that refuses to accept the possibility that Islam may be better understood if approached via philosophical reflection about the meaning of revelation. See Elie Kedourie, Afghani and ᶜAbduh: An Essay on Religious Unbelief and Political Activism in Modern Islam (London: Frank Cass, 1966).

Kedourie can and should be faulted for deciding to judge Jamāl al-Dīn and ᶜAbduh not by what they said or even—despite claims to the contrary—by what they did, but rather by what others said they did or believed (see pp. 2, 6, 16). When due note is paid to Kedourie's account of why Jamāl al-Dīn was deported from Persia, it becomes evident that his book suffers from a unique bias. "Finding himself checkmated by Amin al-Sultan, he took refuge in the Shrine of Shah Abdul Azim, where he remained for seven months, a vocal opponent of the regime, until he compelled the Shah to violate the sanctity of the Shrine by having him seized and deported" (p. 59).

17. Muhammad Iqbāl, Complaint and Answer, trans. A. J. Arberry (Lahore: Ashraf, 1977), pp. 16-19, 67-68; Islam as an Ethical and a Political Ideal: Iqbal's Maiden English Lecture (1908), ed. S. Y. Hashimy (Lahore: Islamic Book Service, 1977), pp. 48-49, 50-51, 75-76, 80-88, 100-2, 103-6, 106-7, 108-9, 112; and Muhammad Iqbāl, The Reconstruction of Religious Thought in Islam (Lahore: Ashraf, 1960), pp. v, 97-98, 165, 168, 179-80, 188-90.

18. Iqbāl, Reconstruction, pp. 3-4, 113-14, 124-25, 126-27, 140-42, 146-48, 155-57, 158-59, 160-62, 162-63, 173-74, 192-93.

19. Abū al-Aᶜlā Mawdūdī, Political Theory of Islam (Lahore: Islamic Publications, 1976), pp. 6, 20-22, 24-25, 37-42; and compare Jean-Jacques Rousseau, The Social Contract, ed. Roger D. Master, bk. 1 (New York: St. Martin's Press, 1978), chaps. 1, 6, 7, pp. 46, 52-55; bk. 2, chaps. 1-4, pp. 59-64; and bk. 4, chap. 1, pp. 108-9.

20. Mawdūdī, Political Theory, pp. 32-33, 33-34, 43-48.

21. Hasan al-Bannā, "Daᶜwatunā fī tawr jadīd" [Our call in a new phase], in Kitāb al-daᶜwa (Cairo: Dār al-tibāᶜa wa' l-nashr al-Islāmiy, n. d.), pp. 9-20, 20-28; idem, "Bain al-ams wa al-yawm" [Between yesterday and today], in Kitāb al-daᶜwa, pp. 44-55, 55-58, 62; and "Le credo des 'Frères Musulmans,'" in La pensée politique arabe contemporaine, ed. Anouar Abdel-Malek (Paris: Editions du Seuil, 1970), pp. 70-73.

22. Hasan al-Bannā, "Daᶜwatunā," pp. 27-28; and idem, "Bain al-ams wa al-yawm," pp. 63-64, 40-41.

23. Hasan al-Bannā, "Bain al-ams wa al-yawm," pp. 65-66.

24. Hasan al-Bannā, "Taᶜālīm" [Instructions], in Kitāb al-daᶜwa, p. 75.

25. Sayyid Qutb, Maᶜālim fī 'l-Tarīq [Signposts along the path] (Cairo: Dār al-shurūq, 1980), pp. 10-12; also idem, Social Justice in Islam, trans. John B. Hardie (New York: Octagon, 1970), pp. 1, 7-8, 10, 13-14, 15, 272-79. In what follows, I draw from Qutb's extended discussion of social justice as set forth in Social Justice in Islam and refer to Hardie's translation despite some minor problems in his rendering of the Arabic (see, for example, Wilfred Cantwell Smith's review of the translation in Middle Eastern Affairs, 5 [1954]: 392-94).

26. Qutb, Social Justice, pp. 17-18, 21-22, 24, 25, 26-27, 28, 31-32, 279-81. The other work in which he discusses the Islamic universal concept in detail is Khasā'is al-tasawwur al-Islāmī wa Muqawwimātuk [Characteristics of the Islamic concept and its constituent elements] (Cairo: Issā al-Halabī, 1962).

27. Qutb, Social Justice, pp. 29-30, 30-44, 45-55, 55-67.

28. Ibid., pp. 69-72, 73-84, 84-86.

29. Ibid., pp. 87-91, 91-93, 93-96, 96-98, 98-99. Hardie's translation of Sayyid Qutb's siyāsat al-hukm in the title and throughout the text of this chapter as "political theory" rather than as "political rule" unduly inflates Qutb's argument.

30. Ibid., pp. 227-28, 240-41, 249-52, 252-76. This last remark occurs in the seventh Arabic edition of the text, which differs in many respects from the edition Hardie translated into English; see Sayyid Qutb, al-CAdālah al-IjtimāCīyah fī 'l-Islām (Cairo: Dār al-shurūq, 1980), p. 287; for a fuller account of his criticism of culture being considered simply human, see p. 276.

31. Ali SharīCatī, On the Sociology of Islam, trans. Hamid Algar (Berkeley, Calif.: Mizan Press, 1979), pp. 39-42, 42-43, 44-45, 46-47, 48-49, 50-53.

32. Ibid., pp. 80-81, 82-83, 86-87, 90-91, 92, 94-95, 121-22, 123, 124; see also Quran 15:26-29, 32: 7-9.

33. SharīCatī, On the Sociology of Islam, pp. 97, 98, 99, 104-5, 106-7, 108-9, 111-12, 114-15, 116-17, 119-20; see also Quran 5:27-31; and Genesis 4:1-15.

34. SharīCatī, On the Sociology of Islam, pp. 48, 52-53, 58-59, 79, 89.

35. Ayātollāh Rūhollah Khomeinī, Islamic Government, trans. Joint Publications Research Service (New York: Manor, 1979), pp. 36-38.

36. Ibid., pp. 6-7, 8-9, 14-15, 18-19, 19-20, 25, 26, 28-30.

37. Ibid., pp. 93-98, 98-99, 99-101, 101-3, 104-9, 112-14, 114-16.

PART III

ISLAMIC RESURGENCE
IN ACTION
Case Studies

6

ISLAMIC MILITANCY
AS A SOCIAL MOVEMENT:
THE CASE OF TWO GROUPS
IN EGYPT

SAAD EDDIN IBRAHIM

Interest in militant Islamic groups was stimulated by a multi-tude of academic as well as existential factors. From a strictly social science point of view, these groups represent a significant variant of social movements that have been proliferating all over the Third World in recent decades. Second, these types of Islamic so-cial movements have not been sociologically studied before. Similar movements (for example, Wahhābīya, Mahdīya, and the Muslim Brothers) have been studied by historians—often a long time after their rise and from a historical perspective. The sociological study of such movements would no doubt complement historical treatises. A sociological investigation, in this context at least, promises first-hand data (through interviews and questionnaires) and a quest for an explanation that anchors these movements in their broader structure.

The emergence of Islamic militant movements in Egypt is of special importance. Egypt is the center of the Arab and Muslim world; vibrations there often radiate to a much broader cultural hin-terland beyond its borders. This has been the case with other politi-cal and ideological currents throughout the last two centuries. The cultural unifiers in the Arab-Muslim world make it possible for this vast area to respond to one center, expecially in times of acute crisis.

Some of the material included in this chapter appears also in "Anatomy of Egypt's Militant Groups," International Journal of Mid-dle East Studies 12 (1981): 423-53. The essay is based on interviews conducted as part of a research project sponsored by the National Center for Sociological and Criminological Research (NCSCR) of Egypt. I would like to thank members of the research team: Sohair Loufty, Afaf Mahfouz, Ibrahim el-Fahham, Adly Hussain, Mohammad Mohi-eddin, and Mona al-ᶜArini.

The sociological study of militant Islamic groups confronts the researcher with a host of obstacles. There are political, ethical, and practical problems in carrying out empirical research on groups that are extremely polemical and whose activities are still unfolding. Both the militants and their antagonists feel a great temptation to use the research undertaking for instrumental gains. Suspicion of the social scientist's motives is unlimited. There is an overall environmental inhospitality to empirical research, even when initial goodwill is established.

Interest in studying militant Islamic groups was translated into a simple research design. Islamic militancy was defined as actual violent group behavior committed collectively against the state or other actors in the name of Islam. Two groups of substantial size met this definition. The first is Shabāb Muhammad (Muhammad's Youth), known in the Arab mass media as Jam^{C}at al-fannīya al-^{C}askarīya (Technical Military Academy Group), and henceforth abbreviated as MA. * The second is Jama^{C}at al-Muslimīn (The Muslim's Group), known in the Arab media as Jama^{C}at al-Takfīr wa'l-Hijra (Repentance and Holy Flight), and henceforth RHF. †

After the arrest, trial, and sentencing of their membership in 1974 and 1977, respectively, the two groups had no legal existence. The two top leaders of MA and the five top leaders of RHF were executed. But many of their second echelon leaders were still in prison. The two groups seemed, from the preliminary information gathered, to be typical of the several others that have been mushrooming under various names since the late 1960s. Many of the leaders of these groups, including the two in question, had some direct or indirect affiliation with the Muslim Brothers, ‡ as will be seen shortly.

---

*In April 1974 this group attempted to stage a coup d'etat. It succeeded in taking over the Technical Military Academy in preparation for marching to the Arab Socialist Union building where Egypt's top leadership had assembled to listen to a speech by the president. The plot was foiled after 11 persons had been killed and 27 wounded.

† In July 1977 this group kidnapped a former cabinet minister for Awqāf (religious endowments), demanded the release of fellow detainees, then carried out its threat to kill him when the release did not materialize. Crackdowns and shoot-outs resulted in 6 dead and 57 wounded around the country. Eventually all the group's top leadership and some 620 members were arrested, of whom 465 stood trial before military courts.

‡ The Muslim Brothers Association was founded by Hasan al-Bannā in 1928. Its avowed principles were the creation of an Islamic society through the application of the sharī^{C}a. It grew gradually, becoming one of the largest mass movements in Egypt during the 1940s.

The data reported here were obtained primarily from interviews inside prison in 1978 and 1979. Some were obtained outside prison from members who were charged but acquitted. The interviews were supplemented by three additional sources of data; questionnaires (14 respondents), writings by the leaders of the two groups, and official documents. In our presentation of respondents' answers to various questions, we were helped by the fact that almost the same words and phrases, the same Quranic verses, and the same hadīth were used by most members of each group in making their points regarding various issues.

Sociologists of social movements are invariably interested in the general societal conditions that give rise to a given movement, its ideology, leadership, recruitment policy, membership profile, internal organization, strategy, and tactics. Some of these aspects are discussed below.

IDEOLOGICAL FRAMEWORK

Much has been written on what Islamic movements are seeking: the building of a new social order based on Islam. This has generally come to mean application of the sharī^{c}a to everyday social life. Islam regards itself as the repository of the will of God, which has to be acted out on earth through a political order. Members of the two militant groups interviewed were no exception in this respect. They subscribed to this objective wholeheartedly. There is no point in repeating here what has been written about extensively elsewhere. [1] Suffice it to say that to these militants, adherence to Islam provides a complete and righteous vision of a healthy society on earth and a heavenly paradise in the hereafter.

A vision of what ought to be, however, is only one part of most ideologies. Analysis of the past, the present, and the unfolding process that links them are often integral parts of ideology. In describing the present, an ideology offers an assessment of the role played by major segments of society. It also points out actual and potential enemies of the new social order envisioned by the ideology.

On most of the principal elements of ideology, a near consensus was found among members of the two militant groups. Typically they started out with axiomatic statements to the effect that man was created for a purpose: to embody the will of God by leading a righteous life and following al-sirāt al-mustaqīm (the correct path). The operational content of such life is described in detail in the Quran and the Sunna. It goes without saying that strict adherence to the five pillars of Islam is an irreducible minimum for every Muslim. But to become a good Muslim, more must be done. Aside from observing the commandments, taboos, and other rituals, a good Muslim sees to it that the will of God in creating mankind is truly fulfilled on the collective level as well. Phrased differently, the righteous Muslim cannot exist individually; he must strive for building and maintaining a righteous community of al-umma (the faithful). Struggling to bring that about is a duty of every true Muslim.

It is this last component of the militants' ideology that sets them apart from others in Muslim societies at present. Creating and sustaining a social order in the moral image outlined in the Quran is problematic, both intellectually and politically. Intellectually, most ruling regimes in Muslim countries, Egypt included, claim to be following the "essence" or the "spirit" of Islam. They may argue to justify what might otherwise seem to be variations in form necessitated by a changing and complex world.[2] Spokesmen for these regimes, including establishmentarian [c]ulamā', would be quite prepared to marshal religious evidence in such intellectual debates. *

Important as it may be, the intellectually problematic is not the most crucial component of the militants' ideology. Rather it is the militants' belief that it is their religious duty to see to it that a truly Muslim social order comes about. Such a belief sooner or later takes on an organizational form leading to an inevitable confrontation with the ruling elite. The objective is to force the elite either to conform to the precepts and edicts of Islam or to step down. In other words, a serious challenge to the status quo is a built-in component of any militant Islamic ideology.

How the two groups view the present is an integral part of their ideology. Both are in agreement that the political system is corrupt and inept. The evidence is abundant. Externally it has been defeated by the enemies of Islam—the Christian West, Jewish Zionism, and atheist communism. The regime made humiliating concessions to them. The system, by deviating from the straight path, has failed to repel external assaults on Dār al-Islām. Internally the regime is oblivious to the sharī[c]a; it has adopted and enforced man-made, Western-imported legal codes. The leaders have not set an Islamic example in behavior and life-style. Nor have they displayed any intention of starting to reinstate Muslim institutions. The inevitable outcome is moral decay, poverty, disease, illiteracy, and radhīla

---

*Husayn al-Dhahabī, who was kidnapped and assassinated by the RHF group, was a typical example of the establishmentarian [c]ulamā' of Al-Azhar. While a minister of religious endowments and religious affairs, he mounted blistering attacks on militant groups, dubbing them as misguided. In that, he echoed the line of the ruling elite toward these groups.

(the spread of vices). In short, all the external setbacks and internal socioeconomic ills of Egypt (and those of other countries in the Muslim world) are fairly and squarely attributable to a corrupt, inept system that has vastly and intentionally deviated from the correct path embodied in the sharī^{c}a. The obverse of this causal proposition is clear: the sure solution for all such problems is a system that commits itself to, and that indeed begins to implement, the sharī^{c}a.

There were some differences between the two groups on these diagnostic aspects of the ideology. The MA condemned the political system in the main. The society at large, though described as decaying and ridden with problems, was not to be blamed. It was viewed as a victim of unscrupulous and "God-fearless" leaders at the top of the political system. Thus, the victimized society was seen as eager but unable to rid itself of its victimizers. The MA's reading of the nature of the Egyptian society with regard to religion is quite interesting. One of the surviving leaders of the attack on the Technical Military Academy stated that "we believe that the Egyptians are basically the most religious of all Islamic peoples. They were so before Islam—from the time of the Pharaohs. They have continued to be very religious. Egypt would therefore be a good base to start the world Muslim revival. All that the religious Egyptians need is a sincere Muslim leadership." This conviction, we believe, had a decisive impact on shaping the strategy of the MA group, as will be shown later.

The RHF does not make the distinction between the political system and the society at large. They are equitable, and each is a manifestation of the other. To the RHF, a corrupt society breeds a corrupt political system, and vice versa. Thus the present-day political system and society in Egypt are beyond redemption. The most frequent term used to describe this state of affairs is a new jāhilīya, that is, a combination of infidelity, decadence, and oblivious ignorance, similar to that prevailing in pre-Islamic Arabia. There are also several doctrinal differences between the two groups, which are reflected in their organizational, strategic, and tactical aspects.

In order to go beyond ideological generalities, several probes about specific issues were built into the research design. In both the questionnaire and the freewheeling interviews, members of the two groups were challenged to answer their critics as to how an Islamic social order would handle some contemporary problems on which the sharī^{c}a is either vague or noncommittal. A sample of typical responses helps put their ideological perceptions in focus.

On the question of women's status, the consensus was that the sharī^{c}a in essence gives women balanced rights and obligations. The militants concede that men have neglected women's rights and have been excessive in extracting obligations. But this results from the overall corruption and irreligiosity of the present social order. They are not against women receiving equal education up to the highest level. They insist, however, that women's rightful place is in the home and that their first obligation is to their husbands and to the socialization of true Muslim children. Women could work outside the home if they had fulfilled their primary obligations and if maslahāt al-umma (the interests of the community) called for it. Significantly enough, the MA was more egalitarian on this issue than the RHF. But the latter had female members, while the former did not. Both groups insisted on al-fitna (the imperative of modesty), al-ghiwāya (protecting women from temptation), and the separation of sexes in public places. The application of hudūd (Islamic legal penalties) with regard to sexual offenses is both necessary and sufficient to ensure these ends. The family was perceived as being the basic unit of Muslim society. Its soundness derives from strict observance of sharīᶜa values and regulations. Authority and protection flow from the male head of a household down to females and the young; respect and obedience flow in the opposite direction. In short, the Muslim family is built around obedience, complementarity, protection, and respect, not around equality, competition, and self-reliance.

On economic issues, both capitalism and communism were dismissed as inhuman and ungodly. But what exactly is an Islamic economic system? Neither group would or could give a complete and coherent picture. One comes away with scattered answers and an overall impression. Excessive wealth and excessive poverty would have no place in a Muslim society—if the faithful are following muharramāt (religious edicts and taboos). The "do's" here include payment of the zakāt (alms tax), fair payments of wages to laborers, hard and honest work by every Muslim, and charitableness (aside from zakāt). The taboos include cheating, tabdhīr (extravagance), iktināz (hoarding), and extracting or receiving usury interest. It is also clear that no single individual or group of individuals should be allowed to monopolize or control public utilities (the analogy from early Islam is water, fire, and grazing land, or al-mā', wa'l-nār, and wa'l-kalā, respectively). Private property, profit, and inheritance are allowed. A Muslim government, however, could and should create what is analogous to a public sector if the interest of the umma requires it.

This last stipulation, interest of the community, seemed to perform two important ideological functions. First, it gives the Islamic state tremendous flexibility to engage in or withdraw from major economic activities. Second, it accentuates the collective or communal nature of the envisioned Muslim society. One never heard anything about the interest of the individual; it was always that of the umma.

Egypt's present economic problems are perceived as the outcome of the mismanagement of resources, application of imported policies, conspicuous consumerism, corruption of top officials, and low productivity. Overpopulation, scarcity of cultivable land and other natural resources, burdens of defense, and the war efforts are not considered causes of or crucial factors in Egypt's present economic difficulties. The militants' blueprint for dealing with Egypt's problems is rather straightforward: austerity, hard work, and self-reliance. Building basic industries and developing appropriate technology are integral parts of Islamic economics.

On the question of classes and stratification, the two groups readily concede social differentiation as an accepted pillar of the Muslim society—as the Quran states, "We [God] have put some of you in classes above others." But the only acceptable mechanism of differentiation is man's labor, not his race, color, or ethnic or family origin. As a matter of fact, this labor-differentiating mechanism determines one's standing, both in this life and in the hereafter. The concepts of ^{C}adl (justice) and al-quistas (equity) are central in the envisioned Muslim society. It is the responsibility of the ruler, commander of the faithful Amīr al-mu'minīn (the Caliph) to see to it that justice and equity are observed. In fact, such is the raison d'être of governance, al-^{C}adl asās al-hukm. Countless episodes were told by members of the two groups of how such principles were implemented and observed by the Prophet and the Rightly Guided Caliphs.

What the militants are calling for in the socioeconomic organizations of Muslim society may come very close to a variety of moderate socialism. But any suggestion to that effect invariably produced an outraged response. Islam is not to be likened to any man-made doctrine or philosophy. It would be more acceptable to them if we were to say that some variety of socialism resembled Islam. The militants would often use words such as al-fuqarā' (the poor), al-masakīn (the wretched), and al-mustada^{C}fūn fī al-ard (the weak on earth) to mean what secular leftists usually refer to by the terms working class, the exploited, or the proletariat. The militants, however, would have an instantly adverse reaction to the latter terms because of their association with imported secular ideologies. By the same token, the militants used words such as al-mufsidūn fī al-ard (the corrupt on earth) and al-zalāma (the unjust) to mean what secularists do when they use exploiters or oppressors.

As to the political system, the two groups expressed their conviction that the head of the community, the ruler, must be selected by the faithful; must be an adult, rational, pious male; and must abide by the sharī^{C}a. In all important decisions, where there is no clearcut ruling in the sharī^{C}a, he must consult his fellow Muslims.

But how is one to logistically organize matters related to selecting the ruler or ensuring consultation with the community? The militants have not worked out the details. When asked if they would go about it in the same way as Western-type democracies, they agreed in essence, although they did not like to use the word democracy and preferred the term shūrā. Both groups stipulated that elected shūrā assemblies would have no legislative powers in matters covered by the sharī^{C}a. Rather, these elective bodies would be responsible primarily for the enforcement of the sharī^{C}a, would choose among alternative interpretations, and would issue rules on matters not directly dealt with in the sharī^{C}a. Elective bodies would have the authority to check on the rulers, hold them accountable, and remove them from office if they failed to carry out their duties. So long as the rulers are dutiful to God and the community, it is the obligation of every Muslim to obey their orders.

The tradition of tolerating an unjust ruler for the sake of preserving the unity of the umma was completely rejected by the MA and RHF groups. In fact, it is the duty of every true Muslim to remove al-zulm (injustice) and dalāla (misguidance), including that committed by the ruler.

How do the militants see the ^{C}ulamā', the learned men of religion? Although there was no uniformity either within or between groups, no one had anything positive to say about the ^{C}ulamā' as a group. Those who expressed indifference toward ^{C}ulamā' tended to view them as being just like any group of state employees—bureaucrats who took no initiative. They saw the ^{C}ulamā' as being committed to observing rituals and formalities rather than to furthering the essence and spirit of Islam. The ^{C}ulamā' were invariably described as babbaghawāt al-manābir (pulpit parrots). Most members of the MA group dismissed them as pathetic cases for whom pity, rather than anger, should be felt. Most RHF group members, however, were openly hostile toward the ^{C}ulamā', especially their top leaders, viewing them as hypocrites and opportunists. Invariably they were described as yuhallilūn al-haram or wa yuharrimūn al-halāl (people who would reverse religious edicts) to suit the whims of the rulers. So much were the ^{C}ulamā' considered a disgrace to Islam that members of the RHF were strongly advised not to pray behind them or in mosques where official ^{C}ulamā' presided.

Underlying this range of negative attitudes by the Muslim militants is their belief that the ^{C}ulamā' and al-Azhar have abdicated their responsibility, have emptied Islam of its sociopolitical component, and have therefore ceased to be qualified to lead the community of believers. Worse still, from the militants' point of view, the ^{C}ulamā' stand in the way of rebuilding a true Islamic social order.

The militants' attitude toward the Muslim Brothers was, of course, more sympathetic. In terms of the religious component of ideology, their reading of history, and their overall vision for the

future, members of MA and RHF expressed no differences with the
Brothers. In fact, they considered themselves a natural continuation
of them. MA and RHF revere the founder of the Muslim Brothers,
Hasan al-Bannā, and the pioneers who gave their lives as martyrs
for Islam.

It was generally with the surviving members of the Brothers
and their current practices that the MA and RHF took some exception.
They considered some of these surviving members as weak, as burned
out, or as having sold out. Some of the early joiners of MA reported
having gone to visit older members of the Brothers, seeking advice
and offering support. They were adivsed to mind their individual
businesses, to stay out of trouble, and to worship God. This was
quite disillusioning to the youngsters, who then decided to form their
own organization.

In closing this discussion of the militant's ideology, it may be
in order to say a word about the intellectual roots of their ideas. By
its own testimony, the MA has been primarily influenced by the literature of the Muslim Brothers, mainly the writings of Hasan al-Bannā
and Sayyid Qutb. Also important in shaping the group's ideas were
the translated works of Abū al-AᶜIā Mawdūdī from Pakistan and Ali
Sharīᶜatī from Iran. The intellectual roots of RHF were far more
complex. They included the above sources, but in addition its leader
Shukrī Mustafā synthesized the works of Kharajites (al-Khawārij),
Ibn Taymīya (1263-1328), Muhammad Ibn ᶜAbd al-Wahhāb (late
eighteenth century), and Jamāl al-Dīn al-Afghānī (nineteenth century).
Curiously enough, Muhammad ᶜAbduh, the most prominent Islamic
reformer, was not among those accredited by the militants.

STRUCTURE AND SOCIAL BASE

It has been argued that following the Arab defeat of 1967, a
tidal wave of religiosity swept Egypt. In an organizational sense,
however, this religiosity remained by and large quite amorphous.
Part of this religiosity took retreatist, mystical, or Sūfī forms—an
individual search for meaning and salvation by turning inward. What
distinguished both the MA and the RHF is precisely their organization
and their outward turning; they sought to change not just their individual lives but the world as well. To be sure, the climate of religiosity enabled the two groups to recruit members and to hurriedly
challenge the Egyptian regime. But their organization, as far as one
was able to trace from their testimony, began with a single man in
each case, and their organizational evolution reflected to a significant
degree the style and temperament of those two men. But the organizational structure and matters of strategy were as much reflections

of their respective ideologies. This was especially the case with regard to their readings of the present state of affairs in the Egyptian society.

Leadership

The MA began on the initiative of Sālih Sirīya, Palestinian by birth. In his mid-thirties, he had a modern education, receiving a Ph.D. in science education. He had been a member of the Muslim Brothers branch in Jordan (more commonly known as the Islamic Liberation party, Hizb al-Tahrīr al-Islāmī). After the defeat of 1967, he intermittently joined various Palestinian organizations, tried to cooperate with various Arab regimes that claimed to be revolutionary (Libya and Iraq), and spent brief sentences in jail. He finally settled in Egypt (1971) and joined one of the specialized agencies of the Arab League in Cairo. It was from that vantage point that he began to attract the attention of some of the religious-minded students. Underground cells, called usar (families) by the group, began to form in Cairo and Alexandria.

Interestingly enough, the initiator of the RHF, Shukrī Mustafā, was also in his early thirties and a veteran of the Muslim Brothers. He had been arrested in 1965, tried, and jailed for a few years. In prison he became disillusioned with older members of the Brothers, as he saw some of them either breaking down under torture during interrogation or engaging in petty fighting. The prison experience, nevertheless, did not disillusion him as far as the Brothers' ideology was concerned. If anything, it made him more of a true believer. The first cell of RHF, in fact, was established while he was in prison. As soon as he was released (in 1971) he launched a steady and relentless effort to expand his movement. Shukrī Mustafā had also received a modern education in Cairo, with a B.S. in agricultural science.

Thus, the two initiating leaders of the two groups had several features in common: age, a modern science education, previous membership in the Muslim Brothers, prison experience, and a disposition toward secret organizing. Personality characteristics of the two leaders could not be directly observed, as both had been hung by the time we started our research. We therefore relied heavily on what their closest lieutenants, that is, the second echelon of leadership, told us. Both leaders were said to have possessed a great amount of charisma. They commanded tremendous respect from their followers, were considered exemplary Muslims, and were emulated. Sirīya also elicited love, and Mustafā elicited awe (some would say fear). None of the interviewed members of the two groups had anything negative to say about their fallen leaders. Both leaders were perceived as extremely eloquent, knowledgeable about religion, well versed in the Quran and hadīth, and highly understanding of national, regional, and international affairs. Both were perceived as virtuous, courageous, and fearless of death, in other words, eager for istishhād (martydom).

Sirīya and Mustafā initiated and organized their respective groups about the same time (in the early 1970s) but quite independently of one another. Somewhat later (early 1974) each became vaguely aware of the other's group. One attempt was made to join forces, but differences in leadership style, ideology, organization, and strategy prevented the idea from being realized.

The leadership style was significantly different. MA was fairly democratic in its deliberations and decision making. An informal executive council of about 12 members was presided over by Sirīya. All points of view were expressed and discussed. Formal voting, however, was quite rare. Consensus was always sought by the leader. His power of persuasion was often decisive in steering the views of the majority in some particular direction. As far as those interviewed could remember, there was only one occasion when Sirīya was unable to sway the council to adopt his point of view. This was the timing of the attempt to take over power and confront the regime. Sirīya, as one of those who was present stated, felt very strongly that the time was not ripe for such an attempt. His argument was predicated on the fact that the regime was still riding a wave of popularity following the October War, that the MA had not perfected its organizational machinery, and that it had not thoroughly prepared a program of action for running the country in case of success. Sirīya estimated their chances of success at the time as no more than 30 percent. The majority (all but one other member) saw otherwise. Even if success was not assured, they argued, their action would be a ghadba li' l-Allāh (outrage for God)—propaganda by deed. The ideological justification for those who wanted to act immediately was the saying of the Prophet, "Any of you who sees a repugnance ought to remove it with his hand; if unable, then by his tongue; and if unable, then by his heart." The political justification was Sadat's apparent moves toward the West and toward an accommodation with Israel, perceived as treasonous acts requiring an immediate reaction. The majority view prevailed, and the leader was obliged to go along in accordance with the shūrā principle, which the group had followed from the beginning.

The leadership style of RHF was quite autocratic. Mustafā was established by his followers as the Amīr jama‘at al-mu'minīn (commander of the faithful group). While he would encourage discussion and dialogue, the final word was always that of the Amīr. The multitude of issues on which he made such final judgments ranged from the personal dealing with questions of marriage and divorce to intergroup and international issues. He was considered by his followers as an authority on matters of doctrinal theology, Islamic jurisprudence, worship, and Islamic social transactions. The followers' perceptions of their leader's generalized competence was steadily reinforced by both leader and followers. Over time, the RHF leader was elevated in their eyes into an almost omnipotent figure. Even after the death sentence had been issued, his followers would not believe that the government could take his life. For several weeks after his actual hanging, his closest followers refused to believe the news. When asked if they thought that Shukrī Mustafā was immortal, they answered in the negative. But they all believed that since God had ordained him and his group to restore Islam, he would not die before accomplishing this "divine mission."

Membership Recruitment

Both leaders recruited followers from among students or recent university graduates. Three recruitment mechanisms were employed: kinship, friendship, and religious ties. RHF relied heavily on kinship and friendship. Mustafā began with close friends (from prison days) and relatives (his brother and a nephew). These in turn would enlist their close friends and relatives as members in the group. MA relied on friendship and religious ties. In the late 1960s and early 1970s, with so many young people increasingly observing religious practices and attending mosques for prayers, members of the first cell formed by Sirīya would look for potential recruits among the worshipers. Typically, the older members would observe young worshipers in the college or neighborhood mosque. If they appeared to be deeply religious (especially as indexed by the dawn prayer), they would be approached to attend religious discussion after regular prayers. During these discussions the potential member was either discovered to be, or could gradually be made to be, politically conscious. Plain religiosity was evident, but the ability to politicize the potential recruit had to be ensured before a person was actually invited to become a member. More significant sociologically, of course, is the social background of the members.

Since only 34 members of both groups (21 MAs and 13 RHFs) were studied our generalizations on the social background of members must be taken with caution. It must be borne in mind that those studied were the most active in both groups, as is evidenced by the fact that the government considered them responsible enough to imprison them.

Regional Background

There were some regional background differences. Most MA members were from Cairo, Alexandria, and the Delta, while most RHF members were from Upper Egypt. This difference is readily explained by the location of the founder's activities. Sirīya operated from Cairo and had a link with Alexandria University. Mustafā, on the other hand, operated from Asyūt, his hometown in Upper Egypt, before moving to Cairo at a later stage. Since recruitment mechanisms were kinship, friendship, and religious ties, it followed that potential members would tend to be in social and geographic proximity.

Age

Aside from these regional differences, the profile of membership in both groups was extremely similar. Age, a crucial variable in most militant organizations, ranged between 17 and 26 at the time of joining as a full-fledged member. The median age for MA was 22 years and for RHF 24.

The leader of MA (Sirīya) was 14 years older than the average age of his followers and the leader of RHF (Mustafā) was 16 years older than the average member of his group. Thus, although youthful in both leadership and membership, all followers were significantly younger than their respective leaders. This may suggest that, even in a radical movement, the age-reverence tradition of Middle Eastern society still operates.

Rural and Small-Town Origins

Another important component of the membership profile is the rural and small-town background of two-thirds of those interviewed (21 out of 34). They were born in villages or small towns and were recent arrivals in big cities when they joined MA or RHF. Most of them had come to Cairo, Alexandria, or Asyūt to enroll in a university after completing secondary school. Fully one-half of those interviewed were living in the city by themselves or with roommates and not with their parental families. Even some of the one-third who were born in urban centers had lived in smaller communities during their early and mid-teens. Five such cases reported moving with their government-employed fathers to smaller communities and living there for several years.

Although women were not represented in our sample, RHF recruited from both sexes. At the time of the government crackdown on the group, some 80 women members were arrested along with several hundred male members. Secondary analysis of the backgrounds of these women indicates that they were mostly relatives or wives of male members of RHF.[3] Interestingly enough, RHF (as indicated earlier) was more literal and dogmatic on women's inequality. The more flexible MA group did not recruit female members.

Class Affiliation

Class affiliation of the membership was hard to establish directly. Broadly speaking it was inferred from the occupation and education of the members and their fathers. There was no significant difference between MA and RHF in this respect. Two-thirds of the fathers (21 out of 34) were government employees, mostly in middle grades of the civil service. Four members had fathers who were in high-level professional occupations (two university professors, one engineer, and one pharmacist). Four members had fathers who were small merchants; three had working-class fathers. Only seven fathers (20 percent) had a university education. A majority of 19 fathers (56 percent) had an intermediate education (ranging from secondary school to less than four years of college). Five fathers had below intermediate certificates and three were illiterate. Although fathers spanned both the educational and the occupational spectrums, the central tendency was decidedly in the middle. It is not unsafe, therefore, to conclude that the class affiliation of most members of these militant Islamic groups is middle and lower middle class.

Achievement and Mobility

The educational and occupational attainment of the members themselves was decidedly higher than that of their parents. All but 5 (29 out of 34) were university graduates or enrolled in college at the time of their arrest. The rest had secondary-school educations. Only 16 (47 percent) of the members were employed, the rest being students. Most of these were professionals (12 out of 16) employed by the government: 5 teachers, 3 engineers, 2 doctors, and 3 agronomists. Three were self-employed (a pharmacist, a doctor, and an accountant), and one worked as a conductor in a bus company. Among those who were students at the time of their arrest (18, or 53 percent), 6 were majoring in engineering, 4 in medicine, 3 in agricultural science, 2 in pharmacy, 2 in technical military science, and 1 in literature.

It is worth noting here that four of the above majors require very high grades in Egypt's statewide high school examination: medicine, engineering, technical military science, and pharmacy. These four majors accounted for 14 out of the 18 (80 percent) who were students. In other words, student joiners of the two militant Islamic groups were decidedly high on both motivation and achievement.

Incidence of Family Cohesion

Most members in both groups came from normal, cohesive families; that is, there was no divorce, separation, or death of either parent. None in either group was an only child, and none reported any significant tragic events in his family history. Seven members (out of 34, or 20 percent) had experienced what may be considered family strain. Of these, three had lost their fathers, with one mother remarrying. Two had experienced a divorce, with one father remarrying. One member had lost both parents and was living with an older brother. One member reported having been "shocked" by the behavior of his Western-educated parents at a New Year's party and had subsequently moved out and was living with a friend.

The typical social profile of members of militant Islamic groups could therefore be summarized as being young (early twenties), from a rural or small-town background, from a middle or lower-middle-class background, with high achievement motivation, upwardly mobile with an education in science or engineering, and from a normally cohesive family. This profile poses theoretical problems, since it is sometimes assumed in social science that joiners of radical movements must in some way be alienated, marginal, anomic, or possessing some other abnormal characteristics.[4] Most of the members investigated would normally be considered as ideal or model young Egyptians.

Membership Control

Both MA and RHF demanded total commitment and ironclad discipline from their members. Decisions arrived at by the MA semidemocratic leadership and orders given by the RHF autocratic leadership were to be carried out thoroughly. Members on varying levels of the organizational structure did so with zeal and joy in the unshakable belief that they were serving the cause of Islam. Thus, the primary control of members' behavior was achieved through their own internal conviction and exhilarating sense of mission.

The RHF, however, employed additional secondary means of membership control. One such mechanism was simply virtual absorption of all the members' time in activities related to the group:

worship, study, proselytizing, exercise, or working in one of the group's economic enterprises.* This tended gradually to insulate the member from the outside society, something that was urged and openly welcomed. Indirectly this total absorption and insulation made the typical member quite dependent on the group for the satisfaction of his spiritual, social, and economic needs. In fact, at a certain point in the evolution of RHF, members were ordered to resign their jobs in the society at large, desert their families, and sever all relations with the outside world. In other words, RHF was to become the members' total and only world.

Both groups were quite keen on preparing their members for maximum personal sacrifice of worldly possessions as well as of life itself. Simply expressed, the member was rigorously conditioned to be a shahīd (martyr). The heavenly rewards awaiting martyrs are boundless. Fear or hestitation to die for Islam is the ultimate betrayal of faithful fellow Muslims. Among other things, it means one's exclusion from their spiritual communion in both lives. Thinking of the joy and rewards of martyrdom is said to make any physical torture by the enemies of Islam quite bearable. Several members reported that the stories they had heard of the torture of the Muslim Brothers in 1966 had had a profound effect on them at the time and on their subsequent decision to join the MA and RHF. The severe torture seems to have marked sharply the dividing line in their minds between a "merciless jāhilīya society and a community of selfdenying faithful."

The threat of being excommunicated from the group should one fail one's fellow members or fail the cause of the movement also acts as a control. In several instances, RHF not only carried out such a threat but also meted out physical punishment to expelled members.[5]

What most of these control mechanisms amount to in the end is no less than an attempt at total resocialization of the members. The individual joiner was asked not only to adhere to the ideas and principles of the group but also to engage in a serious transformation of his own behavior, attitudes, and relationships. In other words, both MA and RHF represented the kind of movements that aim at fundamental, simultaneous transformation of both the individual and society. It was quite evident that the typical member felt and readily expressed a moral superiority to people outside the movement. Their ability to impose self-discipline, in accordance with the commandments and prohibitions of Islam, while others cannot or will not was the source

---

*Most of the RHF enterprises were small scale and still in an embryonic stage at the time of the showdown with the government. These enterprises included bakeries, bookshops, candy-making establishments, and vegetable gardens.

of this feeling. But it was equally evident that, aside from the moral superiority, there was deep joy in defying society and its physical means of coercion. Several who claimed to have been severely tortured, reported having images and dreams of prophets and saints welcoming them to the Garden of Eden or images and dreams of the just Islamic society being established after their pending martyrdom.

STRATEGY AND TACTICS

The two groups, as should be clear by now, have one common objective: to topple Egypt's present social order and establish an Islamic one. It is on questions of strategy that MA and RHF differed the most. Interestingly enough, each group invoked an Islamic principle or precedent to justify its strategy in achieving the ultimate goal of a truly Muslim society.

The MA perceived the majority of Egyptians to be basically religious but helpless victims of ungodly political regimes imposing on them non-Islamic institutions. Such a situation was read as abhorrently sinful, necessitating immediate removal by those who are truly Muslims. One of the Prophet's famous sayings was invoked to justify direct and immediate action. "Ghadba li' l-Allāh" (outrage for God) was the rallying cry for a violent confrontation to topple the regime. Of course, the group had to prepare well for the showdown. The MA leadership believed in meticulous planning for the coup d'etat. Arduous training in the use of arms, infiltration of the army and the police, detailed study of presidential and other elite behavior and daily routines, the construction and study of maps of all important strategic sites in the capital, and the preparation of the first communiqués to be aired on radio and television were all begun long in advance. Several rehearsals of most of the plan were carried out before the final actual countdown on April 18, 1974.

The RHF strategy, on the other hand, was a patient and long-range one. The RHF reading of the situation was quite different from that of MA. It was not just the political regime that was corrupt, but all other social institutions as well. It was not only the rulers who were ungodly and sinful but most members of the society as well. Thus the moral rebuilding had to start from the ground up. RHF strategy was therefore to establish a nucleus community, a miniature society of believers who would act out the true life of Islam. This was to be a genuine alternative to the sinful way of the Egyptian society at large. Establishing this model community was the first step in RHF strategy. After its establishment, this Islamic community of believers would grow in numbers and in spiritual and material strength. Then the true believers would march onward to bring down the already crumbling sinful social order of Egypt at large.

Like the MA, the RHF invoked a precedent from early Islam to justify its strategy. The prophet Muhammad, surrounded and harassed by the jāhilīya people of Mecca, fled to Medina with a few followers and established there the first true Muslim community. [6] As the community gained in strength, it engaged the infidels of Mecca in a series of ghazwāt (battles) and finally conquered Mecca itself. [7] This is the model the RHF was emulating.

Thus, while the MA showdown with the regime followed logically from its strategy, the RHF confrontation did not. In other words, the MA planned its coup, but the RHF, when it clashed with the regime in July 1977, had had no such intention in mind. RHF had a long way to go in implementing the first component of its strategy, that is, building the model community of believers somewhere in an unpopulated hinterland on the edge of the Nile valley. * The groups had barely begun. It is safe to accept the RHF's version that its move in July 1977 was basically a tactical one forced on it by the regime. As the RHF members tell the story, the security forces had arrested several of their brother RHF members and detained them without trial, far beyond what the law allows. They demanded to be tried or set free. When their pleas were ignored, other members kidnapped the former minister of Awqāf, keeping him as hostage till the freeing of their brothers. The deadline set by the RHF passed without a positive response from the government; the group felt it had to kill him as it had warned it would.

In their confrontation with the Egyptian government, the MA and RHF lost many of their cadres, either in actual shoot-outs or in subsequent death sentences. † The remaining leaders were put be-

---

*As RHF members reported it to the research team, "the group debated several places to start its new community of believers." The possible sites included Yemen, Libya, the Sudan, and several spots in Egypt itself. Two sites were actually used by RHF. One was in Mīnya Governorate in Upper Egypt. The second and more important was in the desert strip between Mā^{c}adī Ma^{c}sārah and Hilwān, south of Cairo. The group, however, never moved entirely to either site.

† Three of MA's leaders (Sālih Sirīya, Karīm al-Anadūlī, and Talāl al-Ansārī) and five of the RHF leaders (Shukrī Mustafā, Māhir A. Bakri Zanātī, Ahmad Tāriq Abd al-^{c}Ālim, Anwar Ma^{c}mūn Saqr, and Mustafā A. Ghāzi) were sentenced to death. All but one (Talāl al-Ansārī's sentence was reduced to life imprisonment) were actually executed on November 9, 1976, and March 19, 1978. Of the other 92 MA members tried by the State Security Court, 29 were found guilty and were sentenced to varying penalties (8 years to life imprisonment, 7 to 15 years, 8 to 10 years, and 4 to 6 years). Of the 204 RHF mem-

hind bars. In their retrospective evaluations of what had happened, we found some significant differences between the two groups. MA members were split right down the middle: one-half said that the strategy was correct, that their failure was caused by tactical problems, and that they would do it again.* The other half had come to believe that the strategy was incorrect, the tactics impatient and adolescent. These members felt deep guilt for not having listened to Sirīya and for having dragged him into an action that claimed his life and that of several innocent brothers.

Members of the RHF who were interviewed expressed unanimous approval of their strategy. They regret that the government did not respond to their ultimatum, which triggered the subsequent tragic events. They would do the whole thing all over again.

Almost all members of both groups perceived their present prison sentences as an integral part of their jihād; it was God's testing of their faith and perseverance. None of the ones interviewed had changed his ideology, that is, the conviction that only Islam ensures a just and righteous society on earth. As far as could be inferred from the interviews, both movements were still active, though underground. The initial success of the Islamic revolution in Iran, led by Ayātollāh Khomeinī, has given them a tremendous boost. At the time the interviews were stopped in early 1979, the morale of both groups was high.

But there were signs of other influences from the Iranian example on the strategic thinking of both groups. Popular uprisings as a mechanism to topple the regime were more seriously looked into in late 1978 and early 1979. Till then, such organizational weapons had been perceived by the Islamic militants as essentially communistic. It is worth noting that during 1979 and 1980, a host of Islamic groups

---

bers who were tried, 36 more were found guilty (12 had life sentences, 6 had 10 years with hard labor, and the remainder received sentences varying between 5 and 10 years). See al-Ahrām, December 1, 1977.

*MA members who held this contention claim that one member in the group, who was part of the plan, betrayed them by informing the state security forces of the intended plot to overthrow the regime. Curiously enough, the informant was not taken seriously for several hours, and that enabled MA to implement the first part of its plan successfully, that is, to occupy the Technical Military Academy. By the time the group was ready to move on to the Arab Socialist Union building to carry out the second part of the plan, the authorities had acted on the information and had started a siege and a counterattack on the academy. The reader may check this contention against the official version in al-Jumhūrīya, April 21, 1974.

began to stage sit-ins and campus and street demonstrations, similar
to those of early stages of the Iranian revolution protest activities. *

NOTES

1. See the works of Israel Altman, "Islamic Movements in
Egypt," Jerusalem Quarterly 10 (1979): 87-108; R. H. Dekmejian,
"The Anatomy of Islamic Revival and the Search for Islamic Alternatives," Middle East Journal 34 (1980): 1-12; and R. S. Humphreys,
"Islam and Political Values in Saudi Arabia, Egypt and Syria," Middle East Journal 33 (1979): 1-19.
2. See Sadat's speech in the Egypt's People's Assembly on
May 15, 1980, reported in al-Ahrām, May 16, 1980, in which he
proposes the support of a constitutional amendment to appease the
Muslim groups but in which he insists on separation of religion and
state.
3. See al-Ahrām, July 7, 1977. For more details about those
arrested and their background, see al-Ahrām issues from July 7-20,
1977.
4. This kind of proposition is to be found, for example, in
Eric Hoffer, The True Believer: Thoughts on the Nature of Mass
Movements (New York: Harper, 1951); idem, The Ordeal of Change
(New York: Harper & Row, 1963); and idem, Reflections on the Human Condition (New York: Harper & Row, 1973). Also expounding
similar arguments is Hadley Cantril, The Psychology of Social Movements (New York: Wiley and Sons, 1941); and idem, The Politics of
Despair (New York: Basic, 1958).
5. It was such attempts at penalizing former members that
first drew governmental attention to the potential strength and danger
of RHF. See al-Ahrām, July 7, 1977.
6. For details on this early period of Islam, consult any of the
standard references on the history of Islam, the Arabs, or the Middle
East. See, for example, Fazlur Rahman, Islam (London: Weidenfeld & Nicolson, 1966); S. C. Coon, Caravan: The Story of the Middle East (New York: Holt, Rinehart and Winston, 1958); and Bernard

---

*A typical example of this was reported in al-Ahrām, April 1,
1980, quoting the minister of the interior's account to the People's
Assembly of a student conference that began in a mosque in Asyūt,
then was converted into a march across the city protesting Sadat's
invitation to the shah to reside in Egypt and the peace treaty with
Israel. Islamic groups in other universities staged demonstrations.

Lewis, The Arabs in History (London: Hutchinson University Library, 1950). The act of fleeing from Mecca to Medina marks the first day of the first year of the Islamic calendar.

7. This strategy of the prophet Muhammad is explicitly discussed by Fazlur Rahman in Islam, pp. 18-29.

7

THE ISLAMIC MOVEMENT IN SYRIA: SECTARIAN CONFLICT AND URBAN REBELLION IN AN AUTHORITARIAN-POPULIST REGIME

RAYMOND A. HINNEBUSCH

THE ISLAMIC MOVEMENT AND THE BA^CTH PARTY: ROOTS OF CONFLICT

The Islamic movement in Syria has been shaped in very distinctive ways by its current character as, in large part, a reaction against the ruling Ba^Cth party-state. While in much of the Middle East, Islamic fundamentalism currently expresses nativist and populist rebellion against upper-class-based regimes perceived as clients of Western imperialism, in Syria the Islamic movement is closely linked to the traditionally privileged classes and opposes a regime long regarded as troublesome by the West and currently in the front line of Arab resistance to Israel. The roots of Syria's Islamic movement and of its opposition to the Ba^Cth regime must be sought in four basic factors.

1. The Islamic movement in Syria originated as a nativist reaction against the Western-imported secular state. Under the Ba^Cth, a more rigorously secular regime than its predecessors, it continues to express the aspirations of pious Muslims for a reunion of political power and Islamic morality. The ^Culamā' and traditional urban society have usually been most receptive to this world view.

2. The Islamic opposition to the Ba^Cth is also an expression of a reaction by urban society against a rural-based regime that has damaged its interests. Historically, the cleavage between the city and the village in Syria has been very wide—indeed, one between two worlds: the city, residence of the ruler, landlord, and merchant, held all the power and wealth; the village was a political vacuum, deprived of its economic surplus to support the urban ruling class. Islam itself was chiefly an urban institution.[1] In the 1950s and 1960s,

however, the village made Ba^{C}thism into a vehicle of revolt against the city. The Ba^{C}th recruited from the peasants and rural townsmen outside the clientage networks of the urban establishment, appealing to rural youth with a potent mixture of nationalism and populism. As the army became a major channel of upward social mobility for rural youth, the Ba^{C}th developed a strong following among young army officers. Although the party did in time develop a following in the cities, its quarrels with Nasser deprived it of much of this support. Thus, in 1963, when its officer partisans seized state power for the party, its social color was predominantly rural.[2] In its effort to become entrenched, the party purged from the army and bureaucracy urbanites considered unreliable by virtue of their loyalties to the traditional elite or to Nasserism, thus turning the main institutions of the state into rural strongholds ruling over the city. Subsequently, the Ba^{C}th used state power to impose radical policies favorable to the village and damaging to urban interests. The values of the city were those of traders and rentiers: private enterprise, free trade, real estate speculation. The Ba^{C}th pursued land reform and state socialist policies meant to break the domination of the urban establishment over the economy and the village. The historic ties of the ^{C}ulamā' to the urban merchant community made it natural that Islam, interpreted to exclude socialism, would be used as a vehicle of ideological protest against this assault on urban interests.[3] Thus, to a considerable extent, the cleavage between the Ba^{C}th and political Islam represents a split between the city establishment and the village, Sunnī as well as non-Sunnī.

3. The Islamic opposition also expresses Sunnī opposition to the disproportionate role played by members of the minority communities in the Ba^{C}th leadership. Syria, a "mosaic society," is divided between a majority Sunnī Muslim community (70 percent), traditionally dominant, and several minority communities, long considered less than equal: Christians (11 percent) and several Islamic heterodox sects—the ^{C}Alawites (12 percent), Druze (3.4 percent), and Ismā^{C}īlīs (1.59 percent). While the Sunnī and Christian confessions cut across the urban-rural gap, the Islamic heterodox sects were chiefly rural and, in particular the ^{C}Alawites, traditionally deprived. The Islamic minorities, finding in the Ba^{C}th's brand of secular Arab nationalism an identity that integrated them on an equal basis into the Syrian political community, and very receptive to the party's populism, were disproportionately drawn to the Ba^{C}th. Since the time of the French, who deliberately recruited from the minorities, the army had been an attractive channel of social mobility for these same deprived groups. Thus, when the Ba^{C}th took power, the minorities were already disproportionately represented in the two institutions, the party and the army, that would, together, rule Syria. Subsequently, the

Ba^{C}thization of the army—which, in practice, often amounted to replacing urban Sunnīs with the clients and coreligionists of leading minority Ba^{C}th officers—and intra-Ba^{C}th conflicts in which Sunnīs lost out further enhanced minority ascendancy.[4] This turnabout, in which the historically dominant Sunnī establishment found itself subordinated to a new elite drawn disproportionately from minorities, was bound to result in an enduring hostility: Islamic fundamentalism, denying the legitimacy of rule by other than orthodox Muslims, became a congenial ideological vehicle for it.

4. Up to now, the Islamic movement has been chiefly an expression of urban Sunnī opposition to rural minority rule. In political Islam, the traditional notables, merchants, and ^{C}ulamā' find an ideology that not only authentically reflects their values, but also unites them with a big segment of the traditional urban masses against their Ba^{C}thī antagonists. However, in the late 1970s, it seemed possible that the Islamic movement might become an umbrella for a more generalized opposition of the "ruled" against their "rulers." This would require Islamic leaders to counteract the efforts of the Ba^{C}th to portray itself as a populist regime representing the less privileged social strata by convincingly defining the axis of conflict as one between an unrepresentative, impious, and corrupt minority regime and the Sunnī majority. The Islamic movement could thereby incorporate into its base major, but traditionally unreceptive, parts of society, notably Sunnī segments of the modern middle class and the peasantry. While this would require a major realignment of forces in the political arena, it can by no means be ruled out. The ba^{C}th's authoritarian state had proved capable of absorbing only limited participatory demands, and while authoritarian rule may be accepted if power is used to pursue widely valued goals, the Ba^{C}th, in the view of many Syrians, had, by the end of the 1970s, exhausted much of its nationalist-populist impetus and turned into an increasingly self-serving in-group. Since the Islamic movement has become the major alternative to the Ba^{C}th, the struggle between these two forces for the loyalties of the population will determine the future of Syrian political life. In the following pages, the nature of these political antagonists and the dynamics of their conflict are examined more closely.

THE BA^{C}TH STATE: SECTARIAN
POLITICS AND RURAL ASCENDANCY

The rise of the Ba^{C}th to power resulted in a virtual transformation of the Syrian power structure. An elite predominantly recruited from the Sunnī landlord/merchant bourgeoisie was displaced by a new one of rural, lower-middle-class, and disproportionately minority origins. In place of the old upper-class-based liberal state, the new elite forged an authoritarian, single-party military state, which it sought to base in the lower and middle classes. It excluded all political rivals from participation, concentrated power in its own hands, and tried to use this power to carry out populist and etatist policies, redistributing resources to its own constituency and creating in place of the bourgeois-dominated private market a new state-controlled economy.

Elite Composition

By origin, the Ba^{c}th elite represents a middle-class and lower-class alliance, which generally excludes higher-class elements. Its social center of gravity is distinctly lower middle class: the typical Ba^{c}th leader has come from a peasant, small merchant, or employee family and moved upward through acquisition of some education into a modern profession such as teaching, the military, law, or medicine. [5] Drawn from the village and the provincial town,* the elite reflects the rise of the rural periphery at the expense of the urban center; most notably in the party leadership, but even in the government, the city has been distinctly underrepresented. † In confessional terms, all of Syria's sectarian groups have been represented in the elite, but equally so. At the cabinet level their representation has been roughly proportional to their numbers, but in the more powerful civilian and military party leaderships, the Islamic minorities, especially ^{c}Alawites, have been disproportionately overrepresented and Sunnīs underrepresented. Thus, between 1963 and 1978, in the overall party leadership (the Regional Command), Sunnīs held 58.2 percent of the posts; ^{c}Alawites, 20 percent; Druzes, 10.6 percent; Ismā^{c}īlīs, 6.5 percent; and Christians, 4.7 percent; while in the party military leadership, Sunnī strength fell to 43.4 percent and

---

*Four rural provinces have contributed disproportionately to the elite: Latakia (largely ^{c}Alawite), Suwaydā' (largely Druze), Dīr^{c}a (Sunnī), and Dīr al-Zūr (Sunnī).

†Indicative of the underrepresentation of the two major urban centers, Damascus and Aleppo, is the fact that though these two cities contain 23 percent of the population, and Damascus and Aleppo provinces together, 41 percent, over the period from 1963 to 1978, these two provinces have only contributed 29.7 percent of government ministers and a little more than 11 percent of both the military and civilian segments of the Regional Command. (These figures are taken from Van Dam, The Struggle for Power, pp. 126-29.)

^{c}Alawite representation rose to 37.7 percent.[6] This rural and ^{c}Alawite flavor of the elite has, over time, become more pronounced toward the very apex of the pyramid of power. In the early years of Ba^{c}th rule (1963-66), urban and rural Sunnī and minority elements shared power at the top. Between 1966 and 1970 Sunnī, especially urban elements, as well as Druzes, were purged in a series of intraelite conflicts. After 1970 an ^{c}Alawite, Hāfiz al-Asad, emerged as the clearly dominant figure; and although he deliberately replenished top elite ranks with urban Sunnī elements, his personal following of ^{c}Alawite officers dominated the strategic coercive levers of the Syrian state.

Elite Structure, Conflict, and Change under the Ba^{c}th

The rural petty bourgeois character of the Ba^{c}th elite has given a fairly coherent populist-etatist thrust to its policies and, together with party loyalty, provided it with a reasonable level of solidarity vis-à-vis its urban, largely upper-class rivals. But a multitude of vertical cleavages—personal, ideological, generational, regional, and sectarian—have riven the elite internally; the sectarian division, in particular, because of its deep roots in the social structure, has proved the most durable, if not always the most important, intraelite cleavage. This fragmentation has made for a high incidence of intraelite conflict, frequently involving the use of military force, which has retarded the institutionalization of authority. The fragility of institutionalized authority has only enhanced the importance of noninstitutional ties as the cement of power, but such ties have themselves proved fragile and an obstacle to enhanced institutionalization. Thus, while sectarian loyalties have been critical of the solidity of every Ba^{c}th ruling group, sectarianism has to that very extent defined major lines of intraelite conflict detrimental to leadership teamwork and stabilization of the regime.

Under the first two Ba^{c}th regimes (1963-70), the elite did attempt to institutionalize authority in a set of collegial party organs that specified rules for policy making and elite recruitment and accountability, but because commitment to these norms remained weak, power holders and aspirants had to engage in constant coalition building to maintain and advance their positions. Every available tie and cleavage—not least the sectarian and personal ones—was exploited. Although such coalitions were usually cross-sectarian, when one side lost out and was purged from the elite, sectarian cleavages were aggravated.

During the first Ba^{c}th regime (1963-66), the elite was as broadly representative as it ever was to be. To be sure, the most potent center of power, the party military organization, was led predominantly by rural officers, three of whom were ^CAlawites, two Druzes, and two Ismā^Cīlīs, but there were also four Sunnīs, and the one of urban background, Amīn al-Hāfiz, was the dominant personality in the regime. The civilian party was also dominated by men of rural background, roughly half Sunnī and half minority in origin, but the party's urban elder leaders, Michel Aflāq and Salāh al-Dīn al-Bitār, did retain some power.

The very heterogeneity of the elite, however, made it harder to hold together, and it was soon split by two interlocking conflicts: one largely ideological, generational, and urban-rural in which the party's moderate, older urban leaders confronted younger rural radicals; the other a personal competition between the three ranking party officers, Amīn al-Hāfiz, Salāh Jadīd, and Muhammad ^CUmrān, each of whom, in the end, joined either the moderate or the radical camp. The final showdown was a struggle for personal power, but it also involved a struggle over the regime's course between the moderates, who wished to reach a compromise with the urban upper-class and middle-class opposition, and their opponents, who had a radical populist orientation. Both sides were cross-sectarian coalitions: the Aleppine Sunnī Hāfiz and the ^CAlawite ^CUmrān both tried to mobilize supporters behind the moderate leadership; the ^CAlawite Jadīd led a radical coalition that included powerful Sunnī, but rural, officers—notably Mustafā Talās and Ahmad Suwaydānī—and prominent Sunnī party politicians such as Yūsuf Zuayyin and Nūr al-Dīn al Ātāsī. The radicals won out because the apparent intention of Aflāq and Bitār to reach a détente and perhaps share power with the party's urban rivals, dilute its radical program, and push radical officers/politicians out of politics, threatened broad sectors of the new elite. The decisive factors, thus, were overlapping ideological and urban-rural cleavages. Sectarianism did, however, play an important role because each side tried to exploit it: Hāfiz tried to undermine Jadīd by playing on the resentment and fears of Sunnī officers over minority predominance, while Jadīd was able to mobilize support from minority officers fearful for their positions. In the end, the Sunnīs were more heavily represented in the modern camp and the minorities in the radical camp, with the result that, with the victory of the latter, a disproportionate number of Sunnīs lost their positions and were replaced largely by ^CAlawites. [7]

Under the second Ba^Cth regime (1966-70), the elite was led by an ^CAlawite officer, Salāh Jadīd, and the minority and rural character of the regime was substantially enhanced. Leadership, nevertheless, remained collegial, and Jadīd's main allies in the party, Nūr al-Dīn al-Ātāsī, who became head of state, and Yūsuf Zuayyin, who served as prime minister, were Sunnīs, while Ahmad Suwaydānī, a major Sunnī military collaborator, became chief of staff.

Once he had won out as strongman, however, Jadīd's radical coalition began to fray, and the big divisions did appear to be along sectarian lines. First, Druze officers, led by Salīm Hatūm, disgruntled at what they considered to be their exclusion from the inner circles of power and apparently with the support of much of the Druze party leadership, staged a power play involving the kidnapping of Jadīd. When the defense minister, Hāfiz al-Asad, an ᶜAlawite, threatened to bomb the Druze capital, Suwaydā', and Hatūm sought refuge with the traditional Druze leader, Hasan al-Atrash, the incident took on overt sectarian dimensions. Druze elements in the top elite were decimated when Hatūm's plot collapsed. [8] ᶜAlawites seemed to win out again when, after the disastrous 1967 war, Chief of Staff Suwaydānī was removed, while ᶜAlawite Defense Minister Asad kept his post; the embittered Suwaydānī soon defected to Iraq, taking with him a good many Sunnī followers. [9] While the regime was careful to maintain some sectarian balance by appointing in his place a Sunnī, Mustafā Talās,* by 1970 the ᶜAlawite role in the regime had become yet more pronounced, increasing the feeling among other communities that they had been deprived of their rightful representation.

However, in the most recent intraelite struggle (1969–70) between radical and moderate factions, both sides were led by ᶜAlawite officers—Jadīd and Defense Minister Hāfiz al-Asad, respectively. This conflict, partly a personal power rivalry, also revolved around differences over ideology and strategy. Jadīd continued to enjoy the support of major Sunnī and ᶜAlawite politicians in the party organization, while Asad's base, strongest in the military, also included both ᶜAlawites and prominent Sunnīs—notably Mustafā Talās, Nājī Jamīl, and ᶜAbd al-Rahmān al-Khilfāwī. Once again, both coalitions in the intraelite conflict cut across sectarian lines and were largely cemented by personal and ideological loyalties, but the fact that both sides were led by ᶜAlawite officers indicated for many Syrians the ascendancy of this sectarian community. [10]

The structure of the elite has been substantially altered under the third Baᶜth regime, that of Asad (1971-). Aware of the precariousness of institutionalized authority in the Baᶜth state and of the susceptibility of collegial leadership to factionalism, Asad has personalized and concentrated power in an authoritarian presidency, which raises him above the rest of the elite. His power rests on

---

*Talās was appointed specifically to maintain sectarian balance in spite of the belief that ᶜIzzat Jadīd, an ᶜAlawite cousin of Salāh, was more trustworthy.

several bases. On the one hand, he has constructed a network of personal ^CAlawite clients dominating strategic levers of the military-police apparatus; they not only hold a very large portion of key army and intelligence positions, but also lead several praetorian-guard detachments, including the famous Defense Brigade, which is led by the president's brother Rif^Cāt.

On the other hand, Asad has maintained alliances with Sunnīs. Several Sunnī officers have held key military-security posts in the regime, notably Defense Minister Talās, Chief of Staff Shīhābī, and Nājī Jamīl, longtime air force chief, head of the political department of the armed forces, and political security boss. These men have assumed the role of spokesmen for Sunnī interests in the power structure. They have personal and business ties with Sunnī interests and may constitute the leadership of a Sunnī faction in the regime. Asad also relies on alliances with prominent Sunnī politicians in the civilian party organization, notably Foreign Minister ^CAbd al-Halīm Khaddām, exofficer and frequent Prime Minister ^CAbd al-Rahmān al-Khilfāwī, and party Assistant Secretary-General ^CAbd Allāh al-Ahmar. The prime ministership has remained a Sunnī preserve, and Asad has deliberately co-opted a large number of Damascene Sunnīs into the party leadership in a bid for urban Sunnī support.

In general, Asad has been careful not to ignore the ethnic arithmetic needed to assure each part of Syria's communal mosaic at least a minimum of representation in elite circles. The elite remains under Asad a cross-sectarian coalition and, indeed, even if they so wished, ^CAlawites probably could not rule alone. The demographic facts are such that they cannot make up a majority of the structural bases of the regime—the party, army, and bureaucracy. It does appear, however, that sectarian politics has assumed a greater role in intraelite cleavages since 1970, if only because ideological divisions appear to have greatly diminished. Moreover, under Asad, the power of the ^CAlawites has probably increased again with the subordination of the intraparty political process in which the other sectarian communities were more equitably represented, to an authoritarian presidency held by an ^CAlawite and buttressed by an ^CAlawite clientage network in control of major levers of coercion and virtually immune from accountability. The eclipse in 1978 of Nājī Jamīl, apparently the loser in a struggle with Rif^Cāt al-Asad, lends support to the view that the ^CAlawites constitute the dominant power bloc.* However, the president has been careful not to become

---

*The claim is sometimes made that current top Sunnī officers lack power and are mere fronts for ^CAlawites. Thus, the Ikhwān claims that Talās is only a "puppet in the hands of the ^CAlawites"

identified as the leader of an ^CAlawite bloc and has instead played a balancing, brokerage role between such blocs. He does appear to have sufficiently contained these and other rivalries to give a greater cohesion to the Ba^Cth elite than heretofore, thus fashioning a more stable, albeit no more representative, structure of authority than his predecessors. But institutional legitimacy remains no less fragile, and personal, clientage, and sectarian solidarities no less important as structural cement than heretofore.

The composition and structure of the Ba^Cth elite constitute both an asset and a liability for the regime. The rural lower-class and middle-class origins of the elite have cost it support among the urban population, which considers itself underrepresented at the top. The urban Sunnī establishment considers its subordination to a power elite of lower social status unacceptable; but, though weakened, it has not been destroyed by the Ba^Cth and thus constitutes a counter-elite contesting the regime's legitimacy. On the other hand, the modest social origins of the Ba^Cth elite and its roots in the village allow it to portray itself with some credibility as a popular leadership. ^CAlawite overrepresentation, however, costs the regime considerable legitimacy, although the ^CAlawites, as a relatively cohesive social force with a strong stake in the survival of the regime, are not wholly a liability. At the same time, the heterogeneity of the elite, especially its sectarian pluralism, has detracted substantially from its cohesion. Similar class and village origins and party loyalties have helped to hold it together and have largely deterred sectarian groups inside the regime from the overt alliances with antiregime coreligionists that could destroy the regime. But the modest institutionalization of authority and intraelite competition remain major points of vulnerability, which, particularly in the next leadership-

---

(al-Da^Cwa 30 [September 1980]: 28). A less partisan source, Van Dam, argues that Sunnīs lack the power of ^CAlawites because Sunnī officers do not lead a cohesive faction, and the authority of top Sunnī officers is short-circuited by the presence of ^CAlawites in second-rank commands. While such arguments carry some credibility, in the absence of an objective inside study of the Syrian army, it is impossible to assess the extent to which such dynamics operate. Why Sunnīs should not stick together in the face of the purportedly all-powerful ^CAlawite solidarity is not clear. And if ^CAlawite officers do, in their second-rank positions as division and brigade commanders, short-circuit the authority of the defense minister and chief of staff, what prevents Sunnī officers in third-, fourth-, and fifth-level or lower commands from refusing obedience to their immediate ^CAlawite superiors? (See Van Dam, The Struggle for Power, pp. 89, 103.)

succession crisis, could destabilize the regime. Should such a conflict be along sectarian lines, as seems very possible, it could give the opposition a chance to topple the Ba^{C}th.

Regime Structural Base

The Ba^{C}th regime rests on three overlapping structures: the party, the military-police apparatus, and the state bureaucracy. The party and its auxiliary organizations—peasant, labor, youth, professional, and so on—represent a political machine with a sizable corps of cadres, which penetrates the villages in relatively uniform fashion, constitutes strong points in the cities, and provides the regime with a constituency recruited via a mix of ideological, careerist, personalistic, and primordial ties. In the villages at least, it provides a network of control limiting opposition access to the masses. It is also a web cutting across sectarian cleavages, for although the party apparatus has itself been infected by sectarian rivalries, it nevertheless penetrates the Sunnī as well as minority communities and incorporates into the regime's base many Sunnīs, including religiously pious ones.* Although the authoritarian concentration of power at the center limits the sense of political efficacy the typical party member is likely to feel, the party does provide chances for local power, patronage, and representative channels heretofore mostly absent for the regime's largely rural lower-class and lower-middle-class constituency. [11]

The state bureaucracy, greatly expanded under the Ba^{C}th, represents another network of control penetrating society on which a major segment of the population is dependent for employment or essential services. Ba^{C}th rule has opened up many opportunities for state employment for expeasants who are thus supportive of the regime; however, the Ba^{C}th purge of many urban bourgeois elements in the

---

*The results of an attitude survey given by the writer to mostly Sunnī-Muslim party recruits from villages around Damascus showed that 19. 7 percent expected the Quran and sharī^{C}a to have a large role in legislation, 44.3 percent expected them to have some role, and 36. 1 percent expected them to have no role. This suggests that the regime is able to recruit, even from very pious elements, persons who evidently do not perceive it as an anti-Islamic force and that, for many Sunnīs attracted to the party, the role of Islam in public affairs is not a top priority. See Raymond E. Hinnebusch, "Political Recruitment and Socialization in Syria: The Case of the Revolutionary Youth Federation," International Journal of Middle East Studies 11 (1980): 153.

bureaucracy created resentments inside the bureaucracy, and continuing favoritism on partisan, personal, and especially sectarian grounds keeps them alive.* Since 1970 Asad has tried to accommodate the demands of non-Ba^{C}thists for a greater share of government positions from the ministerial level down, hoping thus to incorporate them into his base.

Given the persistence of strong opposition to the regime and the historic role of the Syrian army as a vehicle of regime change, the capabilities and reliability of the army-police apparatus are decisive factors in the survival of Ba^{C}th rule. The steady expansion in the size and firepower of the military under the Ba^{C}th makes violent opposition to the regime difficult and costly, if not futile, so long as the military remains loyal. The early Ba^{C}thization of the army in which Sunnī upper-class and middle-class officers were replaced by rural, often minority ones, the maintenance of a Ba^{C}th organization in the army, and the later development of an ^{C}Alawite-recruited praetorian guard have helped ensure the regime's control over the military, but have also stimulated discontent among Sunnī officers. Asad, to dilute such resentments, has given non-Ba^{C}thist professional officers greater responsibility. The greater professionalization of the officer corps pursued since the 1967 defeat, the stake it has in maintaining the integrity of the military establishment and of its privileged position in society against a recurrence of the purges that previously resulted from intervention in politics, and the greater difficulty of plotting and mounting a successful coup in a larger army— all work in favor of Asad. But defeat in war, or sectarian strife on a large scale, could split the armed forces and turn part of it against the regime.

This structural base represents a formidable apparatus of control for the regime that has permitted it to penetrate society, organize a significant village base, make a big portion of the salaried middle class dependent on it, and co-opt parts of the urban professional classes into its service. On the other hand, it has been unable to penetrate and organize the masses of the urban quarters significantly. Moreover, regime structures (such as professional syndicates and "popular councils") have shown little ability to satisfy the participatory demands of important portions of the urban upper and middle classes, which, feeling deprived of political power, express themselves politically largely outside of and against the regime.

---

*Many public employees believe, with some reason, that recruitment and promotion depend more on being an ^{C}Alawite or having an ^{C}Alawite patron than on merit.

Regime Policy and Support Base

The nationalist-etatist-populist thrust of Ba^{c}th ideology and
policy appears well suited to forging a broad support base among the
middle and lower classes. It does indeed appear to have generated
some legitimacy for the regime, but owing to the gap between promise and performance (and to the alienation of those whose interests
and ideals have not been served by this orientation), the support base
of the Ba^{c}th regime has probably never embraced more than one-third
of the population.

The regime's Arabism and its militant nationalist stance toward
Israel and the Western powers do appear congruent with the views of
a majority of the Syrian population, but the actual nationalist achievements of the regime have been modest. With the possible exception
of the 1973 war, it has failed to stand up to Israel or even to defend
Syrian territory. Nor has it significantly advanced the Palestinian
cause. It has even been an obstacle to the Arab unity desired by many
Syrians. Moreover, for those Syrians whose national identity is in-
separable from Islam, the Ba^{c}th's secular nationalism has been far
from satisfying. The nationalist legitimacy of the Ba^{c}th regime is
thus somewhat ambiguous.

The Ba^{c}th's populism is best represented by its agrarian policy.
Through land reform, protective legislation, cooperatives, and state
services, the regime has created a stratum of new small owner-
cultivators and buttressed the positions of many others; it has also
significantly expanded opportunities for peasant youth in education
and nonagricultural employment. Through these policies, the Ba^{c}th
has demolished the inegalitarian feudal structure in the countryside,
reduced the peasant's dependency on the landlord, made him more
dependent on the Ba^{c}th state, and generally raised rural living standards. Although there is peasant dissatisfaction with the regime,
the Ba^{c}th's policies do appear to have won it the support of a significant part of the typical village and undercut the position of its traditional rivals. [12]

The regime's etatist policies—nationalization of parts of the
modern sector of the economy and planned state investment in it*—
have promoted a respectable rate of economic expansion, given Syria
the beginnings of a modern agroindustrial base, effected some redistribution of resources from the propertied to the salaried middle and

---

*It is worth noting that the allocation of resources in the state
investment plan has not favored particular regions—for example,
^{c}Alawite Latakia—over others, but seems to derive from rational economic calculations and a desire for balanced development.

working classes, and made these classes more dependent on the
Ba^{c}thist state. The regime has, to a considerable extent, been able
to count on elements of these classes to support it against its rivals.
However, from the beginning, segments of the salaried middle and
working classes were commited to rival political movements—Nasserism, communism, or the Muslim Brothers (hereafter referred to as
as Ikhwān). Moreover, favoritism in personnel policy, especially toward ^{c}Alawites; growing corruption and self-enrichment of the
Ba^{c}thist elite; and the dilution of etatist policies under Asad, accompanied by a serious inflation, which has eroded fixed incomes, have all
further eroded the Ba^{c}th's support among these classes. Ultimately,
the decisive determinant of whether the Ba^{c}th will be able to keep a
support base among these classes or whether they will turn to its
rivals for leadership depends on the Ba^{c}th's ability to sustain economic growth sufficient to absorb new aspirants for nonagricultural
employment. In short, the Ba^{c}th regime does seem to have a popular
base that reaches relatively far into the rural periphery and cuts
across sectarian lines; although it appears to be of limited solidity,
it represents an obstacle to the spread of political Islam.

THE ISLAMIC MOVEMENT

Leadership and Ideology

The Islamic movement in Syria embraces a loose coalition of
groups that share many goals and attitudes but lack a formal overarching organization and a unified strategy. Three distinct, but overlapping, leadership elements can be identified.
The ^{c}ulamā' both individually and as a group have long been a
political force in Syria, pressing Islamic demands on government and
contributing to the Islamic politicization of the population. Traditionally, they have stood against efforts to secularize the state, demanding that Islam be designated the state religion, that the head of state
be a Muslim, that the sharī^{c}a be the basis of legislation, and, more
generally, that leaders of government comport themselves as pious
Muslims.
The assumption of power by the Ba^{c}th—which, as a secular
party led by a Christian, has always been held suspect by the ^{c}ulamā'
—very much alarmed the ^{c}ulamā', and at intervals they have continued to demonstrate their distaste for its secularism. Recruited
chiefly from urban merchant and notable families, many ^{c}ulamā' have
also expressed the interests of their class in opposing Ba^{c}th socialism, which they have held to be an alien import, Marxist (hence
atheistic), and contrary to Islam. In their attacks on the "godless and

socialist" Ba^Cth, they have tried to press religion into the defense of private property.

An outstanding example of a "political ^Calim" is Sheikh Habbanka, an imām from the Midān quarter of Damascus, for a time president of the ^Culamā' association, and reputedly a man of great wealth and prestige. Although Habbanka played an overt role in leading sometimes violent demonstrations against the regime in the 1960s and 1970s, his apparent virtual immunity from arrest seemed to indicate the strength of his popular support. The traditional status of the ^Culamā' as leaders of the urban masses seems to have been little affected by modernization or the efforts of the Ba^Cth to win the lower classes to its side.

A second element of the Islamic movement is made up of more overtly political organizations. Although the Ikhwān is the largest and most prominent of such groups, others such as the Katā'ib Muhammad (Muhammad's Brigades) and the Islamic Liberation party have also been active in Syria. Although there is little hard evidence in the Syrian case, the leadership of these movements has traditionally been thought to be recruited from the middle and lower middle classes, especially merchant families, as well as from the ^Culamā' itself.

Little is known about the Katā'ib Muhammad. The Islamic Liberation party was founded in Jordan by Sheikh Taqī al-Dīn al-Nabhānī and subsequently spread, albeit evidently on a modest scale, to Syria, where it was regarded as more radical than the Ikhwān. [13] The Ikhwān first entered Syria in the 1940s, spread by emissaries of the Egyptian parent organization and Syrian sharī^Ca students returning from study in Cairo. In the 1940s and 1950s, it was led by Sheikh Mustafā al-Sibā^Cī, an ^Cālim from Homs. Under his leadership, the Ikhwān fought for an Islamic state against the French and then fought against secularizing tendencies introduced after independence. For example, it led Muslim forces against secular politicians and Christian churchmen in a conflict over the role of Islam in the 1950 constitution. Although its stance was in some ways conservative, pitting it against both secular nationalists and the Left, its program did include elements of social reform, evidently expressing the aspirations of the urban lower classes. Thus, Sibā^Cī held that the Quran supported state ownership of key industries and a more equitable distribution of wealth than obtained in traditional Syria. The Ikhwān also expressed strong opposition to Western influence in the Middle East and sided with secular nationalists and leftists in the fight against Western-sponsored security pacts in the 1950s. Sibā^Cī went so far as to favor closer relations with the USSR as a means of neutralizing Western interference. [14]

In 1962 Sibā^{C}ī stepped aside, and ^{C}Issām al-^{C}Attār, an engineer by profession, was elected in his place. ^{C}Attār quarreled with the Ba^{C}th soon after its seizure of power and, since 1963, has been forced to lead the movement from exile. In the late 1970s ^{C}Attār still claimed leadership of the resistance to the Ba^{C}th and projected an image of himself as an Islamic radical of the Khomeinī brand, equally opposed to the secular Left, Western imperialism, and all incumbent Arab regimes, republics and monarchies alike. [15] There was some evidence, however, that actual leadership of the movement was passing to a younger generation on the spot.

The group in the forefront of the struggle against the Ba^{C}th in Syria in the late 1970s, calling itself the Al-Taliā^C al-Muqātilā li'l-Mujāhidīn (Combat Vanguard of the Mujāhidīn), has apparently split from ^{C}Attār's group. It was founded and led by Marwān Hadīd—reputedly the leader of the anti-Ba^{C}th Hama uprising of 1964 and the strategist of the assassination campaign against the regime in the 1970s —until his death in prison in 1976. Subsequently, several other figures, such as Sālim Muhammad al-Hāmīd and ^{C}Adnān ^{C}Aqla, also served as leaders until their capture. Currently, a new leadership group headed by ^{C}Adnān Sadr al-Dīn, his lieutenant ^{C}Ali Sadr al-Dīn Baylūnī, a lawyer, and Sa^{C}īd Hāwī, a writer described as "chief ideologist," claim leadership of the movement. In a recently issued manifesto, they attack the Ba^{C}th on a wide range of issues: lack of civil rights and political freedoms in Syria, ^{C}Alawite dominance of the state at the expense of the majority (Sunnī elements in the regime are discounted as puppets), and the turning of Syria into a Soviet satellite. Their goal is an Islamic repulic that, as they describe it, resembles a parliamentary democracy, with freedom of religion, press, speech, a multiparty system (but excluding activity by parties "opposed to Islam"), and with "no clergymen above parliament." Significantly, they hold that "private property will become the base of the economy," apparently envisioning a reversal of Ba^{C}th "socialism."[16] This program appears, more than hitherto, to express the interests and ideals of the bourgeoisie and is notably devoid of the imprint of Islamic populism hitherto associated with the Ikhwān, but this manifesto may represent the views of only one wing of the movement. While little is known about the social composition of the current crop of leaders, this program, the middle-class and upper-class professions attributed to many of them, and evidence that scions of the great notable families damaged by the Ba^{C}th have been increasingly active in the movement suggest that its social base may be gravitating upward in the stratification system.

A third element in the Islamic coalition is a segment of the notable class—landlords and merchants—that has found in Islam a way of expressing its opposition to a regime that has deprived it of wealth and power. These notables have largely played a behind-the-scenes role in the opposition, supplying money and engaging in a number of conspiracies. Ma^{C}rūf al-Dawālībī is an outstanding example of this type of leader. In the 1950s Dawālībī was a member of the upper-class establishment, an Aleppine politician in the ranks of the traditional Sha^{C}b (people) party, as well as a religious sheikh with close ties to the Ikhwān. Throughout this period Dawālībī was a staunch adversary of the middle-class army officers who, at the time, were challenging the rule of the notable class. He also made a name for himself as a radical, outspokenly anti-Western and an advocate of land reform. Called the Red Sheikh, he advocated ties with the USSR to thwart the West and was quoted as saying that Syria would rather become a Soviet republic than to submit to Western pressures to accept Israel. [17] However, in the early 1960s, as prime minister in the "Separatist Regime," he presided over reversals of the land reform and nationalization initiated under the United Arab Republic (UAR). Though he had left the country, he and several other notables were accused of involvement in antiregime conspiracies in collaboration with Saudi Arabia. He is evidently still considered part of the Islamic opposition to the Ba^{C}th.

This brief overview gives some notion of the diversity of elements and ideological shadings embraced by the Islamic movement; it is unclear whether it should be considered one movement or many and to what extent it has been able to act in a unified way.

Organization and Social Base

Historically, the Islamic political movement in Syria never took on the dimensions of comparable movements in neighboring states such as Turkey, Egypt, and Iran. Syria's modern political awakening, led by a Western-influenced notable class including many Christians and originally directed against the Muslim Ottoman Empire, took the form of secular Arab nationalism. Later, as political consciousness spread downward, the Ikhwān appeared and the first attempts were made to organize an activist mass movement behind a vision of Islamic resurgence. But its spread was long contained not only by the clientage networks of the secular-oriented notable parties, but also by the rise of secular middle-class parties, such as the Ba^{C}th, Syrian nationalists, socialists, and communists. In most of these parties, members of minority groups played prominent roles. Indicative of the limited appeal of the Ikhwān to the emerging, salaried new middle class was its historical weakness in the army; in notable contrast to Egypt where middle-class officers had Ikhwān contacts and sympathies, in Syria politicized officers became Syrian nationalists, Ba^{C}thists, later Nasserists, but rarely Muslim Brothers.

Nevertheless, the Ikhwān did carve out a remarkably durable place for itself in the political arena. In the elections of the 1940s and 1950s, it was usually able to elect a handful of deputies from the traditionally popular quarters of Damascus and Aleppo. Later, when Nasserism was sweeping the Middle East and proving to have a very potent appeal to the urban masses, the Ikhwān was very much on the defensive; it nevertheless managed to get 47 percent of the vote in a 1957 contest with a pro-Nasser Ba^{C}thī candidate in Damascus. The Syrian Ikhwān at this time did not develop a disciplined and complex organization comparable to its Egyptian counterpart, but operating in more traditional fashion from mosques, nevertheless exercised pervasive influence in the traditional quarters. [18] Under the UAR, though banned, its influence grew, and in the 1961 postsecession elections, it elected an unprecedented ten deputies to Parliament. [19] But in the years between secession and the Ba^{C}th power seizure, Nasserism remained a powerful rival for the loyalties of the urban masses, and indeed, in the 1962 uprisings against the "Separatist" government, Ikhwān and Nasserist mobs of virtually indistinguishable lower-class social composition battled in the streets. After the Ba^{C}th power seizure, although Nasserism and the Ikhwān sometimes ran on parallel antiregime tracks, they nevertheless divided the loyalties of the urban masses. With the decline of Nasserism in the 1970s, however, and the virtual disintegration of the notable parties, the Ikhwān had outlasted its major rivals for the support of the urban mass; this may help account for its current enhanced strength in Syria's cities.

The evidence suggests that while the scope of support for the Islamic movement has expanded considerably under Ba^{C}th rule in the 1960s and 1970s, it remains quite unevenly distributed among elements of the population. Among the salaried middle class, it enjoys wider sympathy than heretofore, chiefly among elements that, aggrieved at favoritism shown ^{C}Alawites, applaud its challenge to the Ba^{C}th, but few of these seem prepared to support a nonsecular movement actively, especially given their dependence on government employment. Despite its spectacular coup in recruiting the officer who led the murder of military cadets in Aleppo, there is no evidence yet that it has a significant following in the army, a tightly controlled Ba^{C}th preserve; among teachers and bureaucrats, its support seems somewhat stronger, but it is still contained by the Ba^{C}th's own support and other elements of the secular Center and Left. The professional upper middle class, traditionally secular and liberal, has not been particularly receptive to Islamic ideological appeals, but its opposition to the Ba^{C}th and especially to ^{C}Alawite privileges have led it to favor tactical alliances with the Islamic opposition. The Ikhwān does have an activist following on university campuses, especially among sharī^{C}a students, and it enjoys wider sympathy; but the Syrian campus has

yet to be swept by Islamic revival, and campus opposition is as likely
to take a left-wing form.* Urban high school students have shown a
much greater receptivity to Islamic appeals and seem to have provided a good part of the movement's street activists (although the
Ba^{C}th itself has a large youth organization in the high schools). The
Ikhwān is not without a following among the organized working class,
but here also the secular Left, including the Ba^{C}th, has contained its
spread and, indeed, has been able to mobilize workers against Ikhwān-
inspired anti-Ba^{C}th disturbances.[20] As before, then, the strongest
mass support for the Islamic movement seems to come from the traditional urban quarter, that is, from merchants, big and small, artisans, ^{C}ulamā', and the laboring and lumpen proletarian elements under their influence. Since the Ba^{C}th power seizure, moreover, elements of the urban establishment, heretofore linked to the notable parties, have gravitated toward the Islamic coalition.

There are several reasons why these social elements are especially receptive to an Islamic appeal. First, historically, the number
and the influence of the ^{C}ulamā' and the mosque are far greater in the
traditional quarter than in either the village or the modern city; the
^{C}ulama' are themselves largely recruited from merchant and artisan
families based here. Hence, this milieu is most sensitive to the
secular, minority, and in its view, anti-Islamic nature of the Ba^{C}th.

Second, this part of Syrian society was made to pay the heaviest
costs of the nationalist, etatist, and populist policies of the Ba^{C}th.
The land reform and the efforts of the regime to substitute state and
cooperative credit and marketing infrastructures for the old landlord-
merchant networks deprived landlords and merchants (who usually also
own modest amounts of land) of influence and wealth in the villages.
Nationalization of industries, which in a few cases touched artisan
workshops, was seen as an attack on business and property as a whole.
The state takeover of foreign trade and of segments of wholesale trade,
its severe restrictions on imports, and its efforts to set up its own
retail network deprived the great notable families of lucrative sources
of wealth, and because the distribution network reached down from

---

*While there is little hard evidence on political attitudes among
population groups, an attitude survey done at Damascus University
in 1968 gives some idea of campus opinion then. At that time, religion held a very low priority for students, ranking as a value far behind nationalism, although among urban students it found greater favor
than among rural ones. Only 1.9 percent wanted rule by the sharī^{C}a
(see Malakah Abyad, "Values of Syrian Youth: A Study Based on Syrian Students in Damascus University" [Master's thesis, American
University of Beirut, 1968]).

these great compradors to hundreds of petty merchants, threatened
or damaged many others. The government's effort to fix prices and
regulate the market alienated all sizes of merchants. Its militant
policies toward Israel and the West, culminating in the curbs on tour-
ism following the 1967 war, exercised a depressing influence on the
whole sūq (market activity).

Finally, favoritism shown rural citizens, especially ᶜAlawites,
in access to jobs and scholarships antagonizes urban Sunnī opinion.
In addition to the solidarity derived from these threats to its common
interests, the sūq was interlocked with networks of intermarriage and
patron clientage, which helped to transmit traditional and antiregime
values.[21] In the 1970s, Hāfiz al-Asad, through commercial liberalization measures that much improved the business climate, did seem
to ease urban opposition to the Baᶜth, but it seems clear that this
alone has been insufficient to neutralize permanently the animosity
toward the regime of the ᶜulamā', merchants, and notables or to
detach the traditional urban lower classes from their influence. On
the contrary, the scale and duration of antigovernment distrubances
in the 1970s indicate that the Islamic opposition has developed techniques of organization and resistance that can mobilize the traditional
city far more effectively than heretofore.

In other countries in which Islamic political movements attained
significant scale, these movements found a fertile field of recruitment among recent migrants to the city, the half-educated whose aspirations for jobs outside of agriculture were frustrated by an insufficient rate of economic development. In Syria, social mobilization
(acquisition of education, movement off the land) has probably also
been faster than economic growth, and it is reasonable to think that
disaffected urban migrants may well be providing recruits for the Islamic movement. Baᶜth influence in the village might retard such a
development, but once it was under way, such migrants could become
the vehicle for spreading Ikhwān influence into the village itself.

Up to now, however, the Ikhwān, in contrast to the Baᶜth, has
demonstrated no great capacity to penetrate the village, and most of
the peasantry appears to be either linked into the regime's base or politically apathetic. It would be surprising, however, if the Islamic
movement has not been able to establish bridgeheads in the countryside,
especially in villages where it finds sympathetic support from a landlord or tribal leader; where part of the population is split from the
local Baᶜthist group by family, tribal, or localistic rivalries; or
where national-level conflicts between Sunnī and minority elements
inside the regime have seeped down to the village level. It seems unlikely, however, that the historic correlation between the Ikhwān-
Baᶜth cleavage and the urban-rural one has yet been effaced.

REGIME AND OPPOSITION:
THE DYNAMICS OF CONFLICT, 1963-81

From the moment the Ba^{c}th seized power in 1963, it faced powerful, largely urban-based opposition that, even as the new regime
struggled to consolidate itself, mounted two major uprisings aimed
at bringing it down. The first major wave of opposition (in early
1963), was led by Nasserists favoring reunion with Egypt on Nasser's
terms and took the form of massive street demonstrations. But although the Nasserist constituency overlapped with the base of the Islamic movement and the leaders used Islam against the regime,
charging that the Ba^{c}th was reluctant to merge with Sunnī Egypt owing to its Christian and heterodox composition, the Ikhwān, the
^{c}ulamā', and the notables, having no love for Nasser, remained
largely inactive. The divisions among its opponents helped the regime
to weather this first challenge.

The second major uprising (in early 1964), however, embraced
elements from across the political spectrum—socialists, liberals,
and Nasserists, but with the Ikhwān and notable-merchant elements
clearly in the forefront. Resentment among all rival political movements at the Ba^{c}th's insistence on ruling alone helped bring all these
forces together. Unionist sentiment also remained strong. But this
time the main thrust of the opposition was directed against the secular, rural, and minority character of the elite and the radical social
policies it was unveiling. Already, banks and several big industries
had been nationalized, state controls imposed on trade, and a new
land reform decreed; a crisis of business confidence overtook the
sūq, drying up credit and plunging it into depression. The resentment
of the urban establishment at its displacement and subordination to a
regime dominated by lower-status village elements now came to the
forefront as the threat of reunion with Egypt receded. The Ikhwān
saw its prospects, apparently on the upswing a year ago, dashed by
the rise to power of a longtime rival, overtly secular, Christian, and
minority led.

The opposition movement took the form of disturbances in each
of Syria's major cities. Sectarian clashes broke out in Banyās between Sunnīs from the town—both Nasserists and scions of the urban
landlords and merchants who had long dominated the outlying countryside—and ^{c}Alawite Ba^{c}thists from the villages emboldened by the rise
of their comrades to power in the capital. This local overlap of class
and sectarian cleavages and the sudden disjuncture between socioeconomic status and political power were only clearer and more intense
reflections of what was happening at the national level. In Hama, the
Ikhwān, ^{c}ulamā', and great notable families, in tacit collaboration
with Nasserists and disaffected leftists, led an uprising that included

attacks on government buildings, the erection of street barricades, merchant strikes, and denunciations of the "godless" Ba^{c}th from the mosques. Merchants strikes and disturbances spread to Aleppo, Homs, and Damascus. In the capital, the Chamber of Commerce called for the repeal of restrictions on foreign commerce and a guarantee against further nationalization. The regime, alarmed at the rapid spread of opposition across the political spectrum, attempted conciliation, denying it was atheistic and promising credit to small merchants. When this failed, tanks were used against barricades and artillery against a mosque in Hama, killing scores, while in Damascus, Ba^{c}thist militants forcibly opened shops and clashed with the Ikhwān.

In the end the disturbances were repressed. However, the near total convergence of disparate opposition forces against the regime at a time when it had as yet made little headway in organizing a popular base of its own badly shook Ba^{c}th leaders and exposed their political isolation from the population. Only their ability to keep control of the army and the lack of coordination among the opposition forces had permitted them to weather the attack. The uprising strengthened the hand of moderates, such as Salāh al-Dīn al-Bitār, who wanted to seek a détente with the urban opposition, both Nasserists and the conservative establishment. Subsequently, Bitār, a Sunnī and one of the leading Ba^{c}thists least repugnant to the urban bourgeoisie, became the prime minister. In a gesture of appeasement, he promised no further nationalization and sought the cooperation of the business community in the state's development plans. A new constitution, guaranteeing liberal political rights, including the right of private property and inheritance, and specifying Islam as a source of legislation, was promulgated. The regime was thus forced to retreat temporarily from its radical populist-etatist policies, but the failure of the opposition to bring it down when it was most vulnerable, its base most narrow, and the opposition more united than it was subsequently to be, can be counted as a victory, albeit a costly one, for the Ba^{c}th. [22]

In 1965 party radicals, having recovered their balance, launched a major assault on the urban establishment, nationalizing most of the modern industrial sector, all of foreign trade, and segments of wholesale internal commerce, and speeding up the land reform. These measures were motivated not just by their ideological and economic rationales, but by a desire to shift the balance of social power in Syria, to break the hegemony of the upper and upper middle classes over the economy, to snap ties of economic dependency between them and the masses, and to link the masses to the Ba^{c}thī state.

These measures were not only gravely damaging to the business community, but also hurt smaller stockholders and alarmed small merchants and artisans. Another round of disturbances specifically aimed at socialism broke out, involving merchant strikes, protests from the Chamber of Commerce and professional associations, denunciations of the regime from the mosques, and clashes of the Ba^cth National Guard and Workers' Militia with Ikhwān activists. In contrast to 1964, however, this time the opposition was unable to mount a major uprising, since elements on the Left, including some Nasserists, supported the socialization measures, and the opposition appeared to be motivated less by Islam or resistance to dictatorship than by defense of its own special interests. Moreover, the regime's assumption of the power to appoint and dismiss imāms had allowed it to dilute opposition among the clergy and even to foster a group friendly to its aims; thus, the Mufti led a delegation of supportive ^culamā', and even Sheikh Habbanka felt constrained to avoid public identification with the disturbances. When 60 stores were confiscated and several businessmen jailed, the opposition collapsed. [23]

In a major intraparty split in February 1966, the moderate wing of the Ba^cth party was purged by radicals; this change decimated the remaining Sunnī urban middle-class elements in the regime, further enhanced its rural minority character, and signaled a further turn to the Left in policy. Co-optation of communists into government, the forging of a close alliance with the Soviet Union, more overt secularism and antagonism toward the urban establishment, tightened controls over commerce, and growing economic austerity followed. These changes only further alienated conservative and pious Islamic opinion. But, the regime's mounting clashes with the West and Israel may have temporarily disoriented militant Muslim opinion, and it was not until May 1967 that a new round of disturbances occurred.

The occasion of this third outbreak of overt opposition was the publication in an army magazine of an article urging the need to sweep away all the traditions of the past—feudalism, capitalism, colonialism, God, and religion; in their place it proposed "absolute belief in man's ability." This was sufficient cause for the ^culamā' to take to the streets in demonstrations led by Sheikh Habbanka, who denounced the government as "socialist and Godless."* New strikes broke out in the sūq, and for the first time Christian clergymen and merchants joined their Muslim counterparts. The statement of Khālid al-Jundī, head of the Workers' Militia, that in his view religion was indeed the opium of the people poured oil on the flames. The government's response was a typical mix of repression and appeasement. Worker militia forced shops open, made arrests, and mobilized the organized

---

*Rumor had it that Habbanka bought up and distributed copies of the article.

labor movement behind the government. Aware of the need to prevent the opposition from defining the cleavage as one between atheism and Islam, which could only be to its disadvantage, the regime had the writer of the article tried as a CIA agent* and curbed Jundī's inflammatory remarks.[24]

Fueling the animosity between regime and opposition was a covert struggle between the government and the merchant bourgeoisie that went on unabated between 1965 and 1970. Having taken over the heights of the economy, large industry and foreign trade, the regime sought to use its powers to redirect resources away from commerce and consumption into industrial and agricultural investment and to force a resource redistribution in favor of its constituency. Toward these ends, it tried to extend government regulation over the commodity distribution system, fixing prices and profits and limiting imports to essential commodities. But in this it was unable to secure the voluntary compliance of merchants and lacked efficient machinery to impose its policies on the market by itself. The result was shortages, black marketeering and smuggling, and often higher prices as merchants tried to corner the market on scarce commodities. The regime countered by arresting merchants and confiscating stock, which continually unsettled relations between it and the sūq.

The barely disguised hostility of the government toward private business, legal limits on the growth of private enterprises, import restrictions, and the inefficiencies of state foreign trade bodies brought private economic activity to a virtual standstill. Ever intensifying austerity measures, higher taxes and customs, slashes in bureaucratic salaries, clashes between Baᶜthist peasants and landlords over land reform, and a precipitous decline in the tourist trade after the 1967 war all contributed to worsening relations between the Baᶜth and the urban bourgeoisie and its clients. While the government takeover of industry and foreign trade had been expected to snap ties between the mercantile establishment and the urban petty bourgeoisie and lower classes, the inability of the state to effectively replace the former in the market and the conflict between curbs on trade and consumption and the prosperity of the sūq worked against any such realignment of forces.

Had the Baᶜth not suffered defeat in the 1967 war with Israel, a blow that undermined the precarious legitimacy it had heretofore built up, it might have sustained its radical socialist policies. But this defeat demoralized the regime's supporters, encouraged opposition, and caused a split in the elite. A faction led by General Hāfiz al-Asad, which advocated a moderation of the regime's course in the

---

*He was later quietly released.

interests of conciliating its opponents, eventually deposed the radical leadership. In the longer run, the 1967 war marked the eclipse not only of radical Ba^Cthism, but of the whole radical Arab nationalist movement as the dominant ideology in the Arab world, leaving a vacuum that has not yet been filled, and which permits increasing credibility to an Islamic alternative.

Once in power in 1971, Asad pursued policies meant to conciliate and win support from urban society. Manifestly muting the secularism of his predecessors, he tried to portray himself as a pious Muslim, reintroduced abolished religious formulas into public ceremonies, and cultivated the ^Culamā' with honors and higher salaries. Some economic liberalization designed to appease businessmen was launched, limits on the growth of private enterprises were removed, import restrictions were relaxed, and public-sector control of foreign trade was cut back. An economic upswing commenced, and gradually the private bourgeoisie was revitalized. Relaxation of political controls; co-optation of technocrats and non-Ba^Cthist progressives into government; and elections to local councils in which lists led by the ^Culamā', notables, and even Ikhwān sympathizers were allowed to sweep the cities—all were designed to appease the participatory demands of urban society and accommodate it to Ba^Cth rule. Closer ties with Egypt and the mending of political fences with Saudi Arabia, a major Sunnī religious power, pleased major segments of urban opinion.[25]

Events were to show, however, that, although Asad himself was initially regarded favorably by the urban sector as a champion of its interests in an otherwise suspect regime, even under such a liberalizing, conciliatory leadership, rule by the Ba^Cth party remained unacceptable to much of the city. In early 1973 a new round of antiregime disturbances over a proposed new constitution demonstrated the limits of the détente between opposition and regime. In this conflict, two issues were in dispute: the role of Islam and the role of the Ba^Cth party in the state. The religious opposition demanded that Islam be designated the religion of the state, although this had never been the case since independence. The opposition was, however, perhaps most incensed by the designation of the Ba^Cth as the leading party, a provision that it claimed "gives the rights of the people to a small clique." At bottom, the crisis was chiefly an expression of the disappointment of opposition expectations that Asad would dismantle Ba^Cth party rule; at issue was less the wording of the constitution than who rules, for although the change of 1970 had brought new policies and some new faces to the top, the rural and minority character of the power elite had not greatly altered.

The disturbances were led by Sheikh Habbanka in Damascus and the Ikhwān in Hama and Homs; in Aleppo they were joined by "right-wing'' Nasserists demanding a more substantial political union with Egypt and Libya. In Hama violent demonstrations took place, including attacks on Ba^cth party headquarters, while merchant strikes and protests swept the other major cities. While the violent disturbances in Hama were quelled forcibly, Asad tried to contain the opposition by conceding a change in the constitution that would specify Islam as the religion of the president, while bolstering his own disputed credentials as a Muslim through the distribution of copies of the Quran bearing his picture and documents claiming that ^cAlawites were indeed Muslims. This hardly satisfied the hard-core opposition, and disturbances continued until repression sufficient to curb them was brought to bear. [26]

In the years immediately after the 1973 war, Asad's regime seemed, however, to accumulate broader support; the war brought Syrians together and, making Asad a center of world diplomatic attention, increased his personal stature. A new wave of economic liberalization, further easing restrictions on imports and business and designed to "encourage the Syrian commercial tradition" and stimulate an influx of Arab oil money, sparked an economic boom.

By late 1976, however, regime policies were faltering and grievances accumulating; relations between the Ba^cth and urban centers of opposition began again to sour, a disaffection that gradually built up into the antiregime explosions of 1979-80. By the late 1970s, the regime's foreign policy increasingly appeared to be at a dead end. Abandoned by Egypt and prevented by personal rivalries with Iraqi leaders from building an effective new anti-Israeli coalition, the regime proved able to reap few benefits in exchange for the sacrifices of the October war and seemed faced with a choice between capitulation to Israel or an indefinite continuation of no war-no peace. While few Syrians were prepared to accept the former, few relished the latter either; and in fact, elements of the bourgeoisie envied the greater business opportunities enjoyed by Egyptians as a result of their peace with Israel. The regime's intervention in Lebanon—in particular, its drive against the Palestinians and the Sunnī Left, which was generally unpopular—required it to suppress opposition inside, thus weakening the support of its own base, and antagonized segments of Sunnī opinion, which viewed it as an ^cAlawite suppression of Sunnīs in favor of Christians. Most dangerous of all, the intervention seriously exacerbated sectarian cleavages in the army. Once in Lebanon, the regime had impotently acquiesced in the Israeli seizure of southern Lebanon for its Christian clients and the virtual sealing of the border against the fedayeen. On all these grounds, its nationalist credentials, bright in the aftermath of the 1973 war, were again tarnished. [27]

Internally, the regime was also in trouble. By 1977, as Arab oil aid declined, the economic boom petered out; inflation, however, fueled by deficit financing and speculation, remained at unacceptable levels, eroding the relatively fixed incomes of the salaried military and bureaucratic elements of the regime's own base. At the same time, the regime elite, engaged in corrupt practices on a growing scale, was enriching itself. This, and the regime's movement away from historic Ba^{c}th commitments to the Palestine cause and to socialism, weakened its support from its own constituency. Yet, while businessmen profited from the widening economic liberalization, the urban establishment had by no means been converted to the regime's side. Businessmen resented the payoffs required to do business with the state and to negotiate its webs of economic regulation, as well as the taxes exacted to support a mushrooming bureaucratic-military establishment; the old bourgeoisie felt justified in its conviction that Ba^{c}th socialism had never been more than a tool to soak the rich for the benefit of a "new class."

For the little man in the street, the gap between Ba^{c}thist slogans and practice was obviously widening. To Sunnīs, sectarian favoritism and nepotism in the distribution of jobs and scholarships seemed to become increasingly blatant under the influence of the president's brother Rif^{c}āt, whose unsavory life-style, open corruption and sectarianism, and reputation for heavy-handed repression made him the bête noire of the regime. Liberals, through their professional syndicates, began to press for widened political freedoms and curbs on the arbitrary actions of the security police. All this added up to a perceptible erosion in the regime's position as it alienated many of its own supporters on the nationalist Left, yet failed to win compensating support on the Right.

In this atmosphere of malaise, the Ikhwān began its campaign of sabotage and assassinations against members of the regime elite, especially ^{c}Alawites, making several attempts against the president himself. A campaign was also started against Soviet advisers to the Syrian army. By the end of the decade, security seemed to be unraveling at an alarming rate as the Ikhwān demonstrated a capacity to strike on a large scale at targets of its choice. On a more diffuse level, Islamic sentiment and public sympathy for the Ikhwān noticeably expanded.

In addition to undertaking repressive measures, the regime did make efforts to defuse discontent. Twice it launched anticorruption campaigns supposedly charged with bringing wrongdoers to trial, but public cynicism only increased, and the discontent of the business community sharpened when the campaign contented itself with the prosecution of some businessmen and minor officials while leaving corrupt figures in the power elite untouched; it may be that corruption at the top, especially among key military elements, was so pervasive that to have done otherwise would have threatened the very survival of the regime. Ministers could, however, be reshuffled occasionally, providing scapegoats and bringing in "cleaner" faces. Further measures of economic liberalization were also taken to appease merchants, while pay raises were granted to contain discontent in the army and bureaucracy.

Buoyed by the Islamic revolution in Iran and sensing the growing isolation of the Ba^{c}th, Islamic militants accelerated their campaign against the regime.* Assassinations and sabotage were stepped up; in June 1979 the spectacular massacre of more than 50 military cadets took place in Aleppo, an event alarming to the regime because of its scale and because its perpetration by a Ba^{c}thist army officer showed that the regime itself had been infiltrated or, worse, that its own structural base was fraying along sectarian lines. Moreover, most Syrians, while shocked at the massacre, showed little inclination to assist the regime in curbing the terrorism aimed at it. The government responded to the massacre with roundups and executions of Ikhwān members, its second anticorruption drive, and a release of left-wing political prisoners, but it failed to check the deterioration of its position. In August large-scale fighting between Sunnīs and ^{c}Alawites broke out in Latakia (apparently beginning as an ^{c}Alawite reprisal for anti-^{c}Alawite terrorism).

In the spring of 1980, the Islamic opposition staged a major offensive in northern Syria, which took on the character of overt urban guerrilla warfare against the government, as whole quarters slipped out of the control of the authorities. Antiregime merchant strikes and large-scale demonstrations virtually shut down Hama and Aleppo for extended periods, although Damascene merchants decided against a general strike of their own. The ^{c}ulamā' demanded the release of political prisoners, an end to martial law, and the implementation of Islamic law. The professional middle class took the occasion to put forward demands for political liberalization and an end to repression.† The scale, intensity, and duration of this uprising seemed to show the opposition to be broader based and better organized than ever before; moreover, the partial adhesion of the liberal middle class to an Islamic-led movement made the prospect of a generalized antigovernment movement under an Islamic umbrella, as in Iran, more real than any time since 1964. As in Iran, the opposition was hoping to make the scale of civil disturbance sufficient to precipitate a collapse of military discipline or a split in the army that would allow the Ba^{c}th to be toppled.

---

*This was reportedly decided at a secret conference in West Germany in May 1979.

†One report claims it went much further, demanding dissolution of Rif^{c}āt's praetorian guard, the president's resignation, and free elections.

The regime's response took several forms, for the most part hard-line. Repression descended on a scale to match the challenge: a major military force was dispatched to Aleppo to intimidate government opponents; demonstrators attacking government buildings were fired upon; antiguerrilla operations in Ikhwān-controlled urban quarters sometimes degenerated into indiscriminate killings; membership in the Ikhwān was made a capital offense; and a reward was offered for killing its members. Rif^{c}āt al-Asad publicly threatened a bloodbath in defense of the regime. The defiant leaderships of the professional associations were purged. Efforts were made with some success to discredit the Ikhwān by linking it with U.S. and Egyptian efforts to weaken Syria's stand against capitulation to Israel. The regime was also able to play on unease among parts of the population not necessarily sympathetic to the government concerning the Ikhwān's theocratic goals, its use of violence,* and the danger of a collapse of public order. The regime also tried to mobilize its own support base, holding a series of conferences of the mass organizations, particularly the labor, artisan, and peasant unions, which Asad threatened to arm against his opponents. It may not be coincidental that at this time in villages around Aleppo, urban landlords, after clashes with peasants, were reportedly afraid to go to their farms; this may have been a warning to the bourgeoisie that without the protection of the government it disliked, its property rights would prove unenforceable. A government decree ordering employers to raise wages may also have been aimed at creating class cleavages that would put its opponents at a disadvantage.

By the middle of 1980, the uprising had subsided. The army had held firm, and in subsequent months the regime managed to destroy parts of the Ikhwān apparatus. But sporadic assassinations continued. The return of peace to Syria's cities no more signified than ever before urban acceptance of Ba^{c}th rule. [28]

CONCLUSION

The struggle between the Ba^{c}th party and political Islam has profoundly shaped the character of the Syrian political system. The Ba^{c}th regime, in contrast to its predecessors, has proved remarkably durable; deeply rooted in the village, dominating the three biggest

---

*The regime was able to mobilize demonstrations in Aleppo against several acts of Ikhwān violence, such as the killing of the military cadets and the assassination of a respected ^{c}ālim for his supposed friendship with President Asad.

and best organized institutions in society (the army, the bureaucracy, and the party apparatus), it has weathered six major urban uprisings against it. Yet, like authoritarian systems elsewhere, its power, enough to maintain itself and effect a redistribution of resources in favor of its constituency, has been insufficient to destroy the opposition's leadership and mobilize on its side its mass base, to establish institutionalized authority, to absorb broad participatory demands, to reshape society according to a coherent new design, or even to prevent the exhaustion of its own ideological and political energy.

Political Islam, the main alternative to the Ba^{c}th, has proved quite as durable as the regime and, indeed, seems to grow as the regime weakens. It, too, is deeply rooted, albeit in a different part of Syrian society—the traditional quarter, the sūq, the old notables. It possesses wealth, prestige, and the powerful primordial appeal of religion, but ultimately it can only prevail against the great institutions of the Ba^{c}th state by mobilizing enough dedicated people to bring about disintegration of those institutions. The obvious key to this is to effect a realignment of political forces, pitting the whole Sunnī community on the basis of sectarian solidarity, in alliance with all other disaffected elements, against the numerically much inferior ^{c}Alawites entrenched in the regime. This would require breaking the cross-sectarian coalition at the center of the Ba^{c}th state; destroying military discipline and party solidarity; and detaching the peasant, worker, and employee elements of the Ba^{c}th's base.

The chances of such an outcome are nearly impossible to assess, but it does seem beyond the present capability of the Islamic movement, which itself labors under certain liabilities. First, where political Islam has been most successful, it has fused religious zeal with nationalist revolution against a foreign or foreign-dependent regime (as in pre-1952 Egypt, Algeria, Iran, and Afghanistan), but the Ba^{c}th has enough of an indigenous national character largely to deprive Syrian Islam of this weapon; indeed, its attacks on the Ba^{c}th, coinciding at times with those of Israel and the West, call in question its own nationalist credentials. Second, the Syrian Islamic movement —in the origins of parts of its leadership and in its program—probably lacks the populist appeal needed to mobilize the whole society against the Ba^{c}th; indeed, the secular Left, organized workers, the peasantry, and the salaried middle class are bound to be wary of any change likely to return power to merchants and landlords. Third, secular forces in general, as well as Syria's significant minority communities, cannot favor the greatly enhanced role for the clergy and religious law in public life that would result from an Islamic victory. For all these reasons, the most likely prognosis seems to be an indefinite stalemate and, to an extent, paralyisis of the Syrian political system.

NOTES

1. Jacques Weulersse, Paysans de Syrie et du Proche-Orient (Paris: Gallimard, 1946), especially pp. 81-88, 125-26, gives a definitive analysis, which argues persuasively that the urban-rural cleavage was the basic division in Syrian society.

2. Raymond E. Hinnebusch, Party and Peasant in Syria: Rural Politics and Social Change under the Ba^Cth, Cairo Papers in Social Science, vol. 3, no. 1 (Cairo: American University, 1979), pp. 10-19, summarizes the evidence on the rural roots of the Ba^Cth. See also Sāmī al-Jundī, al Ba^Cth (Beirut: Dār al-nahār, 1973), p. 9; Jallāl Sayyid, Hizb al-Ba^Cth [The Ba^Cth party] (Beirut: Dār al-nahār, 1973), p. 29; Mutā^C Safadī, Hibz al-Ba^Cth: ma'sāt al-mawlid, ma'sāt al-nihāya [The Ba^Cth party: its tragedy from beginning to end] (Beirut: Dār al-adāb, 1964), pp. 68-70; and Michael H. Van Dusen, "Political Integration and Regionalism in Syria," Middle East Journal 26 (1972): 123-36.

3. Itamar Rabinovich, Syria under the Ba^Cth, 1963-66 (New York: Halstead Press, 1972), pp. 109-17, 211-12; and Hinnebusch, Party and Peasant, pp. 19-39, 96-103.

4. Nikolas Van Dam, The Struggle for Power in Syria: Sectarianism, Regionalism, and Tribalism in Politics, 1961-78 (New York: St. Martin's Press, 1979), pp. 15-49; and Safadī, Hizb al-Ba^Cth, pp. 68-70.

5. Michael H. Van Dusen, "Syria: Downfall of a Traditional Elite," in Political Elites and Political Development in the Middle East, ed. Frank Tachau (Cambridge, Mass.: Schenkman, 1975), pp. 139-41.

6. Van Dam, The Struggle for Power, pp. 126-29.

7. The account by Rabinovich, Syria under the Ba^Cth, especially pp. 180-208, is the most authoritative, complete, and balanced account of this conflict; see also Munīf al-Razzāz, al-Tajrība al-murra [The bitter experience] (Beirut: Dār al-ghandūr, 1967), especially 109-263; and Van Dam, The Struggle for Power, pp. 51-63.

8. Van Dam, The Struggle for Power, pp. 67-78, discusses this incident. See also Eliezer Beeri, Army Officers in Arab Politics and Society (New York: Praeger, 1970), pp. 159-60. I rely also on an interview with Hamūd Shufī, a prominent Druze Ba^Cth politician (Damascus, 1977).

9. Van Dam, The Struggle for Power, pp. 78-79; also an interview, by the author, with the leader of the deposed leftist-Ba^Cth faction, associated with the newspaper al-Rayah (Beirut, 1974).

10. Martin Seymour, "The Dynamics of Power in Syria since the Break with Egypt," Middle East Studies 1 (1970): 39-46, is the most sophisticated analysis of this complex conflict.

11. See Raymond E. Hinnebusch, "Local Politics in Syria: Organization and Mobilization in Four Village Cases," Middle East Journal 30 (1976): 1-24; idem, "Political Recruitment and Socialization in Syria: The Case of the Revolutionary Youth Federation," International Journal of Middle East Studies 11 (1980): 143-74; and idem, "Rural Politics in Ba^Cthist Syria: A Case Study in the Role of the Countryside in the Political Development of Arab Societies," in Arab Society in Transition: A Reader, ed. Saad E. Ibrahim and Nicolas Hopkins (Cairo: American University in Cairo Press, 1977), pp. 278-96.

12. Hinnebusch, "Rural Politics."

13. George Jabbūr, al-Fikr al-siyāsī wa ^Cilāqatuhu bi'l-siyāsa wa'l-tanmīya wa Masā'iluhu wa musādaruhu fī al-qutr al-^Carabī al-sūrī [Issues and sources of political thought in Syria and its relation to development and politics] (al-Qāhira: Risāla Jāmi^Cat al-Qāhira, n.d.), p. 129.

14. Ibid., pp. 123-24; Patrick Seale, The Struggle for Syria (London: Oxford University Press, 1965), pp. 79, 102, 112, 180; A L. Tibawi, A Modern History of Syria (London: Macmillan, 1969), pp. 386, 391; and Tabitha Petran, Syria (London: Ernest Bonn, 1972), pp. 74, 101, 161-63.

15. "An Interview with ^CIssām al-^CAttār, Leader of Syria's Muslim Brothers," an-Nahar Arab Report and Memo, February 18, 1980, pp. 3-5.

16. "The Moslem Brotherhood," Arab World Weekly, no. 584 (October 14, 1980), p. 13; and interview by Claus Bienfait on Muslim Brothers leaders' broadcast by "Die Welt," Bonn, transcribed in FBIS (Foreign Broadcast Information Service), December 1980, pp. 88-89.

17. Petran, Syria, p. 101.

18. Seale, The Struggle for Syria, pp. 102, 180, 290-91.

19. Petran, Syria, p. 153.

20. Ibid., p. 231.

21. al-Jundī, al-Ba^Cth, pp. 37-40; Rabinovich, Syria under the Ba^Cth, pp. 113-15; and Petran, Syria, pp. 92, 244.

22. Rabinovich, Syria under the Ba^Cth, pp. 109-26; Tibawi, A Modern History, pp. 415-16; Kamel S. Abu Jaber, The Arab Ba^Cth Socialist Party: History, Ideology and Organization (Syracuse, N.Y.: Syracuse University Press, 1966), pp. 89-91; Maxime Rodinson, Israel and the Arabs (Harmondsworth: Penguin, 1969), pp. 155-56; and Beeri, Army Officers, pp. 159-60.

23. Rabinovich, Syria under the Ba^Cth, pp. 139-43; Petran, Syria, pp. 178-79; and Beeri, Army Officers, p. 161.

24. Tibawi, A Modern History, p. 420; and Petran, Syria, pp. 197-98.

25. Moshe Maoz, "Syria under Hafiz al-Asad: New Domestic and Foreign Policies," Jerusalem Papers on Peace Problems (Jerusalem: Davis Institute for Peace, 1975), pp. 5-29; Paul Balta, "The Damescene Gates Swing Open," Le monde, April 22, 1971; and Malcolm Kerr, "Hafiz al-Asad and the Changing Patterns of Syrian Politics," International Journal 28 (1975): 689-706.

26. John Donahue, "La nouvelle constitution syrienne et ses detracteurs," Travaux et jours, April-June, 1973; and A. H. Kelidar, "Religion and State in Syria," Asian Affairs 61 (1974): 16-22.

27. Itamar Rabinovich, "The Islamic Wave," Washington Quarterly, Autumn 1979, pp. 139-43.

28. The foregoing analysis of the crisis of 1979-80 relies on a 1979 field trip to Syria and general press reports, including the following: "Asad's Crisis," Arab Report, July 4, 1979; "Asad Decides to Stand Firm," Middle East Newsletter, April 7-20, 1980, p. 135; "Asad Makes a Show of Fighting Corruption," Middle East Newsletter, February 24, 1980, p. 131; and "Syrie: La regime fait face a un large mouvement de mecontentement," Le monde, December 21-27, 1978.

8

POLITICS AND RELIGION IN KUWAIT: TWO MYTHS EXAMINED

TAWFIC E. FARAH

This chapter addresses itself to politics and religion in Kuwait. It examines two myths that have dominated the discussion and analysis of politics in the Gulf and the Arabian peninsula since the Islamic revolution in Iran. These two myths grew out of certain explanations of what happened in Iran. Somehow Iran was "lost" because the shah forced too much modernization too fast on the people of Iran, who were a traditional people. In reaction to this supposed overdose of modernization, they revolted and sought a return to simpler times— hence the Islamic revival. Somehow modernization was seen as an either-or proposition. Modernization negates traditionalism. One cannot be modernized and traditional at the same time. Moreover, one cannot be modernized and a good Muslim at the same time. Journalists, scholars, and diplomats succumbed to this explanation and became enthusiastic exponents of these myths.

THE SETTING: POLITICS IN A TRIBAL SOCIETY

Politics in Kuwait is not unlike politics in many Gulf states. Kuwait is a small country of 17,833 square kilometers tucked away in the upper Gulf between Iraq and Saudi Arabia. It is a very rich country with annual revenues from the sale of its oil of $21 billion. Its per capita income is about $16,600. Obviously the revenues are not divided equally among the population, half of which are non-Kuwaitis. Yet much of this wealth filters down to Kuwaitis and non-Ku-

This chapter was written while I was a research fellow at the Center for International and Strategic Affairs, University of California-Los Angeles.

waitis alike (albeit in different degrees) through a comprehensive womb-to-tomb welfare program provided by the state, that is, the ruling family the al-Sabāhs. The al-Sabāhs have ruled Kuwait continuously since 1756, a total of 225 years, a fact often ignored by many students of politics in that ministate.

A Kuwaiti, compared with a foreign expatriate, is indeed a member of a privileged and affluent group.[1] He is relatively well-to-do and enjoys one of the highest per capita incomes of the world. (Small pockets of poverty also exist in Kuwait.) He is entitled to free medical care and free schooling (including a university education), and he has a constitutionally guaranteed right to a job.

The al-Sabāhs have been responsive in the political arena as well as in the economic sector.[2] In a region of the world where political freedoms are not the norm, 50,000 Kuwaiti men in March 1981 elected a consultative body, a parliament. Neither Kuwaiti women nor non-Kuwaitis are entitled to vote.

The decision-making process is reserved for an informal coalition of the ruling family, the al-Sabāhs, and approximately 20 leading merchant families. The coalition is dominated by the Amīr (the ruler), Sheikh Jābir al-Sabāh, who is the first among equals, the patriarch of the whole tribe or the extended Kuwaiti family (Kuwaiti society is often referred to in official government pronouncements as "family" or "one family," the ruler being referred to as "the father"). The Amīr is the final arbiter on all political, economic, and social issues.

Yet, access to this small political system is not blocked. Access is gained primarily through personal and informal channels. The functions of interest articulation and interest aggregation are handled by the extended family. An individual is apt to go through a relative or a friend to reach a decision maker. The function performed by the friend or the relative is referred to as wasīta. The decision maker can also be reached directly at the diwānīya or majlis (as it is referred to in other states of the Gulf and in Saudi Arabia). The diwānīya is a men's social institution whose importance in the social, political, and economic life in Kuwait and other Gulf societies cannot be overemphasized. Behavior patterns in the diwānīya, ostensibly an informal gathering of men on a regular basis (a man's private club), are quite formalized. In tribal societies such as Kuwait (even though tribal loyalties are becoming less pronounced than they once were), where maintaining consensus is crucial to the tribe's survival, the diwānīya provides an arena for social intercourse and concomitantly serves the very vital function of providing a framework for settling disputes and arriving at decisions. As urbanization took hold, the diwānīya lost something of its original character and began to reflect the stratifications within the society itself. Today the diwānīya encompasses members of similar social standing, religion, and even age. Thus, a man cannot really choose to join a diwānīya; he is born into one. A group of friends from similar backgrounds may, at their coming of age, join an existing diwānīya of older men or they may form their own. One can be invited to a diwānīya, or eventually become part of it, but subtle and longstanding ties among the members generally characterize diwānīyas.

The structure of the diwānīya is simple: men sit in a loose circle, drink tea and coffee, and talk. Once seated, one stays. Diwānīyas of younger men are more uninhibited. Certain subjects are taboo, while others are approached in prescribed ways. Politics is not taboo. Above all, a diwānīya is where wasīta, connections or influence, become tangible or are felt. One never asks a favor directly; rather a friend or someone who has wasīta approaches the subject in a very discreet manner. Members of a diwānīya form a society that operates for the collective benefit. Appointments are decided, contracts settled, introductions made, jobs awarded—always in subtly understood ways. Thus, the diwānīya's importance far exceeds its purely social aspects.

DATA

The data presented here are extracted from ongoing surveys of political culture in Kuwait, the lower Gulf, and the Arabian peninsula. A stratified random sample was isolated, consisting of 420 undergraduate students at Kuwait University (KU). The total population was 7,300 students. Master lists of the names of all students broken down by nationalities were obtained. Random samples totaling 30 each were isolated. The sample includes students from Iraq, Kuwait, Saudi Arabia, the two Yemens, United Arab Emirates (UAE), Egypt, Syria, Sudan, Somalia, Lebanon, Jordan, Mauritania, and Palestine. Questionnaires were drawn up in Arabic. Each respondent filled out a questionnaire in his classroom. The study was conducted in October 1977 at KU. It was repeated in 1979, 1980, and 1981 without any measurable variance in its original findings reported here. The ages of the subjects ranged from 17 to 24 years with a mean of 21.48 years and a standard deviation of 2.09. Muslims comprised 99 percent of the sample and 63 percent were female; 73 percent considered themselves politically oriented. The questionnaire consisted of 36 items in addition to the usual background questions on sex, age, citizenship, religious affiliation, and national (ethnic) origin. Group affiliations were determined by a scale developed by Melikian and Diab. Two items listed here are illustrative.

1. If to show your loyalty to your nation (a) you were forced to give up your religion permanently, both in private and in public, or (b) you were forced to give up your family and never see them again, which would you choose?

2. If in order to subscribe to a political ideology (a) you were forced to give up your religion permanently, both in private and in public, or (b) you were forced to become a permanent exile from the country to which you belong, which would you choose?

The choice of one alternative in a question meant the subject preferred the other. In the first question illustrated above, for example, a respondent choosing (a) gets a score of 1 for (b), that is, for family.

Most respondents, regardless of sex, ranked religion first in their hierarchy of group affiliations followed by family, citizenship (Kuwaiti, Palestinian, Syrian, and so on), national origin (Arab), and political ideology. Islam, the religion of most Arabs, seems to permeate the lives of our subjects. They ranked it higher than family ($X^2 = 8.20$, $p < .01$). Family was a close second ($X^2 = 8.36$, $p < .01$). Citizenship and political party were not gaining in importance at the expense of religious affiliation.

This last finding holds true for all politically oriented respondents except Palestinians ($X^2 = 3.85$, $p < .05$), Bahraini ($X^2 = 3.82$, $p < .05$), and Southern Yemenis ($X^2 = 4.30$, $p < .05$). The Palestinians ranked being Palestinian (citizenship) first, followed by political ideology, national origin, family, and religion. Politically oriented Bahraini and Southern Yemenis ranked political ideology first, then citizenship, national origin, family, and religion.[3]

Islam was paramount in the lives of the vast majority of Arab undergraduate students attending Kuwait University. It does not seem to make any difference whether the student was from Saudi Arabia or Lebanon, a man or a woman. The only variable that seems to have made a difference was whether the subject was politically oriented or not. Yet, even this variable seems to play a significant role only in the case of Palestinians, Bahraini, and Southern Yemenis.

The Palestinians have lost Palestine, but they do not seem to have lost their "Palestinianism." They identify with Palestine, a lost country and a country to be regained. They also identify with each other. To them it is apparent that their religion, be it Islam or Christianity, did not help them in their conflict with the Israelis on the one hand or fellow Muslims (as in the 1970 war in Jordan) on the other.

Yet this rationale is not applicable to politically oriented Bahraini students. Bahrain has had an active student opposition to its government in the last quarter of a century. As a result, many Bahraini students tend to be highly politicized and ideological.

The Southern Yemenis come from a poor country. It is the only Marxist country in the Arab world. The politically oriented students here are socialized to the point where they accept the need for a political party representing a certain ideology to develop that part of Yemen. Even though Southern Yemen is predominantly a Muslim country, religion is played down by the present government.

These findings were verified by Faisal Al-Salem in a similar survey of 1,334 students from the Gulf.[4] His sample included, among others, 469 from Bahrain (33.7 percent), 111 from Saudi Arabia (8.3 percent), 235 from the United Arab Emirates (16.7 percent), and 287 from Kuwait (20.6 percent). The mean age of the respondents was 17 years. Females comprised 71 percent of the total and 28 percent were males. Their socioeconomic statuses as indicated by the father's occupation were as follows: professional (25.6 percent), merchant (13.4 percent), clerical (16.6 percent), laborer (1.4 percent), retired/unemployed (27.9 percent), and undetermined (15 percent). Islam ranked first in the group loyalties of these individuals (47 percent), followed by citizenship (19.5 percent), and the immediate family (19 percent).

It is important to note that very few of the respondents consider themselves Arabs first. An Egyptian student among the respondents, for example, considers himself a Muslim first, an Egyptian second, and an Arab third. Of course this finding might surprise and anger many Arab social scientists who have accepted Arabism and the supremacy of Arab nationalism as an act of faith.

These findings were supported by the findings of Faisal Al-Salem and Ahmad Dhaher.[5] In Saad Eddin Ibrahim's study on public opinion and Arab unity, Arab unity as an idea appears to be alive and well in many Arab states. However, he did not control for religion in his study.[6]

Not only are these students religious; they are also traditional. Even Western-educated technocratic elites, though probably less traditional than their parents, are nevertheless traditional people with modern wrappings. This phenomenon is described by Fouad Ajami in his piece entitled "The Struggle for Egypt's Soul," where he states, "At the heart of the crisis lay the explosive problem of cultural dualism between an oriental interior and a modern wrapping."[7] The core, or the interior, is and has always been an oriental and a traditional one. This simple and basic fact seems to come as news to many social scientists and area experts who have been weaned on Lerner's The Passing of Traditional Society. After all, Lerner assured us in 1958 that "traditional society is passing from the Middle East because relatively few Middle Easterners still want to live by its rules."[8]

This premise holds that whenever there is a contact between the old ways of the interior and the modern ways of the wrapping (or what Migdal refers to as culture contact theory), inevitably the "new" will triumph (a variation on "How you gonna keep 'em down on the farm after they've seen Paree?").

Obviously, many people "see Paree and then return to the farm."[9] Some even go to Paree but take the farm along. Anne Fuller, in her study of the Lebanese village Buarij, found this to be true.[10] Despite yearly forays from the village to work in the city of Beirut, the stability of the villagers' attitudes, institutions, and behavior did not change. Farah and Al-Salem found that "modern" individuals in Kuwait and Lebanon manage to take apart the modernization package and acquire those characteristics that suit them. To "modernized" Kuwaitis and Lebanese, modernization is not an either-or proposition.[11]

In a study conducted in the spring of 1979 among Kuwait University undergraduates from eight Arab countries who had been identified as modern individuals (that is, they scored 70 percent or better on Inkeles's modernization scale), various questions used by Cunningham and others were asked to determine attitudes about certain traditional cultural issues. Again, these modernized individuals exhibited a number of traditional traits.[12]

In the Middle East, as Michael Hudson has observed, "modernization does not mean destroying the old but simply adding the new."[13] This phenomenon has been referred to as cultural dualism, "bedoucracy," or cultural schizophrenia.[14] It should therefore not come as a surprise to anyone to find that the traditional society has not passed in the Middle East. It persists. It is alive and well. By the same token, Islam has not returned. It has always been there, at times latent, but always there. It has never left.

Even devout Muslims have taken apart the modernization package. They have accepted the technology of the West but rejected all other aspects of Western culture. Saad Eddin Ibrahim drew a sociological portrait of the typical member of al-Takfīr wa'l-Hijra (Repentance and Holy Flight) Society, a fundamentalist Islamic group in Egypt. The profile that emerged from this original study is far removed from the popular image of the uneducated fanatic individual.

> The profile shows that the average member is in his 20s or early 30s, a university student or recent graduate. He is an achiever. His school grades have been better than average. He is interested in discussion, feels deeply about causes, is intolerant of conflicting opinions and is willing to use violence if necessary for ends he regards as noble. He wants Middle East oil wealth to benefit the people of the region. He views most cooperation with the west as neo-colonialism. He comes from the small landowning or middle class and likes to win at whatever he

tries. Surprisingly he is more apt to have an engineering or a science background than one in humanities. He isn't against modern technology but wants control over its introduction so as to avoid violating Islamic principles. [15]

CONCLUSION

It is possible that it has recently become more fashionable for the economic, technocratic, intellectual, and political elites of Kuwait to use and involve Islam in their daily speech. But there has been little if any change in the orientation of the masses. These masses have been and will likely continue to be devout Muslims. Islam has never been moribund or in retreat in that part of the world. Islam prevails in all aspects of social, economic, and political life in Kuwait and has always done so. Islam imposes communal obligations on the faithful in this world. Politics is a function of religion.

Similarly, modernization has never taken hold in the countries of the Gulf. Traditional society has not passed. Some members of the elite might have acquired some modern attitudes, but these modern attitudes coexist with very traditional ones without necessarily being in conflict. Some individuals have taken apart the modernization package; others have wrapped themselves in a modern facade—no more.

NOTES

1. See Tawfic Farah, Faisal Al-Salem, and Maria Kolman Al-Salem, "Alienation and Expatriate Labor in Kuwait," Journal of South Asian and Middle Eastern Studies 4 (1980): 3-40.

2. Tawfic Farah, "Inculcating Supportive Attitudes in an Emerging State: The Case of Kuwait," Journal of South Asian and Middle Eastern Studies 2 (1979): 56-68.

3. For the complete details of this study, see Tawfic Farah, "Group Affiliations of University Students in the Arab Middle East (Kuwait)," Journal of Social Psychology 106 (1978): 161-65.

4. Faisal Al-Salem, "The Issue of Identity in Selected Arab Gulf States," Levant 1 (1980): 20-44.

5. Ahmed Dhaher, "Gulf Youth and the Palestinian Issue," Levant 1 (1980): 63-76.

6. Saad E. Ibrahim, Public Opinion and the Question of Arab Unity (Beirut: Markaz dirasat al-wihdah al-Carabiya, 1980).

7. Fouad Ajami, "The Struggle for Egypt's Soul," Foreign Policy 35 (1979): 21.

8. Daniel Lerner, The Passing of Traditional Society: Modernizing the Middle East (New York: Free Press, 1958), p. 399.

9. Joel Migdal, "Why Change? Toward a Theory of Change among Individuals in the Process of Modernization," World Politics 26 (1974): 190.

10. Anne Fuller, Buarij: Portrait of a Lebanese Moslem Village (Cambridge, Mass.: Harvard University Press, 1961).

11. Tawfic Farah and Faisal Al-Salem, "The Traditionalism and Modernization Dichotomy: The Cases of Lebanon and Kuwait," Journal of the Social Sciences 4 (1976): 38-52.

12. For an overview, see Tawfic Farah, Political Culture in the Gulf (Los Angeles: Middle East Research Group, 1981).

13. Michael Hudson, "Democracy and Social Mobilization in Lebanese Politics," Comparative Politics 1 (1979): 255.

14. In looking at these psychological features, I seek to emulate and borrow from the works of such sensitive students of Arab society as Al-Salem, Ajami, Al-CAzm, Sharabi, Rumaihi, Ammar, Melikian, and Diab. Most of these works will be found in Tawfic Farah and Faisal Al-Salem, Politics in the Arab States: A Social-Psychological Approach (London: Routledge and Kegan Paul, forthcoming).

15. Ray Vickers in the Wall Street Journal, February 11, 1980. See also Saad E. Ibrahim's chapter in this volume.

9

ISLAM AND POLITICS
IN SAUDI ARABIA

FAROUK A. SANKARI

The political culture of the Arab states is rooted in Islam, which has been their predominant religion since the seventh century. In Saudi Arabia Islam plays a more active role in political and social life than in any other Arab state. It can influence political values on three levels: as a religion, as an ideology, and as a symbol of cultural identity.[1] In fact, "only in Saudi Arabia did neo-orthodoxy succeed politically and maintain itself in full force until the present."[2]

This essay examines first the role of Islam in the establishment and maintenance of the Saudi state and then analyzes the role of the ᶜulamā' and other groups in the political system. Thereafter, the analysis tries to determine the significance of the 1979 Mecca events and the extent to which they changed the perceptions of the Saudi regime about the threat to the kingdom.

THE ISLAMIC ORIGINS

Saudi Arabia was established as a kingdom in 1932. Its origins, however, date back to the seventh century, when the Prophet Muhammad became the head of the first Islamic state in Medina. The Prophet administered Islamic law and was also the commander in chief of the state's armed forces. Shortly before his death, Islamic teachings prevailed in Mecca, where the Kaᶜba, the most sacred shrine in Islam, existed. After his death, the Prophet was succeeded by the four Rashīdun caliphs who ruled in accordance with the Quran and hadīth.

The House of Saud

Over a thousand years later the rulers of the house of Saud*
chose the first Islamic state as their model: their intention was to
apply Islamic law and precepts in governing their people. [3] What was
the house of Saud? Saud's immediate ancestors lived near Qātif in
the mid-fifteenth century, and the head of the family then moved into
Najd and founded the town of Darī^Cya near the modern capital of Riyadh. Little is known about the town and its rulers from its founding
until the first half of the eighteenth century, when the history of Arabia
was drastically changed by two men of extraordinary ability who laid
the foundations of the house of Saud. From Darī^Cya emerged a kingdom that today symbolizes Islam in power. The Saudi state has the
largest proved crude oil reserves, estimated at 166.5 billion barrels, [4]
and is presently undergoing rapid economic and social changes.

The dynasty of Saud was from its inception connected with the
Wahhābī doctrine. Sheikh Muhammad Ibn^CAbd al-Wahhāb (1691-1787)
and Muhammad Ibn Saud (reigned 1747-65) formed an alliance and
shared the rule of the new theocratic state of Darī^Cya. The former
bore the title of sheikh, the expounder of religious doctrine; the latter, that of imām, the head of the Islamic community.

^CAbd al-Wahhāb's teachings were adopted by Ibn Saud, and the
house of Saud became the leader of the Wahhābīs. According to ^CAbd
al-Wahhāb, practiced Islam was no longer a pure form of religion because it had deviated from the principles of the Prophet Muhammad.
W. F. Smalley observes that ^CAbd al-Wahhāb felt that Muslims had
abandoned their faith in one God and distorted the Muslim religion
through innovations that ran counter to pure Islam.

> What had most seriously disturbed his monotheistic tradi-
> tionalism was the fact that Moslems everywhere used the
> rosary, dressed in rich garments and jewelry, used tobac-
> co, and even some of the so-called "faithful" were using
> wine. There was, moreover, an almost universal visita-
> tion of the shrines of deceased Moslems, among them the
> shrine of Mohammed at Medina. The religious teachers
> had increased the number of festivals and had indulged in
> debate concerning the nature of God. These things must
> not be. [5]

------

*Throughout this chapter the ruling family of Saudi Arabia is re-
ferred to as Saud. This spelling is followed, since it is more familiar
to the reader. A more precise transliteration is, however, Sa^Cūd.

The Wahhābīs accept only the Quran and the Sunna and reject later theological and mystical developments and interpretations. Muslims who do not accept their views are considered heretics. [6] The Wahhābī rigidity in theology is equaled by its rigidity in the interpretation of ethical precepts in the Quran and Sunna.

The Wahhābī movement drew very little attention from the outside world until 1801, when a Saudi-Wahhābī force crossed into Iraq and damaged the tomb of the Prophet's grandson Husayn, at Karbalā', the holiest place to the Shīᶜite branch of Islam. In 1806 this army defeated the Ottoman Turks and captured Mecca and Medina. But the rapid Saudi-Wahhābī expansion was challenged by the Egyptian Ibrāhīm Pāshā who captured Darīᶜya in 1818 and destroyed it.

By the mid-nineteenth century, the Sauds had recaptured Najd, making Riyadh their capital. Before the end of the century, however, they were defeated again and were forced into exile. Muhammad Ibn Rāshid took advantage of warring among Saudi princes and tried to displace them. ᶜAbd Al-Rahmān ibn Faisal al-Saud, grandfather of the present king, was kept by the Rāshidīs as governor of Riyadh until he fled to exile in Kuwait after an unsuccessful revolt in 1891.

Thus, it seems that the combination of the will to govern and the will to perpetuate Islam made the Saud-Wahhāb alliance unique in desert politics of modern times, so that it could not be defeated for long. In spite of adverse conditions, Wahhābism and the Sauds eventually came to gain supremacy over all Arabia. [7]

ᶜAbd al-Azīz ibn Abd al-Rahmān Āl Saud, known to the West as Ibn Saud, challenged the Rāshidīs in 1902 and began to reestablish the Saud family's hegemony. In a quarter of a century the peninsula was unified, the family promise realized, and a nation-state created and renamed the Kingdom of Saudi Arabia in 1932. Ibn Saud brought together peoples with diverse tribal, political, and economic interests and vast territories with a variety of geographical features. [8] His reign opened a great chapter in the history of the Arabian peninsula, "certainly its greatest since the days when the prophet Muhammad and his successors spread the fame of Arabia through the world with the book and sword of Islam." [9]

POLITICAL AND LEGAL INSTITUTIONS

Saudi Arabia's polity was set off from other systems in the Arab world for three reasons: (1) The country as defined by its present boundaries had emerged as a sovereign state relatively recently (1932), and the state controls huge resources; (2) the Wahhābī school of Islamic thought is dominant in that part of the country where the founders of Saudi Arabia drew their strongest political and military support; and (3) the role the Saudi government assumes vis-à-vis the rest of the Islamic world makes it committed to develop the country as an Islamic showcase. [10]

The religious and national heritage of the Saudi people has been crucial in molding the legal and political institutions of the state. Islam was central when Ibn Saud made himself king. The Sauds have since insisted that the sharī^{C}a governs all, including the king. "It is this comprehensiveness of Islamic law that rescues the monarchy from charges of absolutism and theocracy." [11]

The Sharī^{C}a and Royal Decrees

In theory Saudi Arabia bases its legal system on the unifying force of the sharī^{C}a, which encompasses all civil and religious obligations and is sanctioned and enforced by the state. In Saudi Arabia sharī^{C}a law covers all fields of law: criminal, civil, and international. Though in classical Islamic theory the four sources of sharī^{C}a law are the Quran, the Sunna, ijmā^C (consensus of the religious leaders of the ^{C}ulamā'), and qiyās (analogy), the last two sources were originally opposed though not absolutely rejected by the Wahhābīs.

Of the four major schools of Islamic jurisprudence (Hanafī, Mālikī, Shāfi^{C}i, and Hanbalī), the Hanafī school still predominates in the Hijāz and part of the Eastern Province. The Hanbalī school, the most conservative and rigid school, which was revived by ^{C}Abd al-Wahhāb, rejects all innovation, and uses the Quran and the Sunna as a source of law, however, forms the basis of the Saudi Arabian government as well as of its legal system. It is the responsibility of the king to guard the sharī^{C}a and ensure adherence to its prescriptions.

For all practical purposes, therefore, the sharī^{C}a serves as the central institution of political authority in Saudi Arabia; it is the supreme law of the land, which determines the perimeter of the political process and gives flexibility to Saudi elites in policies not specifically considered illegal. The kingdom has had no experience with written constitutions or constitutionally based representative institutions. [12] In a speech delivered in 1962 before he took office, Faisal said that he was of the opinion that the time had come

> for the promulgation of a fundamental law for the country, based on the Book of God, the Sharia of the prophet and the life of his wise successors. The law clearly sets down the basic principles of government and the relation between the ruler and citizen, organizes the different authorities of the state and coordinates their relation to each other. It also sets down the basic rights of the citizen in-

cluding that of freedom of expression, within the limits
of Islamic faith and public policy. [13]

Apparently, however, King Faisal was not alluding to a written
constitution. For he, like other Saudi rulers, believed that all the
citizen's rights and safeguards, as well as legislation for social justice and security, are contained in the Quran and other sources of
the sharīᶜa.

The most serious effort to write a constitution was made after
the attack on the Grand Mosque of Mecca in November 1979. Crown
Prince Fahd announced that a "basic system of rule" was forthcoming. Thereafter, an eight-man committee under the chairmanship
of Prince Nayyif, minister of the interior, was formed in March 1980
to draw up a 200-article "basic system of rule" based entirely on Islamic principles. [14] As of mid-1981 the committee has not drawn up
a constitution.

The flexibility enjoyed by Saudi rulers gives them the authority
to issue decrees or regulations, not only to enforce the prescriptions
of the sharīᶜa but also to do whatever is deemed necessary for the
welfare of the people. This is the major instrument used in Saudi
Arabia to bring about changes in government, law, and society. It
was by issuing regulations that Saudi kings laid the foundation of the
present governmental machinery and prepared the kingdom for a
rapid rate of industrial expansion and corresponding social reforms.

In this regard, Ibn Saud set a precedent that has been followed
by his successors in varying degrees since he issued the Organic Instructions of 1926, also known as the Constitution of Hijāz. The instructions guaranteed the continued existence of governmental institutions considered to be more advanced than those of Najd. The instructions also established the important principle that secular law
could supplement the sharīᶜa. This was crucial to the evolution of
the modern Saudi state.

Another important precedent set by Ibn Saud in 1931 was the
creation by decree of a council of ministers. This document remained as a general statement of government until the ministerial system was formally institutionalized in October 1953 by a decree creating the Council of Ministers under the leadership of a prime minister.
At first the Council of Ministers had no executive powers; it only made
recommendations to the king, who approved all decisions before they
became laws. The functions of the Council of Ministers were, however, further regulated following Ibn Saud's death in late 1953. Two
decrees were issued on March 17, 1954: the Constitution of the Council of Ministers and the Constitution of the Divisions of the Council of
Ministers. Another significant step was taken by King Saud in May
1958 to provide the legal basis and strengthen the power of the minis-

terial system. This decree revised the council's statute and recognized the council as a formal, policy-making body having both executive and legislative functions. After King Faisal succeeded Saud in 1965, he decreed two important changes: the first united the office of the king and prime minister, which strengthened his position over the Council of Ministers; the second gave the king exclusive power to appoint and dismiss ministers. The present king's formal powers are as extensive as they had been under the reign of his predecessor, Faisal.

The Board of Grievances

As Saudi Arabia was creating a modern governmental machinery regulated by royal decrees, the need was felt by the government for a tribunal that would review various administrative decisions and citizens' grievances. The sharī^{C}a courts, bound to apply sharī^{C}a law, were not in the best position to review legal rules that were outside the sharī^{C}a framework. [15]

The Saudi government fell back upon a traditional Islamic institution, Diwān al-Mazālim (Board of Grievances), which finds its inspiration in ^{C}Abbāsid history, and adapted it to fit modern administrative machinery. Although the institution was not historically integrated into Islamic sharī^{C}a, authors on public law, such as al-Mawārdī and Abū Ya^{C}lā, as well as Islamic historians recognized its existence and described its procedures. [16] The Saudi government created its Board of Grievances in 1955. In principle the functions of the Saudi board are similar to those of its traditional model: "It investigates complaints and adjudicates them under the Board's authority and with the approval of the king." [17] Complaints brought before the board since its creation have varied from those dealing with administrative decisions about pensions, salaries, and dismissals to those dealing with the levying of taxes and fees. [18]

Faisal's Program of Reform

The late King Faisal maximized the use of flexibility, a well-established tradition in Islamic law, by proposing and issuing decrees to prepare the Saudi kingdom for a rapid rate of commercial, industrial, and social reform. After assuming power from his brother, Kind Saud, Faisal's first public act was to issue on November 6, 1962, a ten-point program of reform, which can be summed up as follows.

1. While reconfirming the state's adherence to Islamic law, it promised to issue a basic law (a constitution) and set up a consultative council.

2. It pledged enactment of provincial regulations that would establish local governments.

3. It proclaimed independence of the judiciary and promised to establish a supreme judicial council and a ministry of justice.

4. The judicial council was to consist of 20 members chosen from both the lay jurists and the culamā'.

5. It promised to strengthen Islamic propaganda.

6. It proclaimed the reform of the committees of public morality.

7. It proclaimed the government's solicitude for social matters and education and pledged control of retail prices, establishment of scholarships for students, social security regulations, a law protecting laborers from unemployment, and provision of innocent means of recreation for all citizens.

8. It announced the intention to regulate economic and commercial activities through appropriate legislation, which would ensure progress, economic expansion, and encouragement of capital investment.

9. It pledged a sustained endeavor to develop the country's resources and economy, in particular, roads, water resources, heavy and light industry, and self-sufficient agriculture.

10. It abolished slavery in the kingdom. [19]

Although the program carefully reaffirmed the kingdom's adherence to the basic principles of Islam, it introduced important innovations. Foremost among them was the pledge to establish a ministry of justice and a semisecular judicial supreme council. Second in importance was the intent to reform the committees of public morality and to provide "innocent means of recreation for the masses."

Accordingly, in fulfillment of his pledge to reform the judiciary, King Faisal issued the Judicial Regulations on July 23, 1975. Article 1 clearly indicates Faisal's intention to make the judiciary completely independent and nonpolitical.

> Judges are independent and, in their administration of justice, are subject to no authority other than the provisions of Islamic Law and Regulations in force. No one may interfere with the judiciary. [20]

These regulations provide that the sharīca courts shall consist of the following (in descending order of priority):

1. The Supreme Judicial Council
2. The Appellate Court
3. General courts
4. Summary courts[21]

A large number of important regulations were gradually issued by King Faisal to create a body of laws that will enhance financial and economic progress. Among these are the Regulations for Investment of Foreign Capital (1964), the Regulations for Companies (1965), the Labor and Workmen Law (1969), the Social Insurance Regulations (1969), and the Civil Service Regulations (1971). Faisal's regulations supplemented previous governmental promulgations such as the Regulation on Commerce (1954), the Regulation for Nationality (1954), the Forgery Law (1969), the Bribery Law (1962), and the Mining Code (1963). In an effort to have a complete body of laws regulating business activity, the present King Khālid issued the Regulations for the Procurement and for the Execution of Projects and Works for Government (1977) and the Royal Decree of January 17, 1978, laying down strong controls where an agent was involved in dealing with the Saudi government.

THE ROLE OF THE ᶜULAMĀ' AND OTHER GROUPS

The Kingdom of Saudi Arabia has survived almost intact until the present day. Ibn Saud and his sons Saud, Faisal, and Khālid, who have ruled the kingdom as successive kings throughout the twentieth century, have kept the nation together, mindful of Islam, the sharīᶜa, and the religious leaders. But the major challenge facing the house of Saud has been to reconcile a culture based on Islam with the requirements of a modern state. [22]

The ᶜUlamā'

Saudi kings realized very early that allegiance to the house of Saud as a secular power could not alone retain the loyalty of a tribally diverse and volatile population. The superstructure needed was supplied in a revival of Wahhābism and in giving the ᶜulamā' a feeling of participation and influence on public policy. Hence, since the beginning of the kingdom, Islam and the ᶜulamā' provided a continuing source of legitimation of the Saudi regime. Saudi Arabia's ability to meet the needs of modern legislation was made possible mainly through King Ibn Saud's combination of shrewd common sense and firmness.

Ibn Saud was particularly careful about consulting the ^culamā',
being accessible to them, and to be sure, agreeing with them on fundamental issues of religious life. In 1929, for example, with his approval, the Committee for Encouragement of Virtue and Discourage-
ment of Vice, based on long Wahhābī practice, was formed to eradi-
cate innovations and such dangerous practices as drinking alcohol,
smoking, and singing. At the same time, a decree was issued by him
to guarantee the existing governmental institutions in Hijāz. In 1944
an old sheikh accused the king of impiety in selling Saudi land to the
unbelieving Americans. Ibn Saud summoned the sheikh to a gathering
of the ^culamā' and royal court in Riyadh and asked him to deliver his
charge. The sheikh insisted that the duty of the king was not to help
non-Muslims profit from Muslims.

> Then the King left his throne seat and stood beside Abu
> Bahz and said, "I am now not the King, but only a Mus-
> lim, like you a servant of the Prophet." . . . Showing a
> thorough knowledge of the Prophet's life and traditions,
> the King cited several well-attested cases when the Prophet
> employed non-Muslims individually and in groups. "Am I
> right or wrong?" The judges replied unanimously that he
> was right. "Am I breaking the sharīi law, therefore, when
> I follow in the footsteps of the Prophet, and employ foreign
> experts to work for me? The American at El Kharj, and
> the other foreigners who operate machines, are brought
> here by me and work for me under my direction to increase
> the material resources of the land, and to extract for our
> benefit the metals, oil, and water placed by Allah beneath
> our land and intended for our use. In so doing, am I vio-
> lating any Muslim law?" The judges returned a verdict of
> not-guilty. [23]

The king therefore won the tolerance of the ^culamā' not only by his
respect for the sharī^ca but equally by his willingness and readiness
to involve them in making decisions. This tradition of deference to
the ^culamā' has been continued since the death of Ibn Saud.

The dozen years of King Saud witnessed a ruler unavailable for
consultation, indifferent to public challenges of violating moral codes,
and ineffective in running the affairs of the kingdom with little reference to the ^culamā'. [24] Therefore, the ^culamā' questioned his legitimacy, and the old Wahhābī resistance to change was revived until his
brother, King Faisal, succeeded him in 1964.

The ^culamā' played a clear role in the transfer of power from
Saud to Faisal. They issued a declaration expressing their belief that
the interest of the country demanded a change of power from the for-

mer to the latter. This declaration of ^Culamā' is the only public document that makes any reference to conflict between the brothers. It
says the following:

> May God be praised and bless His faithful follower: In
> view of the current conflicts between his Majesty King Sa'ud
> and his brother, His Royal Highness Prince Faisal, which
> we studied in our meeting held in the month of Sha'aban;
> In consideration of the fact that on 16-8-1383 H. we ren-
> dered our verdict on these divergencies with the aim of
> putting an end to them;
> In view of the fact that it is clear that our verdict has not
> put an end to the divergencies [sic];
> In view of the fact that these divergencies have become
> more serious recently and that they have threatened to
> cause disorder and chaos in the country, with disastrous
> results which only God Almighty could foresee. . . .[25]

The ^Culamā', recognizing that the two brothers were in disagreement,
decided that King Saud should remain the sovereign, but that all his
powers, whether legislative, executive, administrative, or judicial,
be discharged by Faisal without referring anything to Saud. The document is signed by the 12 ^Culamā', the nation's jurisconsults.

On the basis of this document the royal family issued a decision
asking Faisal to take power from Saud. Without exception, all the
important members of the royal family signed the document. Thereafter King Faisal attempted to achieve a partnership with the ^Culamā'
in the pursuit of his policy goals.

It seems that in Saudi Arabia not only do the ^Culamā', who view
themselves as the guardians of Islamic tradition, define the social
guidelines, but they are equally concerned about progress and stability in the kingdom. Their position vis-à-vis modern legislation and
judicial review can be distinguished from that of their counterparts
elsewhere in the Muslim world whom Joseph Schacht accused of "pick-
ing fragments of opinions from the early centuries of Islamic law,
arranging them into a kind of arbitrary mosaic, and concealing behind this screen an essentially different structured idea borrowed
from the west."[26]

The ^Culamā' in Saudi Arabia do not seem to follow such an apol-
ogistic approach. Certain considerations underline their attitudes.
The first is that, according to precedent and Islamic tradition, they
acquire their titles as judges and muftīs by virtue of delegation from
the people in authority. Second, the emphasis in the Hanbalī school
on the Quran and the Sunna has in effect removed many possible objections to new legislation. Finally, the Hanbalī school particularly

emphasizes that the rule saying "things are assumed to be allowable unless there is a proof of their prohibition" is applicable to transactions. As legislation by decree increased, a tendency developed toward creating quasi-judicial institutions to ensure its application. Sufficient coordination exists today between these institutions and the sharīᶜa courts, since the former deal more with the application of decrees, while the latter deal with the application of the sharīᶜa. Yet this is only a matter of emphasis, since both pay due respect to the sharīᶜa and to decree legislation, which is not supposed to be in conflict with the sharīᶜa. [27]

Other Groups

The ᶜulamā', although influential in their own spheres, have little independent political power; they must work through the king to achieve their objectives. Tribal leaders and businessmen do not fare any better. Tribalism as a political force has been subdued. Intertribal warfare has been brought to an end; tribesmen go about their activities in peace, and their leaders are dependent on the king for their political authority and for the welfare of their tribes. One innovation in tribal politics was King Faisal's substitution of economic development projects for traditional tribal subsidies, an innovation continued by the present king. Businessmen also work through the king, the royal family, and the bureaucracy to obtain government contracts and regulatory legislation consistent with their interests.

The Saudi Arabian bureaucracy is not a strong political force either. The bureaucracy's youth is indicated by the dates the ministries were established: Foreign Affairs (1930), Finance (1932), Defense (1944), Education (1953), Commerce (1954), Health (1954), Information (1963), Justice (1970), Higher Education (1975), Industry and Electricity (1975), Planning (1975), and Public Works and Housing (1975). The entire administrative bureaucracy consisted of a few hundred people in the 1940s, 150,000 in the 1960s, and over 200,000 in the 1970s. [28] Saudi bureaucracy is described by one writer as "dropsical, staffed by nepotism and Parkinson's Law and graced with as many niceties of style and rank as the civil service of Whitehall or Washington." [29]

Most members of the Saudi bureaucracy today are drawn from the new middle class. This class began to grow in the late 1940s as a result of dramatic economic and social changes caused by the exploitation of commercial quantities of petroleum and the allocation of financial resources for education and development. The new middle class first gained access to higher levels of the bureaucracy in the 1960s as its numbers increased and more of its members returned

from universities abroad.[30] During the period 1958-64, political activity on the national level was fairly intense, but the primary actors
were a few members of the royal family as the House of Saud remained
the source of political power. Although the new middle class does not
participate in major political decisions, such as questions of succession and the issuance of decrees, it does participate in some of the
economic and social decisions. It is involved in numerous day-to-day
decisions in the middle level of the bureaucracy, and it may have an
impact on Saudi society that cannot be measured now.

The Saudi labor force has seldom influenced policy. Manual
labor is almost totally performed by non-Saudis, primarily by Yemenis. The small numbers of skilled and semiskilled Saudi labor are
employed, for the most part, by the petroleum industry. The minor
occasional disturbances among the oil workers have generally been
sparked by economic rather than political grievances. In 1953,
13,000 of the 15,000 oil workers went on strike demanding better
working conditions and increased wages.[31] The insignificant role of
labor in the Saudi political process can be attributed to at least two
factors. First, because labor unions are prohibited, it is difficult for
labor to organize and mobilize workers to make demands on government or affect public policy. Second, the Saudi labor force is finan-
cially well off by Arab standards, and the government takes a pater-
nalistic interest in the welfare of Saudi workers.[32]

Although the ʿulamāʾ, tribal leaders, businessmen, civil servants, and labor do not have independent political power, there are
organizations in Saudi Arabia that focus on political change. It is
only since the 1960s that any of these organizations gained some popular support. The best known of these movements include the Federation of the Peoples of the Arabian Peninsula, the Saudi Arabian National Liberation Front, the Committee for the Defense of the Rights
of the Saudi People, the People's Democratic party, the Popular Front
for the Liberation of the Arabian Peninsula, and the Popular Democratic Front in Saudi Arabia. These groups seem to appeal to certain
commercial and intellectual elements in the country, which consider
the house of Saud anachronistic, undemocratic, and strongly tied to
the Western powers of imperialism.[33] Some of these groups believe
that the people of the Arabian Peninsula are treated by the Saudi family as slaves. They denounce Saudi oil policy and describe it as de-
pleting the wealth of future generations for little return and creating
an unequal division of wealth between royal family members and the
masses.[34]

As far as one can tell, none of the above movements has obtained
enough support to undermine the Saudi regime. In fact, until the tem-
porary seizure of the Grand Mosque in Mecca by a Muslim fundamentalist group, the royal family had been reasonably confident about its

ability to contain any threat to its position from within the kingdom. This confidence was founded on the assumption that the royal family had acquired claims to legitimacy and the loyalty of its subjects for the following reasons: its reliance on Islam and the approval of the ^culamā' in the development of a modern state; the prestige that traditional Bedouin society accords to the wealthiest, most prolific, and militarily most effective families in its midst; the success of the family in imposing and maintaining unity over the once volatile tribes of the peninsula; and the willingness and ability of the family to distribute growing material rewards to the Saudi people.

However confident the Saudi regime was in its ability to check domestic violence and maintain stability in the kingdom, at the time of the Grand Mosque takeover there were dynamic forces at work that could eventually undermine the regime's status. Among such forces were a growing, dissatisfied secular middle class; the sudden and immense wealth that is bringing rapid technological change; corruption of some members of the royal family; the dissatisfaction of qualified personnel who are unable to enter the high-level bureaucracies and whose innovative ideas are overruled or ignored by their less sophisticated superiors; the monopoly of members of the royal family over the most sensitive cabinet positions—such as foreign affairs, defense, interior, public works, and housing; the absence of political parties, elections, and a parliament; strong identification with the United States; regional discrimination based on giving the most sensitive government posts to natives of Najd, the dynasty's ancestral power base, which is resented by the more educated Hijāzīs;[35] the presence of small but dedicated opposition groups; and, finally, the spillover of the Iranian Islamic revolution.

THE 1979 MECCA EVENT

The November 1979 seizure of the Grand Mosque in Mecca introduced a new element of opposition to the Saudi regime. Those involved in the assault were more than just religious fanatics. Not only did they demand the strict application of and adherence to the sharī^ca, with a ban on television and movies and a prohibition against women working in public places, they also mixed politics with religion by assailing the Saudi ruling regime as being corrupt and inept at ruling as well.[36] Nāsir al-Sa^cīd, a leader of the Union of the People of the Arabian Peninsula, claimed that the invaders of Mecca included elements from various tribal groupings, including the ^cUtayba and Qahtān tribes, as well as ordinary workers, officers from the army and national guard, and students.[37]

When the news of the invasion reached the Saudi capital, King Khālid and other ruling elites at first suspected the invaders were

Shī^{c}īs connected with outside groups. Their suspicions soon faded as they learned that the leader of the group was a Saudi Sunnī zealot. The king sought a fatwa (religious legal opinion) from the ^{c}ulamā' to use military force against the invaders. The sharī^{c}a prohibits the shedding of blood in holy places, but the rule can be suspended if the ^{c}ulamā' agree there is sufficient justification. The ^{c}ulamā' gave the king unprecedented powers to stage a battle within the Grand Mosque. Piscatori observes that the role of the ^{c}ulamā' and the fatwa gave renewed life to the royal family's claim to legitimacy.

> Precisely because the fatwa made clear, in its first para-
> graph, the king's immediate interest in having the support
> of the Ulama and because it made explicit the Islamic teach-
> ing on the need to defend the haram, it helped the Saudis to
> address some of the speculation on the value of their guard-
> ianship and, hence, their stability. By calling on them to
> rescue the holiest place of Islam, the fatwa gave renewed
> life to their primary claim to legitimacy. But it did not
> remove the causes of the revolt, and, as a result, the
> longevity of that claim remains in doubt. [38]

The incident in Mecca has changed the royal family's perception of the source of threats to the country's stability. Before the invasion the Saudi regime's primary concern had been trouble from the outside: from Iraq, South Yemen, and Iran, where Khomeinī's religious revolution was successful. The event in Mecca, however, alerted the royal family to the fact that danger might most easily come from within, not from Palestinian and Yemeni immigrant workers, but from dissident native Saudis themselves.

The persistent concern of King Khālid and other royal family members must be whether below the surface there may be smoldering a national resurgence of the Ikhwān.* This organization was created earlier this century by the founder of the Saudi dynasty, Ibn Saud. The Ikhwān tended to be the most zealous, militant, and fanatic of the Wahhābīs. In Ibn Saud's hands, the "Ikhwān were an elite, confident of their mission of restoring a pristine Islam to the Arab homeland."[39] With the conquest of Hijāz, the Saudi kingdom reached its limits, and, with no more land to conquer, the militancy and harsh fanaticism of the Ikhwān turned inward.

There were signs of tension between the Ikhwān and Ibn Saud resulting from the Ikhwān's use of violence against the established Saudi

---

*This group is not to be confused with the Ikhwān al-Muslimīn (Muslim Brothers) of Egypt and other Arab countries.

leadership in 1916 and from their decision to attack Tā'if on the
Hijāzi frontier in 1924 without instructions from Ibn Saud. Other Ikhwān activities, particularly their resistance to Ibn Saud's attempts to
modernize Arabia by introducing the telephone, telegraph, automo-
bile, and imported machinery, widened the gulf between them and the
king. The continued tension and opposition to the king's policies ultimately resulted in their open revolt in 1929. By 1930 their defeat
was complete, and the crushing of their rebellion marked the end of
radical fanaticism and the removal of a major obstacle to national development.

Since the Ikhwān rebellion of 1929, the royal family has been
threatened more than once by dissatisfaction from within. In June
1969 a major scheme to overthrow the regime was reported. Nearly
300 persons were arrested for complicity in this attempted coup
d'etat, which shook the political system to its core. Implicated were
such influential individuals as the director of the air force academy,
two retired generals, the assistant director of the Institute of Public
Administration, and a number of high civil servants. [40] Other plots
were reportedly uncovered in September 1969 and March 1970. An
attempt was made on the life of King Faisal in June 1974, and he was
assassinated in 1975. Then came the seizure of the Grand Mosque in
1979, which underscored the potential danger threatening a country
steeled by Islam and held in the iron grip of the royal family.

The above attempts have been a product of the same tensions
that appear to be responsible in part for the emergence of extremist
factions like the one that seized Mecca. In a relatively short time,
Saudi Arabia has changed from a tribal society with a primitive economy into a modern state. In the process new institutions have been
established and traditional patterns of life, values, and religious
principles have been strained. The Saudi leadership has taken steps
in recognition of these problems. The pace of economic development
has been slowed, and the Saudi regime intends to keep this moderate
pace under the 1980-85 new economic plan. Internal security measures have been strengthened: gun control, for example, is more
stringent, even for Bedouins, who were previously allowed to possess
guns. In addition, the National Guard, the contemporary outgrowth of
the army of tribal zealots Ibn Saud used to establish the kingdom, has
been enlarged and strengthened. It now numbers more than 50,000,
and its primary function is to preserve domestic order and the dominant position of the royal family. There is some question whether even
a well-planned attempted coup would be successful in the face of the
National Guard, the king's royal guard, and the bands of armed retain-
ers maintained by the key princes, all of which would presumably remain loyal to the regime. [41]

CONCLUSION

Saudi Arabia has the unique advantage of being the birthplace of Islam and of having within its borders the two holiest Muslim cities, Mecca and Medina. It is the only surviving Arab state that is the off-spring of an Islamic revival movement, Wahhābism. The Sauds have relied on Islam to unify the peninsula, structure the Saudi polity, for-mulate national policies, decree new innovations, engage the Culamā' in national decision making, and claim legitimacy to the throne. It thus seems that Islam, a central reality in Saudi life, is not incom-patible with a modernizing monarchy. It is used to serve the monarch and has maintained the regime for half a century.

The Saudi regime tends to be authoritarian, and power remains in the hands of the few. Politics is highly centralized and personalized. In making policy decisions, the king consults with traditionally influ-ential groups—such as key members of the royal family, the Culamā', and tribal sheikhs. Alongside this traditional system, a modern bu-reaucracy has emerged and has become a channel of minor influence for the new middle class.

Saudi Arabia remains one of the few countries in the world with neither parliament nor political parties, neither recognized nor elected national officials. There is no sustained public opposition to government policies. Occasionally, an antimonarchist group, reli-gious or secular in orientation, does appear on the scene to challenge the regime. But to date, no single group has gained popular support. Neither a secularist nor a new fundamentalist alternative seems to be in the offing. There is no indication at the present time that the royal family is vulnerable to challenges from soldiers, students, profes-sionals, or religious zealots.

The Sauds believe they have struck a balance in modernizing a traditional society. They argue that there is much value in tradition and much to be avoided in the new way of life. Islam has had social and political relevance because it is part of the Saudi national and cultural heritage. Should modernization move too far ahead of this heritage, the future of the political system will become more uncer-tain.

NOTES

1. R. Stephen Humphreys, "Islam and Political Values in Saudi Arabia, Egypt and Syria," Middle East Journal 33 (1979): 2.
2. Daniel Pipes, "This World Is Political! The Islamic Re-vival of the Seventies," Orbis 24 (1980): 11.

3. George Rentz, "The Saudi Monarchy," in King Faisal and the Modernization of Saudi Arabia, ed. Willard A. Beling (Boulder, Colo.: Westview Press, 1980), p. 16.

4. Exxon Corporation, "Middle East Oil," Exxon Background Series, September 1980, p. 5.

5. W. F. Smalley, "The Wahhabis and Ibn Saud," Muslim World 22 (1932): 230-31.

6. George Linabury, "The Creation of Saudi Arabia and the Erosion of Wahhabi Conservatism," Middle East Review 11 (1978): 7.

7. Vincent Sheean, Faisal: The King and His Kingdom (Tavistock: University Press of Arabia, 1975), p. 44.

8. Manfred W. Wenner, "The Arabian Peninsula and the Islamic Revival," in Islam in the Contemporary World, ed. Cyriac K. Pullapilly (Notre Dame, Ind.: Crossroads Books, 1980), p. 147.

9. H. St. John B. Philby, "The New Reign in Saudi Arabia," Foreign Affairs 32 (1954): 446.

10. A. M. Sharshar, "Oil, Religion, and Mercantilism: A Study of Saudi Arabia's Economic System," Studies in Comparative International Development 12 (1977): 48.

11. James P. Piscatori, "The Role of Islam in Saudi Arabia's Political Development," in Islam and Development: Religion and Sociopolitical Change, ed. John L. Esposito (Syracuse, N.Y.: Syracuse University Press, 1980), p. 126.

12. Richard F. Nyrop, Area Handbook for Saudi Arabia (Washington, D.C.: U.S. Government Printing Office, 1977), p. 172.

13. Saudi Arabia, Prince Faisal Speaks (Riyadh: Ministry of Information of Saudi Arabia, December 1, 1963), p. 12.

14. Europa Publications, The Middle East and North Africa 1980-81 (London: Europa, 1980), p. 660.

15. David E. Long, "The Board of Grievances in Saudi Arabia," Middle East Journal 27 (1973): 72.

16. Emile Tyan, "Judicial Organization," in Law in the Middle East, ed. Majid Khadduri and Herbert J. Liebensny (Washington, D.C.: Middle East Institute, 1955), p. 268.

17. Long, "The Board of Grievances," pp. 73-76.

18. Samir Shamma, "Diwan al-Mazalim," in Public Administration (Riyadh: Institute of Public Administration, 1967), p. 19.

19. George Lenczowski, "Tradition and Reform in Saudi Arabia," Current History 52 (1967): 101.

20. George M. Baroody, "The Practice of Law in Saudi Arabia," in King Faisal and the Modernization of Saudi Arabia, ed. Willard E. Beling (Boulder, Colo.: Westview Press, 1980), p. 123.

21. Ibid.

22. William A. Rugh, "A Tale of Two Houses," Wilson Quarterly 3 (1979): 65-66.

23. Piscatori, "The Role of Islam," p. 134.

24. J. J. Malone, "Saudi Arabia: Islam in Politics," Muslim World 56 (1966): 293.

25. Sheean, Faisal, p. 117.

26. Joseph Schacht, "Problems of Modern Islamic Legislation," in The Middle East, ed. R. H. Nolte (New York: Atherton Press, 1963), p. 191.

27. Soliman A. Solaim, "Saudi Arabia's Judicial System," Middle East Journal 25 (1971): 406-7.

28. Joseph S. Szyliowicz, "Prospects for Scientific and Technological Development in Saudi Arabia," International Journal of Middle East Studies 10 (1979): 362.

29. Manfred W. Wenner, "Saudi Arabia: Survival of Traditional Elites," in Political Elites and Political Development in the Middle East, ed. Frank Tachau (Cambridge, Mass.: Schenkman, 1975), p. 181.

30. William A. Rugh, "Emergence of a New Middle Class in Saudi Arabia," Middle East Journal 27 (1973): 12.

31. Sydney Fisher, The Middle East (New York: Alfred A. Knopf, 1959), p. 541.

32. Abid Al-Marayati, The Middle East: Its Governments and Politics (Belmont, Calif.: Duxbury Press, 1972), p. 269.

33. Wenner, "The Arabian Peninsula," pp. 152-53.

34. Christian Science Monitor, November 30, 1979.

35. James A. Bill and Robert W. Stookey, Politics and Petroleum in the Middle East and the United States (Brunswick: King's Court Communications, 1975), pp. 29-30.

36. Newsweek, December 10, 1980, p. 50.

37. Christian Science Monitor, November 30, 1979.

38. Piscatori, "The Role of Islam," pp. 135-36.

39. David G. Edens, "The Anatomy of the Saudi Revolution," International Journal of Middle East Studies 5 (1974): 58.

40. Bill and Stookey, Politics and Petroleum, p. 29.

41. Ibid., p. 31.

10

ISLAMIC RESURGENCE OR NEW PROPHETHOOD: THE ROLE OF ISLAM IN QADHDĀFĪ'S IDEOLOGY

ANN ELIZABETH MAYER

In the course of the last few years, while much attention has been focused on the Islamic revival in the Middle East, little concern has been shown for developments affecting Islamic law in Libya, where a program of reinstating the sharī^{c}a, or Islamic law, was inaugurated after the 1969 revolution.

Everywhere in the Middle East where in recent years there has been experience of the Islamic revival, the role of the sharī^{c}a has emerged as a major—if not the major—political issue. Whereas the Westernization of law in Middle Eastern countries was imposed from above at the urging of the elite, the Islamic revival has meant that states have had to deal with popular sentiment in favor of reinstating sharī^{c}a law. However, the decision to reinstate Islamic law in Libya seems to have been made in the absence of any great popular clamor for such a move. Rather, the policy of Islamicizing Libyan law seems to have been the brainchild of Mu^{c}ammar al-Qadhdhāfī, who from the outset has been the dominant ideological and political force in the Libyan regime. Given its origins, the Islamicizing program in Libya was destined to be shaped by Qadhdhāfī's personal conception of the role the sharī^{c}a should play. His dominant position in the regime has if anything been enhanced over his years in power, as one after another of his erstwhile comrades in the Revolutionary Command Council have fallen out with him and been excluded from participation in the government. Since the mid-1970s Qadhdhāfī has moved to impose his particular vision of society in Libya according to the tenets of his The Green Book, the definitive statement of his ideology. In speeches delivered in 1978, Qadhdhāfī began to outline the role that the sharī^{c}a would play in his new "Jamāhirīya," a neologism designating a state where the masses rule themselves. While other states subsequently adopted Islamicizing policies that superficially resembled Qadhdhāfī's policies, it has meanwhile become clear that the relationship between the sharī^{C}a and the state in Libya has been altered in a way that sharply distinguishes the treatment of the sharī^{C}a in Libya from that in the Middle Eastern countries that responded to the impact of the Islamic revival in the late 1970s.

THE CAMPAIGN TO REINSTATE
ISLAMIC LAW IN LIBYA

To appreciate the changes affecting the status of the sharī^{C}a in Libya, it is necessary to recall the status of the sharī^{C}a before the revolution of 1969 and in the first years after the revolution.

Qadhdhāfī's announcement after the September 1969 coup that brought him to power that he intended to reinstate the sharī^{C}a constituted a striking break with what was a well-established trend toward ever greater Westernization in the legal development of all Middle Eastern societies. Since the middle of the nineteenth century, Middle Eastern elites have favored legal changes that led to a steady erosion of the sharī^{C}a in favor of the adoption of laws that derived their inspiration from continental European codes. This entailed a corresponding reduction of the authority of persons trained in Islamic jurisprudence. Persons educated along European lines increasingly came to dominate legislative and judicial activities and, as lawyers, formed an influential, new professional class. So consistent was the progress of this Westernization of the law that it came to seem inexorable. Although Muslim clerics and other traditionally minded Muslims objected to the abandonment of the sharī^{C}a and even formed movements like the Muslim Brethren to campaign for its revival, the Westernized elites who ran the legal systems in Muslim countries remained indifferent to their concerns. The only concessions made to Muslim sentiment in the legal sphere were in the retention of sharī^{C}a law in a few areas like family law and inheritance, where resistance to the importation of Western law proved particularly strong. In the areas where the sharī^{C}a retained its hold, new reforms were undertaken gingerly and with attempts to rationalize them in Islamic terms.

The system that prevailed in Libya at the time of Qadhdhāfī's takeover was largely drawn from French models and was similar to that in countries such as Egypt, Syria, and Iraq, although it also bore traces of Italian influence because of Libya's long exposure to Italian law during the period of colonization. The most important bastion of the sharī^{C}a in Libya was in the area of personal-status law. On October 28, 1971, a law was enacted setting up a commission charged with reviewing existing Libyan law with a view toward eliminating rules that violated the sharī^{C}a and devising projects for reinstating fundamental sharī^{C}a principles. The commission's greatest impact was in the area of criminal law. The five crimes for which penalty, or hadd, was set forth in the Quran were enacted into law, and existing Libyan criminal laws in conflict with the Quranic rules were abrogated. Thus, theft became punishable by amputation of the hand, brigandage by amputation of the hand and foot, fornication by 100 lashes, slanderous imputation of unchastity by 80 lashes, and consumption of alcohol by 40 lashes. However, not all of the traditional features of the sharī^{c}a law regarding these crimes were revived in the new laws. In addition, a few principles of sharī^{c}a law regarding aleatory contracts and interest charges were revived by new enactments, but they were drafted in such a way as to avoid conflict with Western commercial and investment practices. Other, minor changes in the law, such as making the state responsible for collecting part of the Islamic alms tax, or zakāt, were also enacted.[1]

However, not all changes were in the direction of Islamicizing the law. The separate jurisdiction of sharī^{c}a courts was abolished after Qadhdhāfī came to power, leaving only secular courts sitting in sharī^{c}a matters; the venerable Islamic institution of the family waqf, a form of trust set up to provide designated family members with income, was abolished. Some modest reforms in the law of marriage and divorce were enacted with the effect of reducing the sway of the sharī^{c}a and modifying it in its remaining areas of application. These modifications include setting minimum ages for marriage, eliminating most forced marriages, allowing a husband to reduce his postdivorce financial obligations by showing that the wife was at fault for the divorce, and allowing a wife to terminate a marriage over her husband's objections by agreeing to pay him an indemnification set by the court. Thus, despite the publicity given to the reinstatement of sharī^{c}a criminal law in Libya and Qadhdhāfī's own public assertions that his regime was committed to the application of the sharī^{c}a, by 1974, when the trickle of Islamicizing legislation had dried up, the Libyan legal system as a whole was not markedly more Islamic than it had been before, and the Westernizing process was continuing in some areas. However, because Qadhdhāfī still officially championed the cause of the sharī^{c}a as a basis for legislation, it was possible to presume that additional laws reviving the sharī^{c}a were yet to come.

THE ERA OF THE GREEN BOOK

Since beginning the publication of the three parts of The Green Book in 1976, Qadhdhāfī has concentrated his efforts on publicizing and implementing The Green Book ideology. The Green Book did not by its terms preclude further revival of the sharī^{c}a. The first part of The Green Book, the one that deals with politics, includes a section called "sharī^{c}at al-mujtama^c' " in which Qadhdhāfī outlines the legal basis for his new society. The phrase is ambiguous, and the ambiguity is not accidental. In the official English version of The Green Book, the phrase is translated as "the law of society," which has a secular ring. However, a more conventional translation of sharī^{c}a into English would be "Islamic law," qānūn being the term typically used for the secular law. While the English-speaking reader is led to believe that "law" is meant, the reader of the Arabic version will be inclined to think that when Qadhdhāfī is talking of the need for society to be based on this "true law," he means Islamic law. Other aspects of his description buttress the conclusion that the reader of the Arabic version is being quite deliberately led to interpret the phrase sharī^{c}at al-mujtama^c' as referring to the sharī^{c}a. Qadhdhāfī describes this law as one that embraces custom (^{c}urf in the Arabic) and religion.[2] It is a sacred law (sharī^{c}a muqaddasa) with immutable rules that are not subject to change by governments.[3] It distinguishes between right and wrong.[4] These are all characteristics of sharī^{c}a as opposed to conventional positive law. The sharī^{c}a incorporated custom, or ^{c}urf, as a subsidiary source of law. In sharī^{c}a theory, Allāh was the sole legislator, and the two divinely inspired sources, the Quran and the custom, or Sunna, of the Prophet Muhammad were the sources of all law. The state in classical sharī^{c}a theory exists only to administer the sharī^{c}a and to provide conditions under which it can be implemented: it is excluded from any lawmaking function. (This is the majority Sunni position; in Shī^{c}ī theory, divinely inspired imāms can make laws in their capacities as religious and political leaders of their communities.) Furthermore, all acts are classified in the sharī^{c}a according to moral categories with a view to providing the believer with guidance as to what is morally correct behavior regardless of whether compliance with the rules entails any legal consequences.

Why all this circumlocution? Why does Qadhdhāfī not say "Islamic law"? Qadhdhāfī has admitted that since he wants The Green Book to find an audience beyond the Muslim world, he has played down the Islamic character of his concepts to make the book more palatable to non-Muslims.[5] This concern accounts in part for his failure to speak more explicitly of Islamic law as the basis for law in his new society. However, the peculiarities of his description of what constitutes sharī^{c}at al-mujtama^c' may be viewed as preparation for subsequent attempts to promote a new and highly restrictive concept of the nature of the sharī^{c}a and its proper role in Libyan society.

This new concept of the sharī^{c}a was not always part of Qadhdhāfī's ideology. During his first years in power, his own speeches and the projects of the commission charged with revising Libyan law to make it conform to the sharī^{c}a revealed a concept of the sharī^{c}a familiar to Muslims. It seemed that Qadhdhāfī considered the Quran and Sunna to be the sources of the sharīᶜa and that sharīᶜa rules covered all areas of human activity. In the explanatory memoranda that accompanied the new Islamic laws enacted in 1972-74, there were extensive references to the fiqh, the medieval jurisprudence that has been traditionally regarded as the authoritative statement of sharīᶜa doctrine. In contrast, in The Green Book's discussion of the law to govern the new society, there is no reference to Quran or Sunna, religion and custom are treated as equal components, and the ethical character of this "law of society" is emphasized. This shift presaged later developments.

In 1977 Libya adopted a new constitution establishing the people's authority pursuant to the teachings of The Green Book. Article II stated that the Quran was sharīᶜat al-mujtamaᶜ'—with the clear implication that both the Sunna of the Prophet Muhammad and the vast corpus of sharīᶜa law contained in the works of fiqh were excluded from Qadhdhāfī's definition of the word sharīᶜa. Since the very small number of Quranic principles that cover legal questions outside the sphere of personal-status matters had already been enacted into law by 1977, a corollary of this restrictive definition of the sharīᶜa was that the task of reinstating the sharīᶜa was accomplished.

REVOLUTIONARY INITIATIVES
AFFECTING ISLAM

Having redefined the sharīᶜa so as to exclude the major part of it, in 1978 Qadhdhāfī made two important speeches in which he discussed the role that the sharīᶜa would henceforth play in Libyan society. The salient points of these two speeches are first summarized, after which an attempt is made to analyze their significance. *

The first of Qadhdhāfī's two important speeches was made on February 19, 1978, in a mosque in Tripoli on the occasion of a celebration of the anniversary of the birthday of the Prophet Muhammad. Early in Qadhdhāfī's speech he launched into attacks on Christianity of a sort familiar to readers of tracts by Muslim polemicists. Specifically, Qadhdhāfī castigated Christians for elevating Jesus Christ, who was a mere mortal and prophet, to the status of a god. He also criticized them for following the doctrine of the Trinity. Both beliefs he condemned as violating the prohibition of shirk, the Islamic rule that forbids the association of any other being with God. Qadhdhāfī

---

*The summaries are based on the official record of these speeches.

also challenged the reliability of Christian scriptures, contending that the text of the Bible was not an accurate contemporaneous record, having been recorded much later than the events that it describes and having suffered numerous mischievous alterations at the hands of its compilers.[6]

All this turned out to be a preface to a startling criticism of the errors of Qadhdhāfī's fellow Muslims. Muslims were, so Qadhdhāfī charged, as guilty of shirk as their Christian counterparts. Among the proofs that he offered was their obedience to the Sunna of the Prophet Muhammad. That Muslims should follow his example as if it constituted divine law was <u>shirk</u>. The Quran explicitly told Muslims, he pointed out, that the Prophet was merely a vehicle for revelation (Sūra 46:9). Muslims should not seek guidance from him but rather from their own scripture, the Quran, which, unlike the Bible, was accurately recorded, authentic, and reliable.[7]

He also stated that there should be no intermediaries between the Quran and the believer. No one was entitled to get into the minbar (the pulpit) and lecture other Muslims on the Islamic religion. The Quran was written in plain Arabic, and no Arab needed religious scholars to explain what it meant.[8] Not only did Qadhdhāfī reject the authoritative character of the learning of contemporary ^{c}ulamā' he also dismissed as irrelevant the writings of the great medieval scholars of the fiqh. He found special cause for disregarding the views of many of the great early legal scholars who were not of Arab origin; as non-Arabs they had introduced, he claimed, alien and un-Islamic ideas into the fiqh.[9]

Qadhdhāfī's second noteworthy public statement on Islamic law was made on July 3, 1978, in the same Tripoli mosque and again in the context of a religious festivity. In response to a question about whether the source of legislation in Libya would henceforth be the Quran and Sunna or the Quran alone, Qadhdhāfī reaffirmed his position that it would be the Quran alone.[10] This inaugurated a sharp debate between Qadhdhāfī and the ^{c}ulamā' attending the celebration, in which Qadhdhāfī argued that all hadīth, the reports of the Prophet, were unreliable, while the ^{c}ulamā' maintained that the science of the hadīth enabled them to differentiate between those that were reliable and those that were not. They pointed out that there had been an ijmā^c, or consensus, among Muslims that certain standard hadīth collections were trustworthy.* Qadhdhāfī insisted that Muslims had

---

*Once there has been a consensus among Muslim scholars of any generation that a given legal proposition is correct, the proposition is considered to be conclusively established according to the tenets of the traditional fiqh. Only recently have Muslims in significant

no assurance that false hadīth had not been inserted even in these standard collections. In particular, he emphasized that the political factionalism that characterized the first centuries of Islam before the hadīth were recorded in their definitive recensions had provided strong motives for warring groups to invent hadīth to support their causes. He gave examples of hadīth that were clearly the products of the civil war that cleaved the Muslim community when the two factions that were the antecedents of the Sunnī and Shīᶜī sects of Islam fought each other over the issue of succession. As additional proof that the hadīth could not be authentic, he pointed to the existence of conflicting hadīth and conflicts between the hadīth and the Quran. [11]

In this speech Qadhdhāfī also indicated that he did not consider that the fiqh as set forth in the classical law books of the various Muslim schools of law was part of the Islamic religion. These works were, he asserted, no more religious than Roman law or the Napoleonic code, for they all dealt with matters outside the sphere of religion. [12] Qadhdhāfī made clear his view that outside the sphere that he defined as being the concern of religion, The Green Book should be applied. Were the ᶜulamā' to oppose the application of The Green Book on grounds that it conflicted with Islam, which it could not do since the Quran dealt with religion and The Green Book with mundane matters, they could expect the same fate that befell the Turkish ᶜulamā' when they opposed Atatürk's progressive reforming measures and stirred up religious fanaticism against him. Their choice was, he asserted, between The Green Book and a red book, the former a product of Muslim culture and the latter a product of Marxism and atheism. [13] Islam must not become identified with backward institutions like slavery, concubinage, polygamy, exploitation, and the like. If it did, he would abandon Islam. [14]

With regard to their legal implications, these two speeches deal essentially with four major issues: the Sunna as a source of sharīᶜa law; the role of the ᶜulamā', or learned men of religion, as interpreters of the sharīᶜa; the scope and nature of the sharīᶜa; and the relationship between the sharīᶜa and the state. On each issue Qadhdhāfī has staked out a position that is radically at variance with orthodox Sunnī doctrine. Whether he will henceforth be regarded by his co-religionists as a heretic or the herald of a new era in Islamic thought will depend on his ability to bring others around to his positions. Why his positions will not be easily digested is explained in the following outline of the differences between Qadhdhāfī's views and more orthodox Muslim views.

---

numbers begun to challenge the authoritative character of propositions that have been ratified by ijmāᶜ.

Qadhdhāfī's argument that venerating the Prophet and following his example constitutes the grievous offense of shirk can only come as a surprise to his fellow Muslims. In orthodox Islam, the Prophet has never been associated with God as his partner. Instead, he has been consistently treated as a man who was chosen as a vehicle for the revelation, whose inspiration was divine while he remained human. The great deference that Muslims have shown to his example has been based simply upon the conviction that as the man selected by God to be the seal of the prophets, he was a person of the highest morality and thus worthy of emulation. This view is obviously a far cry from the Christian belief in Jesus Christ as part of the Trinity and Christian worship of him as God incarnate, and Qadhdhāfī's attempts to blur this distinction in Muslims' minds is not likely to be effective.

Not content to argue that veneration of the example of the Prophet constituted shirk, Qadhdhāfī also challenged the authenticity of the hadīth. Many of his arguments resemble those used by the opponents of the hadīth in the first centuries of Islam, when a crucial debate took place between the proponents and opponents of the Sunna, al-Shāfiᶜī (d. 820), the famous early advocate of the Sunna as a source of law, was challenged by opponents of the hadīth on grounds that it was wrong to use a source of doubtful authenticity, the Sunna, when there was an unimpeachable source, the Quran, which should be the exclusive source of guidance for Muslims.[15] His opponents also argued that since al-Shāfiᶜī recognized that there were transmitters of hadīth who were unreliable as well as hadīth that were contradictory, he should concede that the whole corpus of hadīth was unreliable, since what was demonstrably true of one hadīth could be true of others.[16] Since the sophisticated legal arguments that al-Shāfiᶜī used to persuade Muslim jurists to recognize the Sunna as a source of law equal with the Quran have been the subject of extensive study, they are not described in detail here.[17] Suffice it to say that al-Shāfiᶜī succeeded, and that for over a millennium Muslims have relied on the Sunna as a source of sharīᶜa law. Indeed, the fiqh, insofar as it invokes the authority of Islamic sources, is largely based on the voluminous hadīth literature. To try to derive a comprehensive system of law from the Quran with its less than 600 verses of legislation would present enormous problems, especially since the greater part of Quranic legal verses is solely concerned with personal-status questions. Thus, discrediting the hadīth entails rejection of by far the greater part of Islamic law, which developed after al-Shāfiᶜī in reliance on the Sunna and which forfeits its Islamic justification if the Sunna is rejected as a source of law.

It is noteworthy that although Qadhdhāfī is in effect demanding a momentous reversal of established legal doctrine, he does not refer to the early Islamic precedents for his positions, presenting them instead as his own fresh insights. This is in sharp contrast to the prevalent approach of Islamic reformers and modernists, who, rather than presenting their views as new, seek to justify them by reference to precedents in the earliest period of Islam before the fiqh congealed in its classical form.

Despite the fact that the Sunna was not definitively compiled until more than two centuries after the death of the Prophet Muhammad in 632, most Muslim jurists have remained of the opinion that the methodology developed by Muslim scholars for evaluating the authenticity of the hadīth is adequate. * In his confrontation with the ᶜulamā', Qadhdhāfī refused to debate technical questions such as the chains of hadīth transmitters, choosing instead to dismiss all methodological arguments on the broad grounds of the inherent unlikelihood that anything recorded over two centuries after the Prophet's death would accurately represent what he had said or done during his lifetime. [19] However, since he did not refute the many technical counterarguments that the ᶜulamā' could present on this issue, it is doubtful that, as far as they were concerned, he carried his point.

Qadhdhāfī also attacked the hadīth on the grounds of their content, but here he was more specific, giving examples of improbable or contradictory hadīth. † For Qadhdhāfī, as for some other critics of the hadīth, the mere existence of hadīth with improbable or con-

---

*It is instructive to note the reaction of an eminent contemporary Islamic scholar, Mawlana Mawdūdī, to the rejection of the hadīth by Pakistani Muslims of the faction known as the munkirīn-i-hadīth, or deniers of the hadīth, whose position provoked a legal-religious controversy. To refute their claims that the hadīth were as a whole unreliable, Mawdūdī had recourse to the traditional methodology used by traditional hadīth scholarship to distinguish unreliable hadīth from those deserving credence. He discussed the various aspects of this methodology, including evaluation of the isnād, or chains of persons who have reportedly transmitted the hadīth; biographical studies of the transmitters; and content analysis of the hadīth. Mawdūdī insisted that the hadīth that passed muster according to the tests of traditional scholarship were genuine. While admitting that some hadīth were fabricated, he denounced the munkirīn-i-hadīth for taking an extreme and unwarranted position in saying that none was to be trusted. [18]

† One of his illustrations concerned two hadīth about the Prophet's favorite wife, ᶜĀ'isha. One hadīth, obviously of Sunnī provenance, said, "Learn half of your religion from ᶜĀ'isha," while the other, just as clearly of Shīᶜī provenance, said, "ᶜĀ'isha lacks intelligence and religion."

flicting contents conclusively establishes the proposition that no hadīth can be trusted. However, most ^culamā' are likely to remain confident that content analysis, which has long been a tool of hadīth criticism, can deal with this problem. Traditional scholarship rationalized apparent conflicts in the hadīth; hadīth in conflict might be held to apply to different problems; a later hadīth might mean that an earlier hadīth had been abrogated; one might be found to be more reliable than the other; missing words could be interpolated in the text of one to represent its meaning more correctly; and so on. Moreover, where the content of a hadīth was inherently dubious, it could be discarded for that very reason.[20] Thus, for the large number of ^culamā' who still rely on the traditional hadīth science, there are many tools for refuting Qadhdhāfī's criticism.

Some modern ^culamā' have themselves questioned the authority of the hadīth within the context of a systematic reappraisal of the inherited corpus of sharī^ca doctrine.[21] Again, it is noteworthy that Qadhdhāfī chose not to cite any modernist critiques of the hadīth in support of his views. In part this may be because few even among the modernists have taken a position as extreme as Qadhdhāfī's general approach, which is to propound his legal ideas as his own creations.

The second issue raised by Qadhdhāfī's speeches is the role of the ^culamā' in interpreting the requirements of Islamic law. Islamic law has been developed by scholars who have mastered the areas of learning traditionally considered necessary to derive rules of law from the sources. Because Islamic law does not recognize the legitimacy of human legislation, qualified legal scholars have enjoyed a monopoly of authority in Islamic law by reason of their role as the sole qualified interpreters of the meaning of the Quran and Sunna. Until this century it was rare for Muslims to challenge the authoritative character of the rules of law worked out by medieval legal scholars. Considering themselves bound by the doctrine of taqlīd, or obedience to authority, they believed that the possibility of ijtihād, or the exercise of independent reasoning to work out the implications of the sources, was precluded in all areas where earlier generations of scholars had elaborated rules.

Qadhdhāfī is far from alone among today's Muslims in his rejection of the authoritative character of the rules in the medieval treatises of fiqh. Although many ^culamā' still insist that today's Muslims remain bound by taqlīd, there has been a mounting tendency among modern scholars and among Muslims generally to discard past solutions to legal problems and to return to the Quran and Sunna in order to devise new rules that will be more suited to the needs of contemporary Muslims.[22] However, Qadhdhāfī does not justify his rejection of the medieval works of fiqh by reference to this well established movement to reopen the door of ijtihād. Instead, he prefers to adduce his own reasons, which most Muslims are likely to find less persuasive than the thesis of the mainstream modernists that the solutions of the past should not bind today's Muslims, who are faced with problems and circumstances that differ radically from those of the past. For example, Qadhdhāfī presents as a reason for discarding the fiqh the fact that so many of the great early scholars were not of Arab origin. This led them, he claims, to inject alien elements into Islam. This appears to be an attempt to mobilize Arab nationalist sentiment as a means of discrediting individuals who have for centuries been venerated for their piety, learning, and outstanding intellectual accomplishments and whose non-Arab origins have long been known and discounted. * Few Muslims would be inclined to revise their opinions of the value of the most venerable works of medieval scholarship solely on the basis of the racial background of their authors, but this may not be clear to Qadhdhāfī, who as a political leader is used to appealing to Arab nationalist sentiment in support of political objectives, where it is more appropriately invoked and probably with greater effect.

If all Qadhdhāfī had done had been to challenge the doctrine of taqlīd, and particularly if he had made that challenge on more familiar and acceptable grounds, his position regarding the Culamā' would not have seemed so radical. However, he is directing his attack not only at the doctrines of the Culamā' of the past but also at any claims by today's Culamā' to possess any special expertise. In order to establish his view of the sharīCa as the authoritative version, Qadhdhāfī apparently felt it necessary to establish that a Muslim untutored in the religious sciences is entitled to interpret the Quran and need not defer to persons with specialized learning. Thus, Qadhdhāfī is led to argue that anyone who known Arabic can read and understand the Quran without any intermediaries to explain the text.[23] This claim is made in the face of overwhelming evidence that understanding Quranic Arabic presents formidable problems for today's Muslims—even for persons with advanced training in classical Arabic, which Qadhdhāfī lacks. Written in verse form in the language of seventh-century Western Arabia, the Quran is so difficult for modern Arabic speakers to construe that it has been necessary to translate it into modern, standard Arabic.[24] The difficulties of deciphering its meaning have led to the development of a vast literature of dictionaries and commentaries but have not ended controversy about how various problematic verses are to be interpreted. Qadhdhāfī's assertions to the

_____

*Since a strikingly high percentage of the greatest early Islamic scholars were of Iranian origin, Qadhdhāfī's attack on the scholarship of non-Arabs is primarily directed at Iranians.

contrary notwithstanding, Muslims will continue to recognize the need
for learned specialists to aid them in interpreting the Quran; and interpretations by untrained persons will continue to lack persuasive
authority.

There is clearly a logical gap in Qadhdhāfī's argument. Why,
if any Arabic speaker can understand the Quran, is Qadhdhāfī pro-
pounding his views as the ones that must be accepted by his fellow
Muslims? His threats to the ^{c}ulamā' of the dire consequences they
will suffer should they oppose his interpretations make it clear that
as a practical matter he will not tolerate disagreement, but he does
not explicitly propose any reason why they should listen to him. The
gap in his argument can be neatly filled if one assumes that Qadhdhāfī
sees himself as a latter-day Muslim prophet, one whose every pro-
nouncement is authoritative by virtue of his special inspiration. Although Qadhdhāfī has not made any such claim, many of his positions
regarding the sharī^{c}a are intelligible only if one accepts the premise
of his prophethood. There is other evidence in his 1978 speeches
that seems to prefigure such a claim, and this is discussed in the
treatment of the remaining issues raised by his speeches.

The third question that Qadhdhāfī addressed was that of the nature and scope of the sharī^{c}a. According to him, the sharī^{c}a as a
religious law covers only such areas as fall within the sphere of religion, a sphere that includes the moral significance of acts and the
afterlife. All other matters lie outside the purview of religious law
with the exception of a few that are covered by specific Quranic rules,
as are some questions of criminal law and personal status.[25] In
Qadhdhāfī's view the Quran, as the law of society in Libya, would
provide criteria for distinguishing between good and evil and incen-
tives for doing good and avoiding evil by offering the reward of paradise for the one and the punishment of hellfire for the other. The
benefit to be gained from adopting the Quran as the law of society
would be that society would thereby be oriented toward doing good and
shunning evil.[26]

In making these claims, Qadhdhāfī expressed an opinion on the
scope of religious law and religious concerns that is more congenial
in a Christian than a Muslim environment. While Christianity has
maintained that worldly affairs are not the concern of religion, Muslims have generally held that their religion offers a comprehensive
scheme for regulating all aspects of human existence. What was
known as "Islamic law" was Islamic in the traditional definitions not
by virtue of the subject matter it covered but by virtue of having been
derived from Islamic sources by qualified scholars according to approved methodology. By far the greater part of Islamic law is concerned with matters that from a Christian perspective would be considered secular (such as constitutional, procedural, criminal, con-

tract, commercial, property, and tort law), but the fact that rules do not concern distinctively religious obligations has not meant that they have been regarded as less Islamic. On the contrary, the fact that Islamic law provides a scheme of guidance for the believer and for the Muslim community in all mundane matters has generally been perceived by Muslims to constitute a particular strength of their religion.

Why did Qadhdhāfī decide to redefine the sharīᶜa as an ethical scheme of other-worldly orientation in the face of overwhelming consensus among Muslims that the sharīᶜa encompasses worldly affairs as well as spiritual ones? One possible explanation is that since he proposes The Green Book as the solution to society's political, economic, and social problems, he felt a need to try to prepare the ground for the acceptance of The Green Book in place of the sharīᶜa as a comprehensive scheme of law. Since it could be anticipated that the ᶜulamā' would challenge The Green Book on many points where it was in apparent conflict with the sharīᶜa as conventionally understood, Qadhdhāfī was apparently inspired to contend that the sharīᶜa must be more narrowly defined in an attempt to obviate any possibility of conflict. The radical and precedent-shattering character of this contention, far from deterring Qadhdhāfī, may have induced him to make it, since on all questions involving the sharīᶜa he seems to favor taking positions that would enhance his status as an innovator.

Another possible explanation is that Qadhdhāfī, who has shown a striking capacity to evolve ideologically since coming to power in 1969 as well as a willingness to borrow ideas from various sources, was prompted to rethink the role that Islam should play in society in the wake of the 1976 Muslim-Christian Dialogue in Tripoli, in which he played a prominent role. Qadhdhāfī showed particular interest in pursuing the question of whether religion could be a viable ideology with representatives of the Vatican and appeared disappointed to learn the Vatican was not a state based on religious law. During the course of the discussion, in which the Muslim representatives extolled the virtues of Islam as an ideology, the Vatican representatives explained their very different notions of the role that religion should play, one of spiritual and moral guidance. The fact that two years later Qadhdhāfī had repudiated the Muslim position to which he had formerly adhered and adopted an opinion closely resembling that outlined by the Vatican representatives at the dialogue prompts questions as to the intellectual parentage of Qadhdhāfī's ideas on this subject. *

---

*At the Muslim-Christian Dialogue Qadhdhāfī appeared to align himself with the traditional Muslim view that Islam offers an all-embracing scheme of regulation.[27]

The fourth question involving Islamic law brought up by Qadhd-hāfī's speeches was not specifically addressed but was implicit in all his remarks. It concerned the relationship between the state and Islam, and in his approach to this question he broke away from the approaches taken by other Muslim leaders. To appreciate the significance of Qadhdhāfī's initiatives, it is instructive to consider the government's role in reforming the sharīᶜa in three countries linked to Libya by history and geography—Turkey, Tunisia, and Egypt.

In the Turkish Republic under Kemal Atatürk, the political leadership took the radical step in the 1920s of reconstituting the entire legal system on a secular basis along continental European lines. Once the sharīᶜa was eliminated from Turkish law, the ᶜulamā' had no role in the legal system. However, Atatürk did not try to impose new sharīᶜa doctrines on the ᶜulamā' and the Turkish populace. His campaign to win support for his reforms was based on secular and nationalistic appeals to Turks to accept the modern laws that were perceived as necessary foundations for national progress and social advancement.[28] Thus, while the sharīᶜa was removed from the sphere of practical application by the action of the state, it continued to exist as an ideal system of religious law whose doctrines were fixed by religious scholars.

In the Arab world, Tunisia has gone farthest in the reform of personal-status law, the aspect of Islamic law that retains the greatest influence in current legal systems in the Middle East. Again, a single political leader—in this case Habīb Bourguiba—was very much the driving force behind the legal reform program. In campaigning for the 1956 Tunisian Code of Personal Status, which went a long way toward eliminating the disabilities that Muslim women suffered under the previous sharīᶜa rules, Bourguiba, like Atatürk, justified law reform as necessary for national progress, arguing that the backward status of women would impede the progress of society as a whole. Official justifications for the reforms were presented in sharīᶜa terms in an attempt to discourage opposition to the reforms on religious grounds. These were prepared by ᶜulamā' who were sympathetic to the objectives of the code and anxious to prove that the sharīᶜa was compatible with progress.[29] That is, the political leadership delegated the task of defending the compatibility of the reforms with the sharīᶜa to persons with recognized competence in fiqh.

Until the late 1970s the government in Egypt did not sponsor any similar, dramatic initiatives to reform personal-status law. In fact, many of the important debates on reform of the sharīᶜa went on among factions and individuals outside the government.[30] The 1979 reforms in personal-status law may owe much to the effort and support of President Sadat's wife Jihān, but even these were the result of a protracted process of consultation and debate and represented a cautious compromise between demands of feminists for change and the insistence of powerful traditional forces that the substance of the sharīᶜa be preserved.

Thus, whether they were aiming at radical or at very modest legal reforms that would derogate from the sharīᶜa, leaders of these Muslim countries avoided acts by the state that would constitute direct tampering with the substance of sharīᶜa doctrine. One must ask why Qadhdhāfī did not follow the same path as Atatürk, whose achievements he obviously admires.

In Qadhdhāfī's sympathetic remarks in his July 3 speech about Atatürk, one senses a shared frustration over the religious fanaticism and obduracy that impede the implementation of programs designed to advance the welfare of the nation. Few leaders in the Arab world have dared openly to advocate the separation of church and state or to mention Atatürk's example approvingly in their public pronouncements, so Qadhdhāfī's presentation of the Kemalist model of a secular state as a reasonable response to political and economic exigencies means that he is taking a relatively radical position on the role that religion should play in a contemporary Muslim society. However, it seems that he cited Atatürk's example—along with the drastic measures that he took when the ᶜulamā' condemned him as an infidel —not because he was prepared to pose as a purely secular leader of a secular state but to remind the ᶜulamā' that they should be grateful to have The Green Book, which allows some place for religion, rather than some other, more radical solution. Qadhdhāfī, however attracted he may be by the Atatürk model, could not have followed it. This is because he is a prisoner of his own theories; he is an Arab nationalist, and he believes that the Arab and Islamic identities are inextricably linked. Thus, he asserts that the Arab revolution must also be an Islamic one.[31] From this it follows that the leader of Arab nationalism must also be the leader of Arab Islam and must offer revolutionary programs for both.

Against this background, the revolutionary nature of Qadhdhāfī's model for legal reform is apparent: his concept of the role the state should play in sharīᶜa reform is unique. It was not just ideological considerations that prompted such personal intervention in sensitive issues of law reform; conditions in Libya facilitated direct involvement by the state in the reformulation of Islam. Aside from the central government, controlled by Qadhdhāfī, there was no group left in Libya after the repression of his opponents in the mid-1970s that could mount any effective challenge to Qadhdhāfī's leadership other than the military. Lacking any professional interest in the outcome of theological disputes and pampered by huge subsidies from the Qadhdhāfī regime, the military was unlikely to make common cause with the beleaguered ᶜulamā'. The political opposition within the country had been decimated by executions, jailings, and exiles. Similar fates had removed Qadhdhāfī's critics within the regime. Private wealth and businesses were in the process of being dismantled and with them the influence of the middle classes. Tribal and regional rivalries impeded the formation of anti-Qadhdhāfī coalitions. The media were obligated to adhere rigidly to Qadhdhāfī's political line. The extraordinary growth of Libya's income from oil and a program of distributing the proceeds to the masses in the form of various subsidies and social welfare projects meant that the lives of average Libyans were improving in the material sense even as they were becoming more dependent on the central government for their basic needs. The ᶜulamā' themselves lacked any strong institutional base from which to mount their opposition. Although he appears to have concluded that Libyans and other Arabs whom he wished to win over would not accept secularization on the Atatürk model, Qadhdhāfī had fewer political constraints limiting his approach to the issue of law reform than did leaders of other states in the region.

In consequence, rather than delegating to liberal ᶜulamā' the task of working out Islamic justifications for desirable legal reforms or simply replacing sharīᶜa rules by secular ones in Libya's positive law, Qadhdhāfī has himself undertaken the role of supreme interpreter of Islamic law. As such, he performs exegeses of Quranic verses—exegeses that he clearly expects other Muslims, including the ᶜulamā', to accept as authoritative.

A revealing example of Qadhdhāfī's approach to interpreting the Quran may be seen in the interpretation that he proposed of the famous verse on polygamy (Sūra 4:3) in his July 3 speech. The relevant verse reads as follows:

> If you fear that you will not act justly towards the orphans, marry such women as seem good to you, two, three, or four; but if you fear you will not be equitable, then only one.

Until this century this verse was held to permit polygamy, the common reading being that it allowed a man to take up to four wives at one time. [32] The most influential modern interpretation was made by the great reformer and Muftī of Egypt, Muhammad ᶜAbduh (d. 1905). He read the verse in conjunction with others to mean that only a man who could treat more than one wife equally was allowed to marry more than one wife, and since equal treatment of more than one wife was a practical impossibility, polygamous marriages were not allowed. [33] This interpretation, while not, perhaps, the most natural reading of the verse, had didactic value, since through it ᶜAbduh was able to communicate the attitude that the unequal treat-

ment that women suffered in polygamous households was condemned
by Islam, and that the man who contracted a polygamous marriage
was perpetrating a wrong. Thus interpreted, monogamy became associated with virtue.

Qadhdhāfī's reading is very different: according to him the
verse is meant to apply solely to those men who are entrusted with
the care of orphaned females. Such men are allowed to marry more
than one of their orphaned wards, and, Qadhdhāfī says, this is the
one exception to an otherwise prevailing Islamic rule that marriages
must be monogamous.[34] This reading of the verse is unusual, and
one must ask why, when the CAbduh reading has gained such currency
in the Muslim world, Qadhdhāfī preferred to propose his own interpretation, which lacked the ethical point that made CAbduh's so attractive. This question is also prompted by the problems that Qadhdhāfī's interpretation involves, resting as it does on technical lexical
and syntactical points such as whether "women" in the verse refers
back to "orphans."[35] Furthermore, he rests this reading on the
premise that there is a general sharīCa rule that marriages should be
monogamous without bothering to explain how he arrived at that conclusion. That he has chosen to propound an ingenious but problematic
reading rather than relying on the widely accepted opinion of a distinguished reformer like CAbduh and that he does not bother to explain whence he derived the proposition that monogamous marriage
is the rule in Islam lead one to conclude that he expects his opinions
on these matters to carry weight precisely because he promulgated
them.

Another Quranic interpretation he offered in his July speech was
of Sūra 9:34, which condemns those who hoard gold and silver to a
painful chastisement. Qadhdhāfī argued that gold and silver were
not to be taken in their literal sense, but that they stood for all forms
of wealth. Interpreting the condemnation of hoarding to mean that no
one was entitled to have more than what was required to meet one's
basic needs, Qadhdhāfī claimed that it was permissible to confiscate
any excess over that amount to redistribute to those in need—a clear
attempt to establish a Quranic authorization for the draconian confis-
cations of property and leveling of wealth called for in the second
part of The Green Book and since implemented in Libya. Since the
sharīCa has traditionally been interpreted to provide strong protection for rights of private ownership and to sanction disparities in
wealth, Qadhdhāfī's interpretation was certain to provoke controversy.

Not surprisingly, one of the Culamā' challenged Qadhdhāfī's interpretation by pointing out that in Sūra 16:71 the following is stated:

> And God has preferred some of you over others in provi-
> sion; but those that were preferred shall not give over

their provision to that their right hands possess, so that
they may be equal therein. What, and do they deny God's
blessing?

Qadhdhāfī's response was to say that in some instances Quranic
verses dealt with the social reality at the time of revelation, a reality
that included stratification by class. Dealing with the reality did not
betoken approval of stratification.[36] Thus, Qadhdhāfī indicated that
in addition to providing his own idiosyncratic constructions of verses
of the Quran, he was prepared to dismiss them as being anachronistic.
While there are Quranic verses that are directed at specific circumstances prevailing at the time of revelation, most of the Quran has
been considered by Muslims to be of general relevance and valid "for
all times and climes." Sūra 16:71 does not seem on its face to be
historically limited, and Qadhdhāfī offered no reasoned explanation
of why it should be so construed. His rejection of its relevance seems
to be of a piece with his denigration of institutions provided for in the
Quran, like concubinage, slavery, and polygamy, deriving not so
much from textual analysis as from his political judgment that they
are retrograde. Implicit in this approach is the notion that where
Quranic provisions are out of tune with Qadhdhāfī's policies, they
are properly dismissed as superseded by the latter.

Of course, it is not unusual for the Quran to be interpreted to
justify different political positions.[37] What is striking about Qadhdhāfī's interpretations of the verses on hoarding and stratification is
his decision to present himself as the final arbiter on the question of
what Quranic verses remain valid for today's Muslims—discarding
those that conflict with his notions of what is progressive—and also
on the question of how the remaining verses are to be construed—
which is obviously to be in a manner that will complement the teachings of The Green Book.

CONCLUSION

Why did Qadhdhāfī chose to promulgate his own interpretations
of the Quran in this way? It seems probable that this unusual behavior results from his high estimation of his own intellectual prowess
and perhaps an evolving, mystical conviction that he has superhuman
inspiration.

From his first years in power, Qadhdhāfī has played the role
of the revolutionary thinker as well as that of revolutionary political
leader. He has courted dialogue with intellectuals from both the
Muslim world and outside it, and he has seen to it that his speeches
and writings are disseminated internationally in many languages. He

has in many respects emulated Mao Tse-tung launching a "cultural revolution" in 1973 and later publishing The Green Book, which in style and name recalls Mao's Red Book. He has often reiterated his conviction that his "Third International Theory," set forth in The Green Book, will ultimately sweep the world, supplanting all other ideologies. Meanwhile, in the preamble to the new Libyan constitution, the "Declaration of the Establishment of the People's Authority" of March 2, 1977, there are a number of references attesting to Qadhdhāfī's absolute ideological ascendancy. His speech inaugurating the 1973 Cultural Revolution and The Green Book are cited as authority, and "the leadership of the revolutionary thinker and teacher, our leader Mu^Cammar al-Qadhdhāfī" is twice acknowledged.

In the course of developing and promoting his ideology, Qadhdhāfī seems to have become disenchanted with conventional approaches to Islam, which lacked the flexibility to accommodate his increasingly radical ideas. Indeed, as early as a speech made on April 28, 1973, to the students of the Benghāzī law faculty, he expressed his impatience and dissatisfaction with the accomplishments of the sheikhs who had been charged with the task of Islamicizing Libyan law. He pleaded with the students to take over the task of deriving new and more suitable laws from the Quran, apparently with no productive result. [38]

Far from diminishing, Qadhdhāfī's misgivings about the feasibility of collaborating with Libya's religious establishment seem to have grown in the following years. His disillusionment with the ^Culamā' may have been due to more than one factor, but the timing of the manifestations of estrangement between Qadhdhāfī and the ^Culamā' suggests that it was seriously exacerbated by their critical reaction to The Green Book. Having offered a revolutionary ideology that, unlike Marxism, left a role for religion, Qadhdhāfī was apparently stung by charges from the ^Culamā' that his policies as set forth in The Green Book were contrary to Islam. In the wake of confrontations between Qadhdhāfī and the ^Culamā' in the spring of 1978, it was unofficially reported that many ^Culamā' had been jailed for their denunciations of Qadhdhāfī's Marxist tendencies.

When they came out in open opposition to The Green Book, the ^Culamā' were competing for the allegiance of the same constituency that has been the mainstay of Qadhdhāfī's support in Libya—the masses of lower-class Libyans, who constitute both the most traditional segment of Libyan society and the one that has benefited most from the changes brought about by the revolution. There is some evidence that religious loyalties among the masses were more ingrained than Qadhdhāfī would have liked, so that the threat to his following and legitimacy represented by the hostile ^Culamā' could not be lightly discounted. [39] Qadhdhāfī apparently believed that he could undermine their authority by besting them in public debates in which he

would challenge their expertise, overwhelm them with the force of
his arguments, and establish himself as the new leader of a revo-
lutionized Islam.

In the years after Qadhdhāfī abandoned his original program of
reinstating Islamic law, the connection between his ideology and the
precepts of Islam became attenuated. Certainly, Qadhdhāfī continued
to evoke Islamic associations even as The Green Book was displacing
the sharī^ca. The book's emerald green cover and its title are sug-
gestive of an Islamic affiliation, green being the color traditionally associated with Islam. Moreover, as indicated, he presents many of his
views as resting on interpretations of the Quran. However, as his
ideology became increasingly radical and idiosyncratic, whether or not
Qadhdhāfī's views on the sharī^ca were accepted as Islamic came to depend on whether Qadhdhāfī was accepted as a new prophet of Islam
whose ideas in The Green Book and whose speeches would take prece-
dence over former sharī^ca doctrines from which they sharply diverged.
This is not to say that Qadhdhāfī has made any formal claim to being a
prophet, but there have been numerous indications that he intends that
Muslims perceive him in that light. An adulatory cult of personality
is actively fostered by the Libyan media. Passages from The Green
Book are reverently and repeatedly intoned in television and radio
broadcasts, much as passages of the Quran used to be read. The
Green Book is used in the manner of a catechism to instruct Libyan
schoolchildren. Sayings from The Green Book are reprinted in Libyan
publications and prominently displayed in public places. The sharp and
seemingly willful breaks with mainstream Muslim opinion represented
by many of the positions taken by Qadhdhāfī on the occasions of his
critical speeches in 1978 also support the conclusion that he intends to
be accepted as a prophet. It would not be surprising if, in his eyes,
one of the gauges of the merits of his ideas was their seeming original-
ity; prophets are, after all, expected to reveal new things, and this
must be doubly so of revolutionary prophets.

Before establishing himself as a new prophet, Qadhdhāfī had to
deal with the fact that the Prophet Muhammad is regarded by Muslims
as the "Seal of the Prophets." As the proponent of a rival scheme of
values, the Prophet Muhammad had to be reduced to a marginal figure
to make room for Qadhdhāfī and The Green Book philosophy. Although apparently unprepared to state outright that he is replacing the
Prophet Muhammad, Qadhdhāfī, by the sumbolism of his actions, is
indicating that this is what he intends to do. It cannot be coincidence
that Qadhdhāfī chose a celebration of the Prophet's birthday in a
mosque to make his speech dismissing the Sunna of the Prophet as
not binding on today's Muslims. Henceforth, if that date is remembered, it should be as the anniversary of the occasion on which Muslims were told to discard the heritage of sharī^ca law based on the

Sunna of the Prophet. Significant, too, is Qadhdhāfī's decision in 1977 to alter the starting year of the Libyan calendar from the date of the Prophet's flight to Medina, where his fortunes prospered, to the date of the Prophet's death. The symbolic meaning seems to be that in Libya the era of the Prophet is in the past.

Not only does Qadhdhāfī need to establish his ascendancy over the Prophet Muhammad to promote his own ideology but by denigrating the importance of the Prophet and His message he also serves the ends of his pan-Arab and regional diplomacy. As is well known, a major tenet of Qadhdhāfī's foreign policy since he came to power has been the need for mergers. He has attempted numerous mergers with other Arab states. He has also tried to entice Malta, whose inhabitants have linguistic and ethnic ties to the Arab world, into closer association with Libya. In many of these attempts he has had to face the wariness of Christian minorities—or, in the case of Malta, a Christian majority—who see in Qadhdhāfī a Muslim zealot inimical to their interests. Thus, Qadhdhāfī has political reasons for wanting to conciliate Christians in Malta, Egypt, and Syria. It is also clear from The Green Book that he sees the existence of religious divisions in the Arab world as a cause of factionalism impeding the progress of unification—of which Lebanon would be the most notable example. In line with his longstanding insistence that Islam is an Arab religion, he has asserted that it is anomolous to have non-Muslim Arabs, that there must be an Arab Islam for the Arab nation to experience rebirth, and that Islam—at least in its early stages—was not really intended for a non-Arab audience. [40] From this, it is not going much further to attack Christian holdouts in the Arab world as standing in the way of an Arab national renaissance.

Qadhdhāfī has evinced a conviction that the differences between Christianity and Islam are minimal and arise merely from some misapprehensions on the Christian side. The Muslim-Christian Dialogue he staged in Tripoli in 1976 with great public fanfare was exploited as an occasion to bring home to the Christian participants their errors and to indulge in heavy-handed proselytizing. One of the main thrusts of the Muslim campaign to convert their Christian brethren was in the direction of getting them to acknowledge the prophethood of Muhammad, a prime stumbling block to Muslim-Christian unity. In line with Qadhdhāfī's position that Christian errors are the product of alterations in the original text of the Bible, participants in the dialogue were pressed to acknowledge the authenticity of the Gospel of Saint Barnabbas. [41] This gospel, which Christian scholars regard as a Renaissance forgery, presages the coming of the Prophet Muhammad, and many Muslims believe that it was excised from the original text of the Bible. If recognized by Christians, it would provide the crucial link between the Bible and the Quranic revelation. Qadhdhāfī and other members of the Muslim delegation exerted pressure on the Christian delegates to make public acknowledgments of the prophethood of Muhammad, indicating that to fail to do so would constitute disrespect for Islam. The official Libyan report of the dialogue even went so far as to distort comments by the Vatican's chief representative, Cardinal Pignedoli, in a way that suggested that he had been brought around to the Muslim position.[42] In fact, the Christians remained obdurate in their refusal to recognize the Prophet Muhammad as the vehicle of divine revelation, and the Muslim side had to be content with a compromise passage in the final resolution in which both sides agreed that honor (takrīm) was due to the prophets and messengers of their faiths.[43] One may speculate on the basis of Qadhdhāfī's behavior at the conference that he was surprised and disappointed at his failure to resolve the differences separating Christians from Muslims.

Despite the failure of his proselytizing at the dialogue, Qadhdhāfī persisted in his propaganda efforts directed at Christians and designed to demonstrate the oneness of the two faiths. However, instead of demanding that all of the concessions be made by Christians, he began to attack facets of Islamic doctrine on the grounds that they were not part of the original, true version of Islam.[44] One is prompted to speculate that having failed in his attempt to win recognition of the Prophet Muhammad in 1976, Qadhdhāfī hoped that in demoting the Prophet from the central position he had enjoyed in Islam, he would remove a major roadblock to the bringing of Christians into the Muslim fold and would thereby encourage them to make an equivalent concession, that of abandoning their insistence on the trinitarian nature of the deity.

As has already been noted, the circumscribed role that Qadhdhāfī allotted to Islam in his July 1978 speech corresponded to the role of the Christian religion that had been outlined two years previously by Vatican delegates. It is possible that his new position—that Islamic law essentially provided a system of moral and spiritual guidance rather than a system of positive law—was motivated by a wish to reformulate Islamic doctrine in a way that would make it more palatable to potential converts from Christianity. If, because of his inspiration, Islam suddenly gained in appeal so that mass conversions from Christianity ensued, Qadhdhāfī's prestige and influence stood to be immeasurably enhanced. This represents an ambitious undertaking, but one that could seem feasible to Qadhdhāfī, who seems convinced that his Third International Theory will sweep the world at the expense of all other theories.

Since Qadhdhāfī's speeches about the sharīᶜa in 1978, Libyan propaganda has concentrated less on issues of Islamic law than on propagating the Third International Theory. In part this may be owing to strong criticisms of Qadhdhāfī's views from many Muslim groups who have been alienated by his attacks on the Sunna and his interpretations of the Quran. That the regime is nervous about this reaction is suggested by the defensive tone of subsequent articles in the Libyan press insisting that lies are being told about the position of the Prophet in revolutionary Libya; denouncing reactionaries who use religion to defend their interests; heaping praise on the Prophet; and arguing that the right way to glorify the Prophet is by following a new, revolutionary version of Islam. [45] This negative reaction may have led Qadhdhāfī to soft-pedal his religious views for the time being, particularly in statements designed for external consumption. With the Islamic fundamentalist upsurge that accompanied the Iranian Revolution spreading throughout the Middle East in the late 1970s, Qadhdhāfī's foreign politics could have become more complicated if his radical policies regarding Islam received much attention. In particular, since Qadhdhāfī has tried to make the revolutionary government of Iran an ally at a time when Libya's international isolation has become embarrassingly apparent, he has every reason to play down his views of Islam in his dealings with the Iranian authorities. The Arab nationalist overtones in his version of Islam, his attacks on the ʿulamā', and his dismissal of the traditional sharīʿa would hardly make him persona grata with an Iranian regime whose dominant figures are Muslim clerics.

Meanwhile, on the domestic scene Qadhdhāfī has pursued the implementation of the tenets of The Green Book with great vigor, and it is clear that these are being treated as the basis for a new system of positive law in Libya. It is likewise clear that Qadhdhāfī's pronouncements are meant to be the basis for a new Islamic law. Whether one accepts the Islamic authenticity of his pronouncements depends on whether one acknowledges his credentials, which seem to rest increasingly on a presumption that he speaks in the capacity of prophet-lawgiver.

NOTES

1. Borham Atallah, "Le droit pénal musulman ressucité," Annuaire de l'Afrique du Nord 13 (1975): 227-52; idem, "L'Acculturation juridique dans le nord de l'Afrique," Indépendance et interdépendances au Maghreb (Paris: Centre National de la Recherche Scientifique, 1974), pp. 159-200; Ann Mayer, "Developments in the Law of Marriage and Divorce in Libya since the 1969 Revolution," Journal of African Law 22 (1978): 30-49; idem, "Legislation in Defense of Arabo-Islamic Mores," American Journal of Comparative Law 28 (1980): 287-313; and idem, "Islamicizing Laws Affecting the Regulation of Interest Charges and Risk Contracts: Some Problems of Recent Libyan Legislation," International Comparative Law Quarterly 28 (1979): 541-59.

2. Mu^cammar al-Qadhdhāfī, The Green Book. Part One: The Solution of the Problem of Democracy (London: Martin Brian and O'Keefe, 1976), p. 31.

3. Ibid., p. 33.

4. Ibid.

5. Mu^cammar al-Qadhdhāfī, al-Sijill al-qawmī, bayānāt wa khutab wa ahadīth al-'aqīd Mu^cammar al-Qadhdhāfī (Tripoli: Matba^cat al-Thawra al-^carabiya, 1978), pp. 462-63.

6. Ibid., pp. 465-66.

7. Ibid., pp. 466-83.

8. Ibid., p. 496.

9. Ibid., pp. 496-97. Among the persons whose authority he expressly denied were Ibn Hanbal, Mālik, and al-Shāfi^cī, each of whom founded a school of law, and the medieval philosophers al-Ghazalī and Ibn Sīna (Avicenna).

10. Ibid., p. 997.

11. Ibid., pp. 997-1009.

12. Ibid., pp. 1017-18.

13. Ibid., pp. 1019-25.

14. Ibid., pp. 1021, 1043-44.

15. Joseph Schacht, The Origins of Muhammadan Jurisprudence (Oxford: Clarendon Press, 1950), pp. 40-41.

16. Ibid., pp. 44-45.

17. This topic is treated in ibid.

18. Charles Adams, "The Authority of the Prophetic Hadīth," in Essays on Islamic Civilization, ed. D. Little (Leiden: Brill, 1976), pp. 24-28.

19. Qadhdhāfī, al-Sijill, pp. 1012-14.

20. For examples of how traditional scholarship dealt with conflicts and contradiction in the hadīth, see Gerard Lecomte, Le Traite des divergences du hadit d'Ibn Qutayba: Traduction annoté du Kitab Ta'wil Muhtalif al-hadīth (Damascus: Instituit Francais de Damas, 1962); and Schacht, Origins, pp. 37-38.

21. J. J. G. Jansen, The Interpretation of the Koran in Modern Egypt (Leiden: Brill, 1974), p. 27.

22. An excellent summary of these developments is found in David Bonderman, "Modernization and Changing Perceptions of Islamic Law," Harvard Law Review 81 (1968): 1169-93.

23. Qadhdhāfī, al-Sijill, p. 496.

24. Jansen, Interpretation of the Koran, pp. 10-13.

25. Qadhdhāfī, al-Sijill, pp. 1027-29.

26. Ibid., pp. 1032-33.

27. Maurice Borrmans, "Le Séminaire du Dialogue Islamo-Chrétien de Tripoli (Libya) (1-6 Fevrier 1976)," Islamo-Christiana 2 (1976): 135-70. Indeed, as late as his February 19 speech, Qadhd-

ḥāfī gave indications of supporting this traditional Islamic view. Qadhdhāfī, al-Sijill, p. 461.

28. Lord Kinross, Ataturk (New York: W. Morrow, 1965), pp. 468, 477-78.

29. Jean Magnin, "Réformes juridiques en Tunisie," IBLA 21 (1958): 77-92.

30. Noel Coulson, A History of Islamic Law (Edinburgh: Edinburgh University Press, 1964), pp. 173-78, 186-88, 195-96, 199-201, 202-5; and Mohamed Al-Nowaihi, "Some Recent Attempts towards More Liberal Interpretation of the Quran and Modernization of Islamic Jurisprudence," Middle East Journal 3 (1976): 64-65.

31. al-Fajr al-jadīd, March 10, 1979.

32. Jansen, Interpretation of the Koran, p. 91.

33. Helmut Gaetje, The Quran and Its Exegesis: Selected Texts with Classical and Modern Interpretations (London: Routledge and Kegan Paul, 1976), pp. 248-51.

34. Qadhdhāfī, al-Sijill, pp. 1030-31.

35. Contrast Qadhdhāfī's simple declaration that Sūra 4:3 should be read his way with the sophisticated analysis of lexical and grammatical points in two classic works, az-Zamakhsharī, al-Kashshāf ᶜan haqā'iq al-tanzīl wa ᶜuyūn al-aqawīl fī wujūh al-ta'wīl (Beirut: Dar al-kitāb al-ᶜarabi, 1947), 1:467; and al-Qurtubī's, al-Jāmiᶜ li ahkām al-Qurān (Cairo: Dār al-kutub al-misrīya, 1937), 5: 11-13.

36. Qadhdhāfī, al-Sijill, pp. 1036-41.

37. Jansen, Interpretation of the Koran, pp. 77-94.

38. Muᶜammar al-Qadhdhāfī, Sijill (Tripoli: Arab Socialist Union, 1973), p. 714.

39. Herve Bleuchot and Taofik Monastiri, "Libye: L'évolution des institutions politiques," Annuaire de l'Afrique du Nord 16 (Paris: Centre National de la Recherche Scientifique, 1978), pp. 170-75.

40. al-Fajr al-jadīd, March 10, 1979.

41. Borrmans, "Le Séminaire du Dialogue," p. 163.

42. Ibid., p. 155.

43. Ibid., p. 157.

44. Qadhdhāfī, al-Sijill, pp. 466-69.

45. al-Fajr al-jadīd, December 17, 1978; and al-Usbūᶜ al-siyāsī, February 9, 1979.

11

REVIVAL IN THE MAGHREB: ISLAM AS AN ALTERNATIVE POLITICAL LANGUAGE

JEAN-CLAUDE VATIN

In general, the Maghreb has not undergone the same type of religious agitation that seized several parts of the Islamic world during the late 1970s. The formerly French-controlled part of North Africa seems to be immune to the contagion of Muslim-inspired movements whether indigenous or imported from the neighboring countries of the Middle East where Allah's religion played a greater role in politics.

The reemergence of Islam as an important factor of social and political activities, although less apparent in the region, is, however, noticeable. Most of the phenomena pointed out by observers are indeed less striking than those that have taken place in other countries like Iran, Pakistan, Saudi Arabia, or Libya. Still there are signs of an increase in religious observances, of governmental concern, and of the recrudescence of popular interest in the Arab-Muslim culture.

Without claiming that the following interpretation would apply to any other part of the Muslim world, the current resurgence in the Maghreb has become clearly marked by the relation between religion and politics, that is between the rulers and the religious convictions of the governed. My main thesis is that Islam has become an alternative political language for dialogues between the people and the political elite. Islam is thus a medium of discourse for the rulers as well as for their opponents and the masses, a language used to convey arguments that sometimes have nothing to do with religion but could not be conveyed through other channels. The reasons for this vary from one country to another, but in most they result from the state's penetration into social activities. Such a use of Islam (which might not be as new as many political scientists think it is) is not similar in the three Maghreb states. What one sees instead are three different ways of nationalizing religion for the benefit of the nation-states.

ISLAMIC RESURGENCE: THE MAGHREB CASE

Curiously, the recent religious manifestations in North Africa have been referred to under the heading of revival, instead of resurgence, the latter being more often used to qualify what has happened in the Muslim world as a whole.[1] The concept of revival implies a reference to a renaissance, to a humanistic renewal of thought, literature, and the arts, and thus has a stronger cultural connotation than the concept of resurgence, which may sound more loaded politically because of possible allusions to a return to prominence. But one should not, however, overemphasize the difference in meanings of the two words, since they appear to be virtually synonymous for most commentators. Nonetheless, it is worth taking note of the various senses of a term so widely popularized and sometimes misused, before examining its application to the Maghreb.

If one considers the word revival as it has been made familiar by numerous commentaries and explanations, one notices it does not convey the same meaning for Muslims as for others. In the Western world, where the concept is strongly associated with fundamentalism, it often suggests a reversion to an earlier stage and carries a somewhat negative connotation. The term Islamic revival can refer to different situations. The term could be used to invoke a new sensitivity to religious values. It could also mean a spectacular upsurge in religious observance. It could refer to a threatening reactivation of religious militancy in a specific part of the world. The Western media have more commonly diffused the last image. The revival is seen in relation to its opposites (tradition, continuity, stability, and the like) as being a rupture with both a certain way of life and a political behavior, that is, as being against a former internal order of things, as well as against the international order. Islam in most cases appears as either a regressive or an aggressive force. Every manifestation of revival is perceived as a challenge to the West.[2] For instance, the press fancies that Muslims are using oil to get recognition and prestige. The Ayātollāh Khomeinī appears to be a new reincarnation of the Mahdī. Despite a general mobilization of their Islamologists, orientalists, and scholars to explain recent developments in Iran, Saudi Arabia, Chad, Malaya, and several other places, most Europeans and Americans still do not understand what Islam is.*

---

*This does not mean that excellent studies are lacking. They might simply not have been properly understood. Louis Gardet's La Cité musulmane (Paris: Vrin, 1969), which provides the reader with a general theory of Islam, is striking. Robert Bellah's Beyond Belief (New York: Harper & Row, 1969), which emphasizes the modernizing

Viewed from the Muslim territory itself, there is a basic un-
certainty regarding the religious revival. For some people, it is
above all else a matter of pride. They think that the Iranian revolution has performed a rare service to the entire umma. They look
forward to a complete rehabilitation of their civilization through it,
and they continue to assert the dynamics of the faith and the vitality
of its way of life.

If some have strongly recommended Islam and the Islamic experience as the only path to authentic development, others have condemned those who advocated a return to a mythical "source" and
glorified the early Muslim community. Although they did not ask for
secularization, they have denounced as fallacies both the restoration
of an unchanged sharī^{c}a law and the implementation of an exemplary
"Islamic city" reconstructed on the Muhammadan model. According
to them, Muslims should not delude themselves into thinking they can
relive their past. On the contrary, they should concentrate on facing
present and future realities.

As for governments, they realized that dissatisfaction could be
given clear and effective expression through the religious vocabulary.
They were afraid of popular puritanism, which demanded them to rule
according to the strict norms of the faith.[3] They still suspected
those who compared their decisions, actions, and conduct with the
exemplary government of the early period and to the Islamic fundamentals. That is why they have strived to divert popular passion and
criticism into other areas, while compromising with some of it.
They have also tried to remove themselves and the rest of their peoples from the ideological agitation and political disturbances that have
unexpectedly occurred in other Muslim countries. Thus, some heads
of states underlined the fact that the Iranian revolution was directly
linked with the dogma of the Twelfth Imām, or that the Ayātollāh
Khomeinī could not play the part of the charismatic leader that the
Islamic community needed to reassert itself.

In fact, interpretations on all sides seem to be characterized
by almost the same misapprehensions and misleading images. Illu-
sions are common. It is an illusion to believe that Muslim revivalism is another one of the long series of cultural and political upheavals that have continuously marked Muslims' aspirations for independence. It is also an illusion to argue that the actual movements

---

aspects of Islam, seems to have been ignored by many scholars. On
the question of Islamic and Maghreb studies in the West, see Jean-
Claude Vatin, "Religion et politique au Maghreb: Le renversement
des perspectives dans l'étude de l'Islam," in Islam et politique au
Maghreb, ed. CRESM (Paris: Editions du CNRS, forthcoming).

have been directly produced by some unique factor, such as the oil revenues or the outcome of the Egyptian-Israeli war of 1973, as if Islamic revivalism were without precedent in modern Islam. There is also the illusion that the old pan-Islamism has returned in a new garb.

If we want to keep our distance from tendentious interpretations, we have to reconsider the concept of Islamic revival. It is almost impossible to differentiate between two aspects of the revival phenomenon: (1) revival as an intellectual concept constructed by social scientists to conceal a complex and ambiguous reality and (2) revival as a variety of manifestations with their own causes and expressions, as a thing-in-itself with a certain autonomy of its own.

This differentiation between a revival in theory and a revival in practice has, however, the merit of helping us distinguish between revival movements, which can be observed and studied, and the whole question of revivalism, which implies a certain attitude of people toward such movements. This establishes a methodological distinction between the actions of reviving, their materialization, and the theoretical problems linked to them. In order to separate the practical appearances of the phenomenon in the Maghreb from its ideology, this chapter will use the word revival to connote the former and the word revivalism to connote the latter.

What is important, then, is to situate the Maghreb cases in a framework of both revivals and revivalism. But the various examples of re-Islamization available for examination today have not provided any detailed typology. What we have are rough, broad categories based on the various experiences of Islamic societies. At each historical stage, we find a certain type of revivalism combined with various revival movements, as for example, the classical pragmatism of the period of the first caliphs; the conservative preservation of the ᶜulamā', which led to political quietism at various times during the Muslim empires; the fundamentalist demand for purification, which was inspired by Ahmad Ibn Hanbal and later by Muhammad Ibn ᶜAbd al-Wahhāb, as well as by the Kharijites; various types of Sūfism, with their marabūts, mahdīs, and religious orders or tarīqas; the reformists who sought a social/religious realignment during the first part of the twentieth century; and the radical austerity of more recent leaders of Islamic movements.

Several scholars have produced broad classifications that could be helpful here. Among others, a Tunisian sociologist, Abdelwahab Bouhdiba, devised one according to the four rites of the sunnism.[4] More recently, John Voll has also differentiated four styles or patterns of action and response within the Islamic historical process.[5] We now have sets of variables related to the kind of revival movements that have taken place since the first Islamic century, the initiators of such movements, the political authorities in office and their reactions to various events, and so on.

One aspect of Islam that most typologists do not seem to take into account is its multiple forms of expression. Thus, we are simultaneously confronted with several tendencies within the same Muslim community. At any given moment these could include secularists and fundamentalists; quietists and militants; conservatives, liberals, and socialists; traditionalists (Mawdūdī), nationalists (Ziya Gökalp), and communalists (Fazlur Rahman); secularists (ᶜAli ᶜAbd al-Rāziq) and revolutionaries (ᶜAli Sharīᶜatī); reformers (Afghānī and Sayyid Ahmad Khān) and revivalists (Muhammad Iqbāl); agitators (Hasan al-Bannā) and conciliators (ᶜAbduh).[6] There are representatives of almost all the above-mentioned categories in each Islamic territory.

Even further, different tendencies exist within the same group. Sūfism provides a good example, as it has been throughout the decades divided into a militant ecstatic religion on the one hand, and a more quietist and scripturalist one on the other. We find a similar dichotomy among the fundamentalists. On one front, a conservative subtendency fostered a rigid and purist version of Islam by means of a return to the early Islamic society, while on another, a radical counterpart launched similarly puritanical programs for transformation, but at the same time espoused a complete modernization and political activism through a renewed interpretation of Islam.[7] With regard to the reformists, we have the inheritors of the post-World War I generation like ᶜAlāl al-Fāsī in Morocco, who continued to press for the practical adaptation of Islam. But a new generation is on the rise, with greater demands, a sharper vocabulary, and a certain aptitude for manipulating populist slogans and putting pressure on the state, all of which serves to launch a second Nahda (renaissance). The old orthodox itself is still alive, but no caliph remains, and modern governments in the Middle East and North Africa are forming new relations between religious and political spheres. The "new fundamentalism" is evident in fresh developments on all sides. What Fazlur Rahman called a "neofundamentalism," or what G. H. Jansen named the "rethinkers" as opposed to the "reiterators" serves as illustration.[8] Others refer to a "new reformism" or a "new orthodoxy." All these trends can be found in the postcolonial Maghreb.

What has been called the "Islamic resurgence" within the Maghreb conceals a large variety of manifestations ranging from the Atlas of South Morocco to the city of Tunis. The recent increase of religious fervor, the obvious appeal to return to the sources and regulations of the Quran, to the strict application of the sharīᶜa, and to the restoration of the original spirit and virtue of the umma, have taken shape according to the specific characteristics of countries in which Islam is at once a faith and a code. Thus, within the "world market of Islamic values," the Maghreb possesses characteristics of its own. And, within the Maghreb, in each of the three countries, Islam as a belief, as a set of practices, and as a collection of laws includes different aspects that reflect the various ethnic groups and social strata as well as the relations between the elite and the masses. These variables also depend on the kind of believers in question— simple practicing Muslims and activists, free thinkers and proselytes, reformists and radicals, theologians and thaumaturgists, saints and scholars. Their personal involvement with religion and the relation between that involvement and their society's obligations and needs also come into play.

The somewhat classical religion of Morocco, the more reform-ist version of Algeria, and the modernist example in Tunisia have common salient features. The most obvious one is the overwhelm-ingly Sunnī composition of the Maghreb. This is Sunnism of the Mālikī legal school that has always accorded decisive weight to con-sensus; and it includes a small Hanafī minority and small enclaves of schismatic Kharijites, such as the Djerba island in Tunisia and the Pentad Mzabi cities of southern Algeria. Within this common region, however, there are differentiating features. Morocco prof-ited more from the Moorish retreat from Spain after the Catholic reconquest than did its eastern neighbors. Moreover, it was not subject to Ottoman domination, so that several dynasties of sultans were able to reign there. Algeria and Tunisia were subject to Otto-man rule for three centuries and governed by a minority of Hanafīs sent by Istanbul, with the Ottoman sultan acting as both a political suzerain and a religious leader.

A second common feature among the Maghreb states is their experience of colonial domination, although each was governed ac-cording to different principles. It is generally overlooked that about one-tenth of Morocco's territory was under the control of another Catholic European country, Spain, and, that additionally there existed the international zone of Tangier.

There is a striking similarity in the reaction to French influ-ence, which occurred in three successive and somewhat different steps during and after the colonial occupation. During the first stage of French occupation, Islam was called upon to rally the militants against the infidels. Armed resistance, which started in Algeria just after 1830, lasted until the so-called Rīf rebellion a century later. Throughout this period, the opposition was led by rural lead-ers and often supported by religious orders. After World War I, resistance to the French was divided into two broad movements: pro-secular on the one hand and proreligious on the other, the latter hav-ing been initiated by reformist Culamā', especially in Algeria.

In each case, when independence was declared, men of religion, Culamā' and sheikhs, imāms and scholars were passed over by the nationalists. Moreover, because of the educational system established by the colonizers, the only personnel available to fill the vacuum created by the departure of the French were the Western-trained administrators and teachers. Thus, those with the legitimacy that derives from technological skill were able to unite with those whose legitimacy was political in nature. They created a modernist elite existing somewhat apart from the Islamic legacy. Here again, Morocco is something of an exception, as is discussed later.

Since there, the religious groups have felt deprived of any political influence. In order to regain it, they have tried either to make alliances with the politicians or to put pressure on them. One of their favorite techniques has been the old reformist ᶜulamā' approach of developing the national consciousness of a cultural and religious identity, while insisting on the use of Arabic. On that basis, they were able to criticize the way mentalities had been Westernized through the importation of Western techniques. In societies in which social cleavages were becoming more obvious, the argument was not without effect on the lower strata of society. The religious groups, or those who made use of the Islamic vocabulary for political purposes, either presented an idealized version of the old Muslim tradition or fostered a purist return to religion. They also emphasized the ability of the Islamic model to achieve a solution for existing problems. This backlash against the Western world is recent, and it mixes ambivalent elements including some xenophobia, extremist glorification of the past, and a demagogic appeal to popular frustration.

Strangely enough, no original religious thinker, no great theologian, no class of ideologists, prophets, or intellectuals, to use Lewis Feuer's terms, has emerged since the liberation.[9] The official interpretations of Islam by the appointed ministers of religious affairs and the grand muftīs, or the political leaders, on one side, and the spokesmen of the fundamentalist movements on the other, evidence no real philosophical revival. The first group finds its reference in the reformist tradition now embodied in the state apparatus. The second borrows most of its arguments and slogans from Muslim thinkers from abroad: Mawdūdī or ᶜAli Sharīᶜatī. There seems to be a gap between the generations, that of, say, ᶜAlāl al-Fāsī, the Moroccan; Malek Bennabi, the Algerian; Muhammad Talbi, the Tunisian; and that of the younger scholars. There are well-known representatives of bilingual intellectuals, including Abdelkebir Khatibi, Mohammed Lababi, and Abdallah Laroui in Morocco; Hicham Djait, Abdelwahab Bouhdiba, and Bechir Torki in Tunisia; and Mohammed Arkoun, Ali Merad (both living in France), and Mohammed el-Mili in Algeria. These figures proclaim a second Nahda (Laroui) or a new "applied Islamology" (Arkoun), but they are scholars, professors, and commentators, not the Islamic rethinkers that a religious revival would normally produce.

Contrary to the situation in other Muslim countries, in the Maghreb no movement has managed to convey the ideology of fundamentalist Islam. No political party, no organization has been allowed to build itself on religious bases. In the Maghreb, there is no equivalent to the Jama^{c}āt-ī Islāmī of Pakistan, or the Masjūmī party of Indonesia. There is also nothing similar to the Sudanese Socialist Union in which former members of the Muslim Brothers are openly participating. Nor is there an association such as the Society of Muslim Brothers created by Hasan al-Bannā in Egypt. The Istiqlāl party in Morocco plays a very limited role in this respect despite its efforts. As to the traditional religious orders of the Maghreb, they seem to have lost most of their traditional impact. And the three governments have seen to it that change will not occur.

Another element common to the whole Maghreb is that Islam has now become the language both of the state apparatus (and of those who control it) and social and political protest groups. Religious dissent from official Islam, then, might indicate political resistance to government decisions and reflect conflicts on specific policies.

The popular religious revival, whose strength has been overestimated (because it is feared) by Western observers, has revealed itself in several, sometimes contradictory, ways. For modern Maghreb societies, the appeal to Islamic sources and forces is linked with their need to solve various impending crises—of identity, of adaptation to change, of religious leadership and political legitimacy, and of economic discontent and social unrest. The means the governments pretend to use to solve these crises have been questioned. As there is no real, autonomous political sphere, Islam has served as an alternative. This explains why, on the one hand, governments have done their best to occupy and control the religious domain and why, on the other hand, minorities and periphery groups have tried to oppose such a monopoly. This also explains why opposition movements use Islamic discourse to convey their criticism and to stir popular support and why the states attempt to thwart such practices.

MOROCCO: SYMBOLIC AND PRACTICAL
POWER OF A MONARCH

The most striking characteristic of Moroccan politics is the part played by the king. * The sultan, whom the colonial power had

---

*"The Moroccan Monarchy, to begin with, is not just the key institution in the Moroccan political system. That, one would naturally expect. It is also . . . the key institution in the Moroccan religious

tried to eliminate by sending him into exile, returned to the throne with greater popular support than ever before. The religious legitimacy he had traditionally enjoyed was maintained and strengthened by his new political charisma as a hero who had led the resistance against the French. Between November 1955, when he returned from exile, and his death in February 1961, Muhammad V restored his dynasty to power, giving it an even greater control over the whole society. As a sovereign, he enjoyed the privileges of both a traditional "Commander of the Faithful" and a modern political leader or za^{c}īm. This made him both a symbol of continuity and an agent of change. Muhammad V succeeded in portraying himself and imposing his authority as the representative of the crucial institution: one that received its power from God and from the people at the same time. His son, Hasan II, followed the same track, and the three constitutions of 1962, 1970, and 1972 have confirmed the extraordinary privileges of the head of the state, now the king.

The whole political system is dominated by a man who has learned to manipulate both religious and national symbols and to enhance his own position as both actor and director. The king is at the same time caliph, sultan, and head of the executive. The royal leadership during Hasan II's reign has also implied that the king could intervene directly in the political sphere regarding government policies. The immediate consequence of this is evident in the monarch's tendency to sharply limit or stop altogether the activities of any other political force whose popular base might make it appear a potential adversary. Hasan II has never ceased to clash with the political parties and trade unions, especially the Istiqlāl, the Union Nationale des Forces Populaires (UNFP), and the Union Marocaine du Travail (UMT). Neither the resistance of the UMT during the riots of Casablanca in March 1965, nor the several strikes that have taken place since then, nor the political parties themselves (even when they united under the common banner of the National Front in 1970) have been able to check or even to balance the king's hegemony in both the symbolic and the political fields.

There may be several reasons for this. An important one, as Rèmy Leveau has shown so well, is that the Moroccan monarchy quickly recognized that it was much safer to enlarge its social base and political support by allying with a social class that, though it lacked political legitimacy (partly because it had been associated with

---

system, which is perhaps a bit more surprising, at least in the middle of the twentieth century." See Clifford Geertz, Islam Observed: Religious Development in Morocco and Indonesia (Chicago: University of Chicago Press, 1968), p. 75.

the French during the protectorate) still retained its economic pow-er. [10] The rural elites could in fact help the king resist the demands of the urban middle class and thwart modern pressure groups and parties. This de facto alliance between the monarchy and the rural elites has had its impact upon the monarchy's use of Islam. Because the king's most faithful clients are in the countryside, he tends to in-sist on maintaining the aspects of Islam that suit them best. Addres-sing himself to a more traditional part of society, he is inclined to insist on symbols that are consonant with a rather conservative view of religion. [11] This might also explain why the references to Islam have been so consistently clear, in the three constitutions as well as in the day-to-day life, and why religious and political vocabularies overlap naturally.

As far as official ideology is concerned, the monarch is thus partly a prisoner of his own political supporters. The failure of the ambitious industrialization plans is a recent example of this. Be-cause such an economic change would probably have led to an altera-tion of the social hierarchy, plans for building smaller industries in-stead have been put forward by the experts. What Clement H. Moore pointed out in 1971 remains true: "Islamic consciousness, confined to the surface structure, continues to exercise a veto power over the whole realm of ideology and action."[12] This is mostly because of the special relations the king maintains with a fraction of the population. If indeed there has been a complete fusion of religion and politics at the top of the political hierarchy, this fusion no longer occurs within the national culture. At that level, there even seems to be a separa-tion between religious norms and values on the one hand and political life on the other.

One reason for such a phenomenon may be that in Morocco, Is-lam is not directly linked to a national ideology of transformation as it is in Tunisia and Algeria, where radical or modernist interpreta-tions of the Muslim traditions have produced a new dynamism. Hence, while there is a greater religiosity among people in Morocco, there is a lesser concern for politics. Another reason might be that in Morocco, which suffered less than Tunisia and Algeria from the ef-fects of colonial destruction and, unlike Algeria, has not had to use popular mobilization for industrialization, the traditional culture has remained more intact. Islam has not been questioned vigorously and so Morocco has probably not needed the kind of political reactivation that both Tunisian and Algerian leaders have used. This is clearly demonstrated in children's religious education books, for instance, which refer to classical Islam only.

The sultanic authority can legitimately run the political machine. A common belief in the authority of Amir al-Mu'minīn, the Comman-der of the Faithful, tends to keep part of the people away from political battles for the control of power, and a widely shared consent to the use of an Islamic code in which there is almost no separation between faith and life, prayer and activity, religion and action exists. Thus, the Moroccan system presents two characteristic features. First, a powerful executive authority is concentrated in the hands of a man who has never hesitated to use the religious laws for political purposes. We saw this with Muhammad V when he forced the courts to dissolve the Communist party in 1959 or to condemn two Ba^{c}thists to death in 1962, to give but two examples. [13] Second, this does not imply that the sovereign has complete control over the Islamic domain; the government intervenes in juridical and educational matters as with the operation of Quranic schools in October 1968 and the nomination of teachers in rural madrasa (religious schools) by the Ministry of Religious Endowment and Islamic Affairs, but it does not claim to monopolize the whole domain of religious belief and activity. A certain liberalism allows limited nongovernmental initiatives.

Religious opposition expressed itself violently in 1971 when the insurgent cadets at Sukhirāt smashed all the symbols of wealth and consumption (food, alcohol, jewels) and threatened to kill the king and his guests. Among the people who seem rather dissatisfied with the dependent orientation and politics of their country are youths, [14] intellectuals, students, and representatives of the lower strata of the middle class. These groups would certainly like to see the "true," "original" Islam restored and transformed into a new set of principles to help the people find original solutions to the crises around them. Among these groups, a certain element, especially in the countryside, in the Rīf, or in the Middle Atlas may join conservative fundamentalists similar to the Muslim Brothers. Alternatively, they may join the tarīqa (brotherhoods), whose influence may either spread beyond the limits of North Africa, * or be more localized, like the Bou Tchich, which is influential among university students and workers, especially in Casablanca. Still others will look for some radical fundamentalist movement that could help to rebuild a stronger Moroccan community, through the development of a new kind of political religion under the leadership of ^{c}Abd al-Sallām Yāsin, the editor of al-Jama^{c}a (the community) or ^{c}Abd al-Karīm Mu^{c}tī and Ibrāhīm Kamāl, president and vice-president of the Moroccan Islamic Youth Movement.

---

*Some members of the Egyptian-based Society of Muslim Brothers "are said to have played a leading part in the student demonstrations in Morocco against the presence of the ex-Shah of Iran in that country." See G. H. Jansen, Militant Islam (New York: Harper & Row, Torchbooks Library Binding, 1979), p. 151.

In Morocco, there is an alienated social consciousness that tends to express itself through religious and political means. There are ideologues ready to manipulate the concepts for political purposes while looking for supporters among dropouts from the educational and economic systems. These are facing the state, which is also using religious symbols to formulate and justify its own objectives. The Moroccan government does its best to consign them to a marginal position; to make them look outdated and reactionary; to implicate some of the most representative leaders in criminal affiars; to suspend al-Jama^ca and ban meetings; or to contrast national Mālikī orthodoxy to the bigotry, intolerance, and charlatanism of a handful of extremists. The government relies on a strong bureaucratic structure (but not on the army, whose officers have twice attempted to assassinate the monarch) and on the league of the ^culamā'.[15] It is also able to mobilize nationalism (as it did throughout the Saharan conflict and the Green March), Islam, and Arabism by sending troops to Egypt to participate in the 1973 war, for instance. It can go as far as trying to circumvent and appropriate for its own use the fundamentalists' principles.

Morocco differs from the rest of the Maghreb primarily because Islam occupies a largely autonomous sphere. The use of tradition belongs to the system and is a part of it, not a sign of opposition. Furthermore, some traditional institutions are still organized and run as they were before, though they have adjusted somewhat to change: the Qarawīyīn in Fes provides an orthodox education for the local elites; the Ministry of Religious Endowment is still taking care of the habūs (religious endowments), which have disappeared in the other two countries; some personalities, such as Sheikh Makki Naṣīrī, president of the council of the ^culamā' of Rabat-Salé and member of the Council of the Regency, fulfill traditional functions. The chances of the repoliticization of Islam are few, and even if this happens, it might take place within the system and not turn into a counterpoliticization.

This implies that the second stage of fundamentalism (the first being that of the Salafīya movement rejecting the "old" Islam, that of the Saints and Sūfīs), that is, the movement in favor of an Islamic way of modernization, might express itself differently in Morocco than in the neighboring countries of North Africa.

ALGERIA: STATE REFORMISM
AND POPULAR RELIGION

Algeria has had a long tradition of cultural resistance to foreign control.[16] Islam and nationalism were tied during the colonial period and have become closer since the 1930s. During the colonial period, religion was the only language used by a large number of people against the system imposed by the French. The Muslim code made it possible to create a local means of discourse and expression with which to oppose the official political code, which was European or at least controlled by the Europeans.

In the 1930s the ᶜulamā' drew on the old Islamic common background to build up a program of renovation and to help the revival of the Arab-Muslim Algerian identity. Their challenge to colonial domination rested on cultural bases and offered the whole Algerian community renewed values. In a sense, they helped transform passive into active opposition, although they never advocated open rebellion themselves. [17]

After the war of liberation (1954-62), reformist Islam was recognized as the established religion and almost no one questioned its position. This happened because in the conflicts over political leadership all the contenders had appealed to the main source of legitimacy, to the commonly shared vocabulary—religion—as the symbol of national liberation. While fighting one another, Ben Bella, Ben Khedda, Mohammed Khider, and the rest had each tried to rid himself of political rivals by demonstrating that the others were no longer following the national code, which had religious implications. By doing so, they "sacralized" their language with reformist formulas, which tended to become the political language of modern independent Algeria.

During Ben Bella's presidency and more openly after the June 1965 coup, the state, to reinforce itself, tended to impose a similar type of control over religious activities as that put into practice by the French. Following the example of the colonial state, the national state tried not to allow any kind of autonomy either to local culture or to associations and organizations based on Islamic principles.

The message of modernization and the decision to impose socialism and to promote economic development (implying among other things a marked centralization of power and a dominant state bureaucracy) had to be passed on to the people through the same, well-accepted language. There would be no real independence, it was proclaimed, without socialism and no socialism without Islam. The less legitimacy the men in power had, or thought they had, the more they referred to state reformism and national Islam as justification for their choices and decisions. Islam was quite compatible with modernization according to the reformist doctrine of the ᶜulamā', which stressed a puritanical observance of the Quran and a transformation of society at the same time. That is why technocratic orthodoxy has made itself legitimate by claiming that it alone could lead both in upholding religion and in modernizing the country. The intercessor between God and development is no longer a saint, a prophet, or a muftī, but rather, the state apparatus.

State reformism, or national Islam in Algeria, now means that the state monopolizes religious affairs. It has nationalized Quranic schools, madrasas, and institutes (1976), and it appoints imāms, muftīs, members of the Supreme Islamic Council, and qādīs (judges). It issues a constant stream of propaganda and enforces religious principles for political purposes. If necessary, it makes a political ideology of religion, as Ali Merad has recently shown.[18] The consequence is a nonpluralist state tolerating neither political parties nor those social classes seen as disruptive elements threatening the national consensus, the amalgam of unified "citizens, workers, brothers."[19]

Until now, national ideology has tended to veil the development of various social cleavages. More than anything else, Islam has served to enforce national unity. But the deprived stratum of the lower middle class may find within a new puritanism some argument to contest the privileges of the ruling class. Such criticism may also gain some support among the growing number of the "rejected," those overlooked by a rapidly modernizing Algeria.

Despite this continuous strengthening of the government and the nationalization of Islamic ideology to the benefit of the state, the central authority is still being censured and criticized, and Islam is being used as a means to argue about various aspects of the government's general orientation and about particular policies and political decisions.* In practice, some groups demand a return to a more orthodox Islam that would be compatible with modernization and even revolution. Among these groups there is not much demand for a return to mysticism as synonymous with marabūtism or the cult of the saints.

The public debates over the National Charter in 1976 revealed that the compromise between those who control the state apparatus (administrators and bureaucrats who have technical competence) and those who have political legitimacy (political leaders and party men) is not completely accepted by the people. For them, puritanism is a kind of opposition to the "Islamic deviationism" of state reforms, which they attacked on the grounds that it helps to cover and protect

---

*What is striking about most of the historical literature devoted to Islam in Algeria is the permanence of disputes between religious groups and the central power. A main characteristic has been the lasting opposition to central administration either based almost directly on religious arguments or using Islam at least as a means to contest the legitimacy of governmental authorities. It would thus be extraordinary not to have any form of Islamic protest now.

practices that lead the country, through constant amendments, to abandon its basic principles. *

At the moment, the political class claims a threefold legitimacy: (1) the religious—which has led to state reformism; (2) the political—derived from the war of liberation and embodied in the party and the army; and (3) the technical—which is demonstrated through industrialization. Its alliances with the bourgeoisie and with the "Mamlūks" have not been seriously questioned since 1965.[20] But a conflict may be arising over religious legitimacy. People are beginning to realize that pure Islam is not compatible with a modern, social organization that tends to lead to the adoption of foreign traditions. There were signs of opposition coming from groups appealing to the spirit of Ben Bādīs (leader of the Association of Reformist ᶜUlamā' between the two world wars) to establish their criticism of the official positions. But each time, the regime, which presented itself as the only legitimate heir to the greatest figure of Algerian reformism, claimed that any outward opposition to its policy on religious grounds would be contrary to the interests of the nation. Thus, whenever criticism originated in the countryside, the political groups in command declared that those who were expressing their displeasure were in fact trying to return to traditional practices, to superstition, to neopaganism through the cult of saints, and the like.

To take but one example, in the summer of 1968 there was a crisis in the eastern area near Mostaganem, along the coast, where the Alouia (a branch of the Sciadlia brotherhood), according to El-Moudjahid of July 20, 1968, wanted to give expression to popular dissatisfaction. The state-run newspaper declared that Algeria would return to obscurantism and mysticism if such people were allowed to talk on behalf of the peasants.

But most matters could not be dismissed so easily. In that same year, for instance, when it appeared that a majority of the people seemed to be in favor of birth control, the question of family planning became a controversial issue between the government and traditionalists. Sheikh ᶜAbd al-Rahmān al-Jilālī condemned birth control openly, and the Islamic Superior Council, though it was more cautious, shared this view.[21] El-Moudjahid again declared that opponents did not understand the true principles of Islam, but the minister of health and population and President Boumedienne had to re-

---

*The excessively speedy modernization of industry, for instance, has led to close contact with Western markets and to effective economic dependence. Such technocratic Westernization goes along with a Westernization of morals in the cities and of manners within the ruling elite.

treat.[22] This was a typical subject on which the state was forced to respect the sharīᶜa precepts as put forward by the conservatives.

A new association did its best to make use of the existing narrow margin of freedom and to advocate a strong respect for Islamic law. The al-Qiyām society, through its periodical Humanisme Musulman and through meetings, made every effort when President Ben Bella was in office to invade the political field and make its members recognized as the new reformists. It even pushed a bit further after Ben Bella's fall, trying to appear as the true guardian of pure Islam, as well as of governmental ethics. As a matter of fact, it undermined the legitimacy of people in office. The periodical was banned, and the society was dissolved in 1966. As its members were still active and meeting together, the ruling party, Front de Libération Nationale (FLN) opened a direct campaign that ended in al-Qiyām being outlawed in 1970.[23] Less than one year later, the official press reported the arrest of 13 "devout activists" who had created a subversive organization to force people to respect Islamic principles according to the literal terms of the Quran and the Sunna. El-Moudjahid did not mention whether those extremists were former members of the al-Qiyām association, but some could easily have participated in its activities.[24] Others may well have joined the movements of the Ahl al-Daᶜwa, which has developed in towns like Algiers, Constantine, Ghardaia, and Médéa.

More recently, two kinds of puritanism have developed. First, the orthodox, conservative fundamentalists profited from the national debates on the draft of the National Charter in 1976 by being allowed to give their own interpretation of what a pure return to Islam should be. Since then, their spokesmen have laid stress on every element that might force the state to put into practice a religious policy that would answer their demands. Maintaining that Article 2 of the 1976 constitution proclaimed that Algeria was a Muslim country, they have asked for a systematic Islamization. Furthermore, the Iranian revolution has helped them get rid of the pejorative label of reactionary. Muslim militants in Teheran have demonstrated that fundamentalism could call forth a revolution. The Algerian activists argue that what they require fits with the ideologies and policies of a modern country and with a program of social and industrial transformation.

Apparently, militants are collecting money in Algeria itself or receiving funds from other Muslim countries like Saudi Arabia to finance religious education. * Thus, they tend to develop an organized religion parallel to that controlled by the government. They try to

---

*The entire system of education was nationalized in 1976. However, there are still private Quranic schools in the countryside.

build a spiritual and moral force into an influential pressure group.
If the occasion presented itself, they would take a further step and
test governmental capacities. In December 1979, for instance, Muslim students who had gone on strike requested that mosques be made
available inside the university. At the Faculty of Law, they occupied
a large lecture room that they transformed into a mosque; neither the
dean nor the rector dared to change it back to a lecture room.

Second, the radical fundamentalists, including a dynamic minority who think that Islam and socialism can really fit together and
that Boumedienne's policy should be carried on, have their own interpretation of Islam. They repeatedly refer to what is said in the
National Charter about a progressive Islam, to remind the leaders
what their duties are. This movement is also looking for popular
support among those who think that the traditions of the war of liberation and of modernization should be maintained.

The state has been trying to draw a line between its concessions
to the Islamists and its political control of religious institutions. Its
main problem at the present time is to keep its monopoly over the
entire religious sphere, which is endangered by the extension of a
"private" Islam having its own mosques and imāms, and which is
probably going to ask for its own schools. One of the government's
answers to private Islam is a project that, if promulgated, will allow
the government to regain control of the entire field. New Islamic institutes have been created; 10 of them are functioning already, preparing about 500 students for the imāmate. In the near future, there
will be one such institute in each wilāya (province) and a postgraduate
institution at the top, so that students will not have to go abroad to get
a diploma. * It is quite possible that after the system has been extended to the whole country, nobody will be able to lead the prayer in
a mosque without being graduated from one of these institutes. Important enough gains and losses are at stake in this project that it
could lead to an open confrontation. Furthermore, an overorganized
state education of imāms could, in the long run, lead to the creation
of some kind of institutionalized clergy similar to the one that exists
in Iran, for instance.

There exist other ways the state can check or counterbalance
the Islamists' activities. One is to use the police to keep an eye on
the private Islam. Another is to abstain from making decisions that
could appear provocative. That is probably why the family code,

---

*This institute for theological studies, which would be able to
compete with the well-known universities of the Islamic world, would
be located in Constantine, close to a new mosque that has been under
construction for several years.

which could arouse controversy, has never been published. The
present campaign of moralization, initiated by President Chadli Ben-
jedid himself, whose purpose is to purify the morals of the political
and technocratic class, is a demonstration that the state is applying
Quranic principles to its own personnel.

In 1981 the government seems to have mastered the situation
as far as the two kinds of above-mentioned religious criticisms are
concerned. But this does not mean that a part of the petty bourgeoisie—which was not so keen on taking up the extreme conservatives' cause, but which on the other hand feels it is being deprived
of the benefits of modernization—will not develop some kind of opposition based on religion. There are signs of a renewed religiosity:
young people going to the mosques, girls wearing the "Muslim sisters" dress, private mosques being built, an increasing Islamic conformism in the cities and in the countryside, which has suffered from
the changes industrialization has brought as well as from the failure
of the agrarian revolution. The opposition can easily be checked by
the state apparatus, which seems able to distract or thwart it. Nothing indicates either that the new critics will automatically turn into
opponents or become traditionalists and conservatives. But every
time some dissatisfaction spreads out apropos to the Arabization of
cultural or ethnic minorities (at the University of Algiers during the
winter of 1979-80, in Kabylia in early 1980 also), we see various attempts by the radical fundamentalists to profit from the occasion.
The present managerial state might not be competent to deal with
these ideological questions.

TUNISIA: BOURGUIBISM VERSUS
RELIGIOUS RADICALISM

In Tunisia, Islam has been linked with politics for a long
time.[25] The Neo-Destour party and Habīb Bourguiba played a prominent part in making Islam a crucial element of nationalism during the
colonial period. Soon after independence in 1956, they launched a
campaign against the religious establishment, that is, against traditional Islam and the members of the Old Destour with whom it was
said to be linked. In the two following years, the government enacted
several laws and undertook other initiatives aimed at weakening the
sheikhs and the ʿulamā'.[26] Religious courts were suppressed, and
the influence of the Zaytūna Mosque and the Quranic schools was
weakened. Justice and education were unified. The habūs were
seized by the regime and redistributed. Religious practices, such
as pilgrimages, the fasting of Ramadān, and ceremonies and social
traditions linked with religious observances, were played down. A

progressive secularization seemed to have taken place. This reduction of traditional Islam was organized by the state for its own benefit. Even the Constitution of 1958, which proclaimed Islam the religion of the state, tended to sanction the priority of the state over religion in practice.

During the 1960s, this dominance together with the presidential interventions for adapting Islam to the necessities of modernization, led to a certain kind of sanctification of both the state and its leader, the founding father of the republic. Tunisians faced what David Apter called political religion, in other words, a religion enunciated by the state to help unify the people.[27] Such a sacralization resulted in a ritual of a new type: Islam has since been dealt with through a political intercessor. The religious apparatus (the personnel of the mosques, the Islamic hierarchy, Grand Imām, Muftī of the Republic, and so on) became an administrative body and an ideological intermediary of a central power eager to increase its intervention in the religious sphere year after year. The consequence so far has been the ritualization of political religion and a reactivation of Islam as the state religion.[28]

There have been several ramifications to this new influence of politics over religion. For example, just as those in power have increased their activities within the Islamic domain, including the related institutionalization of the clergy, so too have the people found ways to escape the official religion and return to interpretations and practices of their own. In addition, reinforcement of the state religion could, paradoxically, lead to its weakening. The leaders have recently noticed this danger. They have consequently given serious consideration to such a possibility and modified their policy and their attitude toward Islam accordingly.

What is most striking in the early 1980s and apparent in governmental speeches and decisions is the backing off from certain modernist measures adopted 20 years before. This has been brought about by the Islamic resurgence among the Tunisian population and especially among the lower middle class in both the cities and the countryside. Such a revival might portend a political threat. In fact, observers have already predicted the formation of a religious sphere distinct from the one defined by politicians. Although such a tendency is still confined to the legal arena, it might well develop into a form of political criticism kept alive by both social and economic difficulties as well as by political instability. The government is not quite ready to face it. The government somehow believes that it has eliminated all religious opposition since the "old turbans" and conservative fundamentalists have lost their appeal. Before 1970 at least, with the exception of the popular demonstrations in Qayrawān in 1961, there had been no serious criticism of a religious nature. *

Following the period in which Ahmad Ben Saleh initiated agricultural and commercial cooperatives and later the return to a liberalized economy, a new type of criticism originating with the radical fundamentalists of the al-Ittijāh al-Islāmī movement appeared. There are several former Muslim Brothers (referred to in Tunisia as Khuwānjīya) officials who call them Islamicists, but they do not constitute a well-organized body. The Association for the Preservation of the Quran was originally comprised of a group of militants doing their best to make themselves known and to exercise some influence over the people. They aimed at exploiting the symbols of Islam for the purpose of a return to orthodoxy and austerity by way of puritanism and a transformation of society by means of a systematic appeal to the original Islamic culture, without reference to foreign experiences or ideologies, especially those of the West.

There has been a moral and a political crisis in Tunisia recently. Everyone is worrying about who will succeed Bourguiba, and people are dubious about the strength of the regime and its capacity to maintain national unity, institutional balance, and economic stability. Souhayr Belhassen, in three articles that Mark A. Tessler echoed in the Maghreb Review, depicted very well both the manifestations of and the actors within a new kind of Islam.[29] The followers are now asking for access to mosques and the right to hear preachers who have not been subsidized by the government. They have requested special locations for praying in places of work. They have recruited supporters among students and intellectuals at the university as well as in popular districts of the cities. They also have leaders: Rāshid Ghanūshī, ᶜAbd al-Fātih Mūrū, Hasan Ghūdbānī, and several young imāms, to name but a few. These men share a certain resentment toward a state-run religion. They question Bourguiba's charisma, which has turned into a personality cult, and they have even dared criticize some of his decisions.

The program of the so-called Islamic movement is unclear and ambiguous, as the Islamic government it clamors for has not yet been very well defined. But they are not without legitimate argument when they cite some of the country's current problems: economic unrest, widening gaps between classes, increasing selfishness and self-ag-

---

*Opposition was supposed to express itself within the Destourian Socialist party. Moreover, political critics usually had come from the Youssefists, the Communists, the Baᶜthists, the Nasserists, or the pro-Western liberals, none of whom had much to do with Islam or any interest in using Islam as a political weapon.

grandizement of the upper class, nepotism and corruption within the administration, Westernization of morals and public culture, and the like. They too have their means of expressing themselves: through a return to puritanism and its moral conduct and through propaganda for the reconstitution of the sharī^{c}a costume for women. They can also engage in political activism, as they did in a café in Sfax during the Ramadān in 1977, at the University of Tunis in 1979, or in the lycées and at the university again in February and March 1981. They may augment not only the number of their recruits but also their influence by increasing the number of Islamic-oriented associations, publishing more books, broadening the circulation of relevant records and cassettes, and increasing the sales of such periodicals as al-Ma^{c}rifa (Knowledge) or al-Mujtama^c (Society). When it was said that the monopoly of the Parti Socialiste Destourien (PSD) might come to and end and multipartism be allowed, Hasan Ghūdbānī even announced the possible formation of an Islamic party of the Shūrā.

For the government, there is a latent danger that a populist Islam might claim its association with a foreign radical movement, such as the Ba^{c}th, and find political support among a population for whom the traditional sense of religiosity and piety is so vivid. It is conceivable that populist Islam could help a particular personality or group to challenge the privileges of the political class. The trade union, the Union Générale Tunisienne du Travail, might be a case in point, although during the brutal confrontation of January 1978, religious feelings did not play a great part. In this instance, a certain underlying fear among trade unionists seemed to be slowing any impulse to mix with fundamentalists. Another example may well be seen in the candidate to Bourguiba's succession, who will be looking for a popular base in order to broaden his influence over the long term. Here Muhammad Masmūdī is a more striking prototype than Ben Saleh. Finally, although most of the extremists came out squarely against Qadhdhāfī, some of them may be inspired or influenced by his policies in Libya.

The government has been reacting very cautiously. It has tried to cut off the Islamic movement's social support instead of taking extreme measures, although it has banned its publications. * On the one hand, the police have been keeping a close eye on private mosques and the leaders of al-Ittijāh al-Islāmī; they have arrested some of the supposed leaders of the early 1981 agitation among the youth. On the other, the government has, in general, appeared much more tolerant and, in particular, more patient about implementing the modernist

---

*In December 1979 the monthly al-Mujtama^c was banned for three months.

Islam. The Gafsa incident of January 27, 1980, * has led to, among other things, a governmental program of constructing new mosques and restoring old ones. By answering but a part of the Islamicists demands, the regime is using one of the oldest tricks of the trade, geared to undermine the fragile structure of a movement, hoping that, under normal circumstances, it will not be possible for a group that lacks a real social base, a proper organization, or a strong ideology to pose a serious threat to a powerful and unchallenged state. †

RESTORATION OF A FORCE:
FOUR LEVELS OF COMPARISON

I would like to emphasize four factors: (1) the present analogies between the Maghreb and the rest of the Islamic world, (2) the links between Islamic revival and social change within each nation-state, (3) the use of the Islamic code to express political opposition, and (4) the conflict between nationalization and internationalization of Islam.

First, the states and societies of the Maghreb share several phenomena with the rest of the Islamic world. For example, the Islamic resurgence in the Maghreb has been indirectly influenced by developments in Iran since the fall of the shah. It has also expressed itself through an increase in various individual practices, namely, a greater respect for religious rituals and activities, more frequent attendance at the mosques, and an exteriorization of some religious practices, especially among the young people. ‡ That is new, if we

---

*A Libyan-trained group of Tunisians, some of whom were natives of the city—which happened to be the birthplace of a strong opponent of Bourguiba's policy, the late Saleh Ben Youssef—with a minority of young people attacked the mining town of Gafsa in the south and staged a day-long uprising before being arrested.

† We have been referring mostly to urban Islam. A good study of rural Islam (in Khrumiria) is Wim M. J. Van Binsbergen, "Popular and Formal Islam, and Supra-Local Relations: The Highlands of North-Western Tunisia, 1800-1970," Middle Eastern Studies 16 (1980): 71-91.

‡ Especially among girls who go to the lycées and the university not with the traditional veil but with the dress of the "Muslim sisters." An increasing amount of funds are collected by local informal groups, which raise money to build private mosques close to the official ones and to distribute stipends to imāms who are not appointed by the government but who are selected by the people. The growing number of

remember that until recently Moroccans, Algerians, and Tunisians
thought more in terms of national unity than in terms of Muslim community and, generally speaking, did not attach as much importance to
religious practices as most of the other Muslims in the world. People who did not formally respect ritual demands were not criticized
as much by their coreligionists. Public opinion is apparently changing and Muslim conformism seems to play a greater role than before.
Islam is tending to become the cultural and religious frame of reference.

Furthermore, despite the fact that there is no equivalent to
any situation of the "Iranian type," there are now more people who
advocate a complete transformation of their societies in compliance
with the instructions of the Quran, the teachings of the Islamic precepts, and the historical experience of the Muslim civilization.

Such a revival is no more a novelty in the Maghreb than in most
of the other countries. The return to orthodoxy has always been a
part of the Muslim tradition. And this has been particularly true in
a society where a cosmological ideology led life and faith to be so
strongly interwoven. Furthermore, in the Maghreb, Islam played an
important part in national liberation and was presented afterward as
the instrument of salvation. Finally, in the Maghreb, in Algeria
perhaps more than in the other two countries, economic and social
developments have created dissatisfaction, a sense of imbalance and
insecurity, and a fear of what could happen next, which echo some
of the feelings expressed in other Muslim countries.

Second, the Islamic revival is closely linked with the stressful
problems of change and adaptation, which the three countries of the
Maghreb are still facing. The Islamic language thus becomes a
means to cope with moral anxiety, social disequilibrium, cultural imbalance, ideological restlessness, and problems of identity produced
by the economic transformations of the postindependence period.
People do not think that precolonial or colonial society was more
harmonious, but they see that national autonomy has profited a minority whose mobility might be a direct threat for the other classes.
Moreover, centralization, the concentration of decisions within a few
hands, the bureaucratization—all that could be alluded to as the French
colonial legacy—have had a decisive influence on public opinion.
Most people have ambivalent feelings toward the state apparatus. On
the one hand, they despise a state that is so much like the colonial
one, which was essentially repressive. On the other, they expect
that very state to solve all their problems and to bring them social

---

personal donations are also highly significant. New networks of religious popular support are emerging, although they are difficult to spot.

equality through common access to jobs, houses, education, and the like.

These increasing expectations have tended to sanctify the state and to help it to create and develop new sources of loyalty at the national level, to the detriment of local links. But national solidarity, which had been very strong in the years before independences, is more recent than local solidarity, and it does not fulfill the same functions as the old bonds. The ideology of the core polarizes peoples' beliefs and at the same time destroys the ideologies of the intermediary groups. In the same way, parliaments, political parties, trade unions, governments, and modern institutions in general do not serve as substitutes for traditional institutions. Furthermore, a state-controlled culture and a national system of education do not replace the old centers of education and socialization without damaging effects. One of the most striking consequences is probably the coexistence of different systems of identities and solidarities that compete with one another instead of performing complementary roles. Even some of the most appealing decisions made by the governments seem to endanger the future by introducing reforms that are seen as enlarging the gap between the social strata. Islam is thus, for many people, the most efficient symbol, a positive reference to unity and stability, to the idea that order will be kept when change is introduced. The recrudescence of both religiosity and Muslim militancy has a lot to do with a common need for security.

Third, the Islamic revival has also expressed itself through various manifestations of dissent, focusing on the state's monopoly of the Islamic language. It is true that in the three countries the defense of governmental actions through Islam has been going on for some time. Thus, we witness three varieties of popular radicalism against the nationalization of religion. Now, perhaps for the first time since independence, social organization, political institutions, and economic policies are judged in terms of Islamic expectations. In addition, there exists a small group of individuals who think that their religion is already too strongly state organized. They conclude that the requirements of personal piety (personal relation with God) are not met and declare that the state's interference is inadmissible.

Although in each country radicalism arises from the same deprived stratum of the middle class, which fears it will be the next victim of modernization, and has articulate spokesmen (schoolteachers, local imāms, students), members of other strata are joining in the chorus. This connection arises out of a fundamental contradiction within the official language of the state itself, which makes use of two versions of Islam: the modernist one, to prepare for change, and the traditional or conservative one, applied to the preservation of the national community. Sometimes, the governments insist on change and find some argument in the Muslim tradition to support it; sometimes they praise order and lay stress on another aspect of the creed or cultural legacy. Most of the time, they answer popular demands either by maintaining their complete control over one field (such as economic development in Algeria) and letting Islamicization rise in another (such as personal matters) or by mixing the two systems of reference in political discourse. Another device is to reform the Islamic institutions that are at the government's disposal—muftīs, Islamic councils, High Council of the ᶜUlama'—in such a way that they can play an intermediary role between the masses and the government. This goes along with keeping complete control over the system of religious education and the mosques and with manipulating the concepts sometimes to maintain traditions and political order and sometimes to introduce reforms and initiate social mobilization. Each of the three governments can also be directly repressive. It is open to each to ban periodicals published by extremists, put the leaders into prison, forbid private mosques to do any teaching, and so on. *

One should note here that the demands are not so much to create an Islamic state (no one really knows what a purely Islamic state would be in terms of administration, economic policy, and social organization designed to meet modern needs). The people who make such requests do not propose an alternative. Rather they suggest that the central authorities should find their own ways to bring modernization without becoming estranged from their original Muslim sources and without giving up their freedom by appealing to other ideologies or borrowing from other social systems. For these critics, Islam is the reference for judging the governments' performances as they procure foreign capital, ask for foreign advisers and teachers, and acquire technology from the industrial countries; and for evaluating the foreign policy of the country.

Fourth, we are witnessing different types of opposition to what could be called Islamic internationalism. Whether Islam gives the state its stamp or the state commands religion is still an open question. But in either case Islam is used to reinforce both the state and the nation. This creates a somewhat paradoxical situation. The ten-

---

*There are limits to the state's intervention, as it must also demonstrate its adherence to Islam. In Tunisia and in Algeria, the government has been keeping a close eye on popular Islam, especially on the private mosques and imāms who criticize its decisions in their sermons. But it does not go as far as forbidding them to preach, or putting them in jail.

dency to quote the Quran and the Sunna, which is seen in the political elites of the nation-states, has had an indirect but striking effect: the establishment of three rival centers in North Africa (four if we include Libya), each of them claiming that its policies are based on the most accurate interpretation of Islamic precepts.

What has been noticeable since 1962 is a competition for moral and political leadership within the Maghreb itself and sometimes beyond its frontiers. Muslim solidarity has not been able to prevail over national interests. The Algerian-Moroccan conflicts of 1963 and more recently in regard to the Western Sahara are the most striking demonstrations. The Green March is certainly the best example of aggressive nationalism mixed with militant Islam. It even looked like a Moroccan jihād, although it was aimed at attacking another Muslim country. The Gafsa attack by a Libyan-subsidized party of Tunisian opponents in 1980, although it remained localized, proved that the radical Libyan regime had found both an echo among some Islamic movements in Tunisia and support from elements in the native populations critical of President Bourguiba's "Westernized" regime.

Libya's leaders present themselves as divine instruments of a new fundamentalism that should be internationalized to allow the entire umma to be politically and ideologically reunited, especially by means of eliminating the noxious influence of the conservatives, namely the Saudis. Qadhdhāfī's propaganda is thus aiming at destabilizing traditional regimes, especially that of Morocco. Hasan II gave the revolutionary Libyans some ammunition when he welcomed the banished Shah of Iran, an act that aroused discontent in Morocco. The king's statements declaring Khomeinī's regime anti-Islamic and the Iranian imām himself a dissenter from established Muslim dogma (he went so far as to ask "his" ʿulamā' to give a fatwa [a religious legal opinion] condemning the Ayātollāh in 1980) did not receive general approval. Libya's radio, which praised the Moroccan officers who attempted the Sukhirāt coup in 1971, is still broadcasting over the whole North African territory. Even the Algerians now fear Libyan initiatives on the Saharan fringe, such as the direct military intervention in Chad and the support given to the Sahrāwī leaders.

CONCLUSION

The "return of Islam"[30] in North Africa has expressed itself in very different ways: an evident regeneration of a culture, a profound renewal of religiosity, a political exploitation of the Islamic vocabulary by governments that use it to reinforce their legitimacy and to strengthen their power, and a use of religion by a political opposition that is often left with no other means of expression. Instead of trying to place these forms along a scale going from conservative fundamentalism to extreme radicalism, we should try to understand the way in which they provide a meaningful response to today's Maghreb. *

In Tunisia, the delegitimizing of the Islam of the Culamā' and the breach with the Islamic tradition—presented as a regressive force in order to allow for the development of a modernized society —has led to cultural and political destabilization. The Atatürk model, as interpreted by Bourguiba, has not permitted the transformation that would have suited the majority of the population. The Muslim revival is, then, a partial response to an aggressive secularism that has not borne its expected fruits.

In Morocco, the reinstitutionalizing of Islam through the king and the Culamā' and the accent put on the official religion accord with a more secular reinstitutionalization, such as that of the local elected councils, the political parties, and the trade unions. The central power is trying to reinforce its religious base together with its social control in order to check the criticism of popular fundamentalists.

In Algeria, the delegitimizing of traditional Islam was followed by the nationalizing of reformist Culamā' theories. But the excessively rapid modernization engineered by the technocrats has the appearance of practical secularization, and state-organized Arabization that of a counter-Islamization. The balance between radical socialism and reformist Islamism, between efforts to modernize and the preservation of Muslim identity, has been difficult to maintain. The Islamic revival is thus partly a response from a lower class that is sounding the alarm because of its dread of the future.

The most striking common element is that the Maghreb states now seem less influenced by the revivification of the Islamic faith and code than the other way around, that is, the nation-states have put their mark on Islam. Islam, then, refers to the state's current right to existence rather than to its justification in history. Although there are several reasons for believing that the states are strong enough to continue such practices, this does not necessarily mean that they will continue indefinitely. Radical fundamentalism is not

---

*Elis Goldberg, in speaking of the Muslim Brothers in Egyptian society in the 1930s and 1940s, says they "appeared to be not only a positive response but the only meaningful positive response to what was occurring then." See Elis Goldberg, "Bases of Traditional Reaction: A Look at the Muslim Brothers," Peuples mediterranées 14 (1981): 80.

strong enough to create a movement capable of mobilizing popular Islam under its banner. However, if other forces were successful in appealing to popular Islam in order to support their political views, puritanical Islam could then be used as an ideological weapon against the governments.

NOTES

1. See, for instance, Patrick Blum, "Islamic Revival Fuels Maghreb Discontent," Middle East Economic Digest 24 (1980): 6-8; Richard Hrair Dekmejian, "The Islamic Revival in the Middle East and North Africa," Current History 456 (1980): 169-79; and Susan E. Marshall, "Islamic Revival in the Maghreb: The Utility of Tradition for Modernizing Elites," Studies in Comparative International Development 14 (1979): 95-108.

2. Adapted from the title of the book edited by Altaf Gauhar, The Challenge of Islam (London: Islamic Council of Europe, 1978). See also Alford T. Welch and Pierre Cachia, eds., Islam: Past Influence and Present Challenge (Edinburgh: Edinburgh University Press, 1979); and Jacques Bergue, L'Islam au défi (Paris: Gallimard, 1980).

3. Michael Walzer, The Revolution of the Saints (Cambridge, Mass.: Harvard University Press, 1965), p. 2.

4. Abdelwahab Boudhiba, "L'Islam maghrébin: Essai de typologie," Revue tunisienne des sciences sociales 4 (1965): 3-30.

5. John O. Voll, "The Islamic Past and the Present Resurgence," Current History 456 (1980): 145-48, 180-81. See also Hamid Enayat, "The Resurgence of Islam: The Background," History Today 30 (February 1980): 16-22; and Leila Ahmed, "The Resurgence of Islam: The Return to the Source," History Today 30 (February 1980): 23-27.

6. These taxonomic categories are selected from Fazlur Rahman's Islam 2d ed. (Chicago: University of Chicago Press, 1979).

7. On the ambivalent character of fundamentalism, see R. Stephen Humphreys, "Islam and Political Values in Saudi Arabia, Egypt and Syria," Middle East Journal 33 (1979): 1-19. On the broader subject of the relation between puritanism and political activity, see Walzer, The Revolution of the Saints; and Christopher Hill, Puritanism and Revolution: Studies in Interpretation of the English Revolution of the 17th Century (London: Mercury, 1962).

8. G. H. Jansen, Militant Islam (New York: Harper & Row, Torchbooks Library Binding, 1979), p. 134.

9. Lewis S. Feuer, Ideology and the Ideologist (London and New York: Harper & Row, Torchbooks Library Binding, 1975), pp. 197-210.

10. Rémy Leveau, Le Fellah morocain défenseur du Trône (Paris: Presses de la Fondation Nationale des Sciences Politiques, 1976), pt. 2. See also John Waterbury, The Commander of the Faithful: The Moroccan Political Elite. A Study in Segmented Politics (London: Weidenfeld and Nicholson, 1970).

11. On rural Islam in Morocco, see Ernest Gellner, Saints of the Atlas (London: Weidenfeld and Nicholson, 1969); idem, "Pouvoir politique et fonction religieuse dans l'Islam marocain," Annales E.S.C. 25 (1970): 679-713; Dale Eickelman, Moroccan Islam: Tradition and Society in a Pilgrimate Centre (Austin: University of Texas Press, 1976); Jean-Francois Clement, "Mouvements islamiques et représentations de l'Islam dans la Tensift," in Islam et politique au Maghreb (Paris: Editions du CNRS, forthcoming); and Henry Munson, Jr., "Islam and Inequality in Northwest Morocco" (Ph.D. diss., University of Chicago, 1981).

12. Clement Henry Moore, Politics in North Africa, Algeria Tunisia and Morocco (Boston: Little, Brown, 1969), p. 282.

13. See Muhammad's Memoirs: The Challenge (London: Macmillan, 1978), especially after the traumatic endeavor of the military at Sukhirāt, when the king declared on August 4, 1979, that the social disparity between rich and poor was increasing, which was "intolerable in a country like Morocco, of which Islam is the rightful constitution," that is, in a land where there should exist neither inequality nor wickedness. And there are other examples of the king's efforts to command the Islamic sphere: his appointment to the presidency of the Al-Quds committee, in charge of discussing the problem of Jerusalem, in May 1979; his explicit support of the PLO; and the breach of diplomatic relations with Cairo after the Camp David agreements. See Rémy Leveau, "Islam officiel et Islam populiste," in Annuaire de l'Afrique du Nord 1979 (Paris: Editions du CNRS, forthcoming).

14. See P. Lambert, "Point de vue sur les jeunes Marocains," L'Afrique et l'Asie moderne 117 (1978): 57-62.

15. Leveau, "Islam officiel et Islam populiste." The institutionalization of the Culamā', religious advisory councils in charge of helping the governor implement a policy in compliance with the Islamic (official) code at the provincial level, and the High Council of the CUlamā', at the top, might be efficient; the Culamā' could become the intermediary body that the king needs as far as religious affairs are concerned. The regimenting of the scholars might also cut them off completely from the popular Islam.

16. Jean-Claude Vatin, "Religious Resistance and State Power in Algeria," in Islam and Power, ed. A. S. Cudsi and Ali E. Hillal Dessouki (London: Croomhelm, 1981).

17. On the role played by the reformist Culamā', see Ali Merad, Le réformisme musulman en Algérie de 1925 a 1940. Essai d'his-

torie religieuse et sociale (Paris: Mouton, 1967); Fanny Colonna, "Cultural Resistance and Religious Legitimacy in Algeria," Economy and Society 3 (1974): 232-52; Ernest Gellner, "The Unknown Apollo of Biskra: The Social Base of Algerian Puritanism," Government and Opposition 9 (1974): 277-301; Ahmed Nadir, "Le mouvement réformiste algérien: Son rôle dans la formation de l-idéologie nationale" (Doctorat d'Etat, University of Paris, 1967); and Jamil Abun-Nasr, "Islam und die Algerische National Identität," Die Welt der Islams 18 (1978): 178-94.

18. Ali Merad, "L'idéologisation de l'Islam dans le monde arabe contemporain," in Islam et politique au Maghreb (Paris: Editions du CNRS, forthcoming).

19. Hubert Gourdon, "Citoyen, travailleur, frére: La deuxiéme constitutionalisation du systéme politique algerien," in Développements politiques au Maghreb, ed. CRESM (Paris: CNRS, 1979), pp. 99-292.

20. What Ernest Gellner called the "Mamluks of the Modern World," that is, those who possess military and administrative skill. See Gellner, "The Unknown Apollo of Biskra," p. 303.

21. Algérie actualité, January 28-February 2, 1968; and Al Sha^cb, April 23, 1968.

22. El Moudjahid (the reference here is to the French edition of the newspaper), April 17, 1968.

23. Révolution africaine, February 14-20, 1970.

24. El Moudjahid, January 29, 1970. On these questions, see Jean Leca and Jean-Claude Vatin, L'Algérie politique: Institutions et régime (Paris: Presses de la Fondation Nationale des Sciences Politiques, 1975), pp. 304-15.

25. See Mohammed H. Cherif, "Hommes de religion et pouvoir dans la Tunisie de l'époque moderne," Annales E.S.C. 34 (1980): 580-97.

26. On the Tunisian ^culamā', see Arnold Green, The Tunisian Ulama, 1873-1915: Social Structure and Response to Ideological Currents (Leiden: Brill, 1978); and idem, "A Comparative Historical Analysis of the Ulama and the State in Egypt and Tunisia," Revue de l'Occident musulman et de la Méditerranée 29 (1980): 31-54.

27. Quoted in Michel Camau, "Religion politique et religion de l'état en Tunisie," in Islam et politique au Maghreb (Paris: Editions du CNRS, forthcoming.

28. Ibid.

29. Souhayr Belhassen, "L'Islam contestataire en Tunisie," Jeune Afrique 949 (March 1979): 82-84; 950 (March 1979): 65-68; 951 (March 1979): 89-92; and Mark A. Tessler, "Political Change and the Islamic Revival in Tunisia," Maghreb Review, 1980, pp. 8-19.

30. Quoted from Bernard Lewis, "The Return of Islam," Middle East Review 12 (1979): 17-31.

SELECTED BIBLIOGRAPHY, 1970-81

The objective of this bibliography is to provide students of Islam in the Arab world with a list of the primary books and articles in English and French published during the period 1970-81. The material included here covers a number of issues: ideology, law, economics, and politics.

Abu Saud, Mahmoud. "Islamic Banking—The Dubai Case." Outlines of Islamic Proceedings of the First Symposium on the Economics of Islam in North America. Indianapolis: Association of Muslim Social Scientists, 1977.

d'Afflitto, I. Camera. "At-Takfir wa' al-Higrah et l'Integralismo Musulmano in Egitto." Oriento moderno 58 (1978): 145-53.

Ahmad, K. , ed. Islam, its Meaning and Message. London: Islamic Council of Europe, 1976.

Ahmed, Ziauddin. "Socio-Economic Values of Islam and Their Significance and Resurgence to the Present Day World." Islamic Studies 10 (1971): 343-55.

Altman, I. "Islamic Movements in Egypt." Jerusalem Quarterly 10 (1979): 87-106.

Aruri, N. "Nationalism and Religion in the Arab World: Allies or Enemies." Muslim World 67 (1977): 266-79.

Ayoob, M. "The Revolutionary Thrust of Islamic Political Tradition." Third World Quarterly 3 (1980): 269-76.

Ayubi, Nazih N. M. "The Political Revival of Islam: The Case of Egypt." International Journal of Middle East Studies 12 (1980): 481-99.

Azzam, S. , ed. The Muslim World and the Future Economic Order. London: Islamic Council of Europe, 1979.

Beck, L., and N. Keddie, eds. Women in the Muslim World. Cambridge, Mass.: Harvard University Press, 1978.

Beling, W. A., ed. King Faisal and the Modernization of Saudi Arabia. Boulder, Colo.: Westview Press, 1980.

Berger, M. Islam in Egypt: Social and Political Aspects of Popular Religion. New York: Cambridge University Press, 1970.

Berque, J. "Tradition and Innovation in the Maghrib." Daedalus 102 (1973): 239-50.

Boisard, M. A. "On the Probable Influence of Islam on Western Public and International Law." International Journal of Middle Eastern Studies 11 (1980): 429-50.

Borthwick, B. "Religion and Politics in Israel and Egypt." Middle East Journal 33 (1979): 145-64.

Branbati, Ralph. "The Recovery of Islamic Identity in Global Perspective." In The Rose and the Rock: Mystical and Rational Elements in the Intellectual History of South Asian Islam, edited by Bruce Lawrence, pp. 159-95. Durham, N. C.: Carolina Academic Press, 1979.

Brett, Michael. "Islam in the Maghreb: The Problem of Modernization." Maghreb Review 3 (1978): 6-9.

_____. "Mufti, Murabit, Marabout and Mahdi: Four Types in the Islamic History of North Africa." Revue de l'Occident musulman et de la Méditerranée, 1980, pp. 5-15.

Brett, Michael, ed. Northern Africa, Islam and Modernization. London: Cass, 1973.

Campbell, R. Marxism and Other Western Fallacies: An Islamic Critique. Berkeley and Los Angeles: University of California Press, 1980.

Chamie, J. "Religious Groups in Lebanon: A Descriptive Investigation." International Journal of Middle Eastern Studies 11 (1980): 175-87.

Chaprā', U. M. "The Economic System of Islam." Islamic Quarterly 15 (1970): 3-18, 91-96, 143-56, 237-51.

Charnay, Jean-Paul. Sociologie religieuse de l'Islam. Paris: Sind-
bad, 1977.

Cherif, Mohammed H. "Hommes de religion et de pouvoir dans la
Tunisie de l'époque moderne." Annales E. S. C. 35 (1980): 580-
97.

Colonna, Fanny. "Saints furieux et saints studieux dans l'Aurès, ou
comment la religion vient aux tribus." Annales E. S. C. 35
(1980): 642-62.

Cudsi, A. S., and Ali E. Hillal Dessouki. Islam and Power. London:
Croomhelm, 1981.

Curtis, M., ed. Religion and Politics in the Middle East. Boulder,
Colo.: Westview Press, 1981.

Dekmejian, R. H. "The Anatomy of Islamic Revival." Middle East
Journal 34 (1980): 1-12.

_____. "Islamic Revival and the Arab Israeli Conflict." New Outlook
23 (1980): 9-12.

_____. "The Islamic Revival in the Middle East and North Africa."
Current History 456 (1980): 169-79.

Dessouki, Ali E. H. "Arab Intellectuals and al-Nakba, the Search
for Fundamentalism." Middle Eastern Studies 9 (1973): 187-96.

Edens, D. G. "The Anatomy of the Saudi Revolution." International
Journal of Middle East Studies 5 (1974): 50-64.

Eickelman, Dale F. "Ideological Change and Regional Cults: Mara-
boutism and of "Closeness" in Western Morroco." In Regional
Cults, edited by R. P. Werbner. New York and London: Academic Press, 1977.

_____. Morrocan Islam: Tradition and Society in a Pilgrimage Cen-
ter. Austin: University of Texas Press, 1976.

_____. "Religious Tradition, Economic Domination and Political
Legitimacy, Morroco and Oman." Revue de l'Occident musulman et de la Méditerranée 29 (1980): 17-30.

_____. " A Review of Morrocan Islam." Maghreb Review, vol. 2
(1977).

Enayat, Hamid. "The Resurgence of Islam, 1: The Background." History Today 30 (1980): 16-22.

Entelis, J. "Ideological Change and an Emerging Counter-Culture in Tunisia." Journal of Modern Asian Studies 12 (1974): 543-68.

Esposito, J. L., ed. Islam and Development: Religion and Sociopolitical Change. Syracuse, N.Y.: Syracuse University Press, 1980.

Fakhry, Majid. "The Search for Cultural Identity in Islam: Fundamentalism and Occidentalism." Cultures 4 (1977): 97-106.

Gauhar, A., ed. The Challenge of Islam. London: Islamic Council of Europe, 1978.

Geertz, Clifford, Hildred Geertz, and Lawrence Rosen. Meaning and Order in Morrocan Society: Three Essays in Cultural Analysis. New York: Cambridge University Press, 1979.

Gellner, Ernest. Muslim Society—A Sociological Interpretation. New York: Cambridge University Press, 1981.

_____. "Post Traditional Forms in Islam: Turf and Trade and Votes and Peasants." Daedalus 102 (1973): 191-206.

_____. "Pouvoir politique et pouvoir religieux dans l'Islam Marocain." Annales E.S.C. 25 (1970): 699-713.

Gilsman, Michael. Saint and Sufi in Modern Egypt. New York: Oxford University Press, 1973.

Green, A. "A Comparative Historical Analysis of the Ulema and the State in Egypt and Tunisia." Revue de l'Occident musulman et de la Mediterranée 29 (1980): 30-54.

Griffith, William E. "The Revival of Islamic Fundamentalism: The Case of Iran." International Security 4 (1979): 132-38.

El-Guindi, F. "Religious Revival and Islamic Survival in Egypt." International Insight, 1980, pp. 6-10.

Hanafi, Hassan. Religious Dialogue and Revolution. Cairo: Anglo-Egyptian Bookshop, 1977.

Hassan, Farooq. The Concept of State and Law in Islam. Washington, D. C.: University Press of America, 1981.

Humphreys, S. "Islam and Political Values in Saudi Arabia, Egypt and Libya." Middle East Journal 33 (1979): 1-19.

Ibrahim, Saad Eddin. "Anatomy of Egypt's Militant Islamic Groups: Methodological Note and Preliminary Findings." International Journal of Middle East Studies 12 (1980): 423-53.

Israeli, Raphael. "The New Wave of Islam." International Journal 34 (1979): 369-90.

Jansen, G. H. Militant Islam. New York: Harper & Row, Torchbooks Library Binding, 1979.

Kedourie, Elie. Islam in the Modern World and Other Studies. London: Mansell, 1981.

Khalid, Detlev V. "The Phenomenon of Re-Islamization." Aussen politik (German foreign affairs review, English edition) 29 (1978): 433-53.

Kramer, M. Political Islam. Washington Papers, no. 73. Beverly Hills and London: Sage, 1980.

Lewis, B. "The Return of Islam." Middle East Review 12 (1979): 17-31.

Linabury, G. "The Creation of Saudi Arabia and the Erosion of Wahhabi Conservatism." Middle East Review 11 (1978): 5-12.

Marshall, Susan E. "Islamic Revival in the Maghreb: The Utility of Tradition for Modernizing Elites." Studies in Comparative International Development 14 (1979): 95-108.

Mayer, A. "Islamicizing Laws Affecting the Regulation of Interest Changes and Risk Contracts: Some Problems of Recent Libyan Legislation." International Comparative Law Quarterly 28 (1979): 541-59.

Mitchell, R. P. The Society of Muslim Brothers. London: Oxford University Press, 1969.

El-Naggar, Y. "The Religious Phenomenon in Modern Egypt." Islamic Quarterly 15 (1979): 133-42.

Al-Nowaihi, M. "Problems of Modernization in Islam." Muslim World 65 (1975): 174-85.

_____. "Some Recent Attempts towards More Liberal Interpretations of the Quran and Modernization of Islamic Jurisprudence." Middle East Journal 3 (1976): 59-70.

O'Kane, Joseph. "Islam in the New Egyptian Constitution: Some Discussion in Al-Ahram." Middle East Journal 26 (1972): 137-48.

Pipes, D. "This World Is Political: The Islamic Revival of the Seventies." Orbis 24 (1980): 17-39.

Pullapilly, C. K. , ed. Islam in the Contemporary World. South Bend, Ind.: Cross Road Books, 1980.

Rabinovitch, Itamar. "The Islamic Wave." Washington Quarterly 1 (1979): 139-43.

Said, Edward W. Covering Islam. New York: Pantheon, 1981.

Samson, Henri. "La laicité dans l'Algérie d'aujourd'hui." Revue de l'Occident musulman et de la Méditerranée 29 (1980): 55-68.

Shina, Pessah. "Traditional and Reformist Mawlid Celebrations in the Maghrib." In Studies in Memory of Gaston Wiet, edited by Ayalon M. Rosen, pp. 311-43. Jerusalem: Hebrew University, 1977.

Sivan, E. "How Fares Islam?" Jerusalem Quarterly 13 (1979): 33-46.

Smith, D. E. Religion and Political Development. Boston: Little, Brown, 1970.

Solaim, Soliman B. "Saudi Arabia's Judicial System." Middle East Journal 25 (1971): 403-7.

Tessler, M. A. "Political Change and the Islamic Revival in Tunisia." Maghreb Review 5 (1980): 8-19.

Van Dom, Nikolas. The Struggle for Power in Syria: Sectarianism, Regionalism and Tribalism in Politics, 1961-1978. New York: St. Martin's Press, 1979.

Voll, John O. "The Islamic Past and the Present Resurgence."
Current History 456 (1980): 145–48, 180–81.

Warburg, G. "Islam in Sudanese Politics." Jerusalem Quarterly 13
(1979): 47–62.

Vatikiotis, P. J. "What Is an Islamic Revival?" New Society, February 15, 1979, pp. 354–56.

Zghal, Abdelkader. "The Reactivation of Tradition in a Post Traditional Society." Daedalus 102 (1973): 225–38.

INDEX

ABOUT THE EDITOR AND CONTRIBUTORS

ALI E. HILLAL DESSOUKI is Associate Professor of Political Science at Cairo University in Egypt. During his academic career, he has taught at McGill University, the American University in Cairo, the University of California-Los Angeles, and Princeton University.

Dr. Dessouki has written extensively in Arabic and English on Arab politics. In English he has been editor of, and contributor to, Democracy in Egypt, Islam and Power, and The Iraq-Iran War; co-author of The Political Economy of Income Distribution in Egypt and The New Arab Order; and author of Canadian Foreign Policy and the Palestine Problem.

His articles have appeared in Middle East Forum, Muslim World, Islam and Modern Age, Middle Eastern Studies, Social Problems, Indian Journal of Politics, Journal of South Asian and Middle Eastern Studies, and Armed Forces and Society.

CHARLES E. BUTTERWORTH is Associate Professor in the Department of Government and Politics at the University of Maryland, College Park. He has taught at the University of Bordeaux, the University of Grenoble, and the Ecole Pratique des Hautes Etudes in Paris. His research interests lie primarily in the field of political philosophy and have resulted in books such as Averroes' Three Short Commentiares and Jean-Jacques Rousseau: The Reveries of the Solitary Walker, as well as such articles as his "Philosophy, Stories, and the Study of Elites," which appeared in an earlier Praeger volume, and his recent "Frantz Fanon and Human Dignity."

TAWFIC E. FARAH is President of the Middle East Research Group (Fresno, California) and Editor of the Journal of Arab Affairs. He has taught at the University of California-Los Angeles, California Polytechnic State University, and Kuwait University. His recent publications include Aspects of Consociationalism and Modernization: Lebanon as an Exploratory Test Case and Political Behavior in the Arab States.

RAYMOND A. HINNEBUSCH is Assistant Professor of Political Science at the College of St. Catherine in St. Paul, Minnesota. He previously taught at the American University in Cairo.

Dr. Hinnebusch has authored _Party and Peasant in Syria_ and coauthored _Political Elites in Arab North Africa_. He has published a number of articles on Syria and Egypt in such periodicals as the _Middle East Journal_, the _International Journal of Middle East Studies_, and _Social Problems_.

R. STEPHEN HUMPHREYS is Associate Professor of History at the University of Wisconsin-Madison. He has previously taught at the State University of New York at Buffalo and at the University of Chicago and was a Fellow of the Institute for Advanced Study, Princeton, New Jersey, in 1980/81.

Dr. Humphreys is author of _From Saladin to the Mongols, Approaches to Islamic History_ (forthcoming) and several articles appearing in _Studia Islamica_, the _Middle East Journal_, and _History and Theory_.

SAAD EDDIN IBRAHIM is Professor of Sociology at the American University in Cairo. Previously, he taught at De Pauw University and the University of California-Los Angeles. He has written extensively on the sociology of Arab countries and his articles have appeared in _International Journal of Middle East Studies_ and _Journal of Conflict Resolution_. He has coedited and contributed to _Arab Society in Transition_ and has authored a book, _The New Arab Social Order_ (forthcoming).

ANN ELIZABETH MAYER is Assistant Professor of Law at the Wharton School of the University of Pennsylvania. She has written extensively on legal developments in the modern Middle East in articles published in U.S. and European journals and has contributed chapters to several books dealing with related topics.

DANIEL PIPES is Research Associate with the Department of History at the University of Chicago. Previously, he taught at Harvard and at the University of Chicago. He is the author of _Slave Soldiers and Islam_ and has written widely in the U.S. press on Middle East politics and Islamic affairs. He is now writing a study on Islam in modern politics.

FAROUK A. SANKARI teaches political science at the University of Wisconsin-Oshkosh. He is the coauthor of _The Middle East: Its Government and Politics_, _Arab Oil: Domestic Transformation and International Implications_, _The International Relations of the Middle East and North Africa_, _OPEC_, and _The Middle East Crucible_.

ISMAIL SERAGELDIN is presently at the World Bank as Division Chief in charge of Urban Projects for Europe, Middle East, and North Africa. For the preceding four years, he was Chief of the Technical Assistance and Special Studies Division of the World Bank. He has published widely on developmental problems of the Muslim countries, generally, and of the Middle East, specifically, and is presently coauthoring two books: <u>Problems of Labor in Saudi Arabia</u> and <u>International Labor Migration in the Middle East and North Africa</u>. He is also editing the proceedings of the International Symposium, "The Arab City: Its Character and Islamic Cultural Heritage," due to appear in 1982.

JEAN-CLAUDE VATIN is a Senior Researcher at the French National Center for Scientific Research (CNRS), Paris and Aix-en-Provence. He has taught at the University of Algiers and was a Fellow of the Institute for Advanced Study, Princeton University. His publications include <u>L'Algérie: Politique, histoire et société</u>, <u>L'Algérie politique institutions et régime</u>, and <u>L'Algérie des anthropologues</u>. He has also edited <u>Culture et société au Maghreb</u>.

Books written under the auspices of
THE CENTER OF INTERNATIONAL STUDIES
PRINCETON UNIVERSITY,
1954-81

Almond, Gabriel A. The Appeals of Communism. Princeton University Press, 1954.

Kaufmann, William W. , ed. Military Policy and National Security. Princeton University Press, 1956.

Knorr, Klaus. The War Potential of Nations. Princeton University Press, 1956.

Pye, Lucian W. Guerrilla Communism in Malaya. Princeton University Press, 1956.

Cohen, Bernard C. The Political Process and Foreign Policy: The Making of the Japanese Peace Settlement. Princeton University Press, 1957.

Weiner, Myron. Party Politics in India: The Development of a Multi-Party System. Princeton University Press, 1957.

Corbett, Percy E. Law in Diplomacy. Princeton University Press, 1959.

Knorr, Klaus, ed. NATO and American Security. Princeton University Press, 1959.

Sannwald, Rolf, and Jacques Stohler. Economic Integration: Theoretical Assumptions and Consequences of European Unification. Translated by Herman Karreman. Princeton University Press, 1959.

Almond, Gabriel A. , and James S. Coleman, eds. The Politics of the Developing Areas. Princeton University Press, 1960.

Kahn, Herman. On Thermonuclear War. Princeton University Press, 1960.

Butow, Robert J. C. Tojo and the Coming of the War. Princeton University Press, 1961.

Knorr, Klaus, and Sidney Verba, eds. The International System: Theoretical Essays. Princeton University Press, 1961.

Snyder, Glenn H. Deterrence and Defense: Toward a Theory of National Security. Princeton University Press, 1961.

Verba, Sidney. Small Groups and Political Behavior: A Study of Leadership. Princeton University Press, 1961.

Modelski, George. A Theory of Foreign Policy. New York: Praeger, 1962.

Paret, Peter, and John W. Shy. Guerrillas in the 1960's. New York: Praeger, 1962.

Almond, Gabriel A., and Sidney Verba. The Civic Culture: Political Attitudes and Democracy in Five Nations. Princeton University Press, 1963.

Burns, Arthur L., and Nina Heathcote. Peace-Keeping by United Nations Forces. New York: Praeger, 1963.

Cohen, Bernard C. The Press and Foreign Policy. Princeton University Press, 1963.

Dunn, Frederick S. Peace-Making and the Settlement with Japan. Princeton University Press, 1963.

Falk, Richard A. Law, Morality, and War in the Contemporary World. New York: Praeger, 1963.

Knorr, Klaus, and Thornton Read, eds. Limited Strategic War. New York: Praeger, 1963.

Rosenau, James N. National Leadership and Foreign Policy: A Case Study in the Mobilization of Public Support. Princeton University Press, 1963.

Sklar, Richard L. Nigerian Political Parties: Power in an Emergent African Nation. Princeton University Press, 1963.

Black, Cyril E., and Thomas P. Thornton, eds. Communism and Revolution: The Strategic Uses of Political Violence. Princeton University Press, 1964.

Camps, Miriam. Britain and the European Community 1955-1963. Princeton University Press, 1964.

Eckstein, Harry, ed. Internal War: Problems and Approaches. New York: Free Press, 1964.

Paret, Peter. French Revolutionary Warfare from Indochina to Algeria: The Analysis of a Political and Military Doctrine. New York: Praeger, 1964.

Rosenau, James N., ed. International Aspects of Civil Strife. Princeton University Press, 1964.

Thornton, Thomas P., ed. The Third World in Soviet Perspective: Studies by Soviet Writers on the Developing Areas. Princeton University Press, 1964.

Falk, Richard A., and Richard J. Barnet, eds. Security in Disarmament. Princeton University Press, 1965.

Ploss, Sidney I. Conflict and Decision-Making in Soviet Russia: A Case Study of Agricultural Policy, 1953-1963. Princeton University Press, 1965.

Sprout, Harold, and Margaret Sprout. The Ecological Perspective on Human Affairs, with Special Reference to International Politics. Princeton University Press, 1965.

von Vorys, Karl. Political Development in Pakistan. Princeton University Press, 1965.

Black, Cyril E. The Dynamics of Modernization: A Study in Comparative History. New York: Harper & Row, 1966.

Eckstein, Harry. Division and Cohesion in Democracy: A Study of Norway. Princeton University Press, 1966.

Knorr, Klaus. On the Uses of Military Power in the Nuclear Age. Princeton University Press, 1966.

Bienen, Henry. Tanzania: Party Transformation and Economic Development. Princeton University Press, 1967.

Gordenker, Leon. The UN Secretary-General and the Maintenance of Peace. New York: Columbia University Press, 1967.

Hamilton, Richard F. Affluence and the French Worker in the Fourth Republic. Princeton University Press, 1967.

Hanrieder, Wolfram F. West German Foreign Policy, 1949–1963: International Pressures and Domestic Response. Stanford, Calif.: Stanford University Press, 1967.

Kunstadter, Peter, ed. Southeast Asian Tribes, Minorities, and Nations. Princeton University Press, 1967.

Miller, Linda B. World Order and Local Disorder: The United Nations and Internal Conflicts. Princeton University Press, 1967.

Rosenau, James N., ed. Domestic Sources of Foreign Policy. New York: Free Press, 1967.

Wolfenstein, E. Victor. The Revolutionary Personality: Lenin, Trotsky, Gandhi. Princeton University Press, 1967.

Young, Oran R. The Intermediaries: Third Parties in International Crises. Princeton University Press, 1967.

Bader, William B. The United States and the Spread of Nuclear Weapons. Indianapolis: Pegasus, 1968.

Black, Cyril E., Richard A. Falk, Klaus Knorr, and Oran R. Young. Neutralization and World Politics. Princeton University Press, 1968.

De Visscher, Charles. Theory and Reality in Public International Law, rev. ed. Translated by P. E. Corbett. Princeton University Press, 1968.

Falk, Richard A. Legal Order in a Violent World. Princeton University Press, 1968.

Gilpin, Robert. France in the Age of the Scientific State. Princeton University Press, 1968.

Ullman, Richard H. Britain and the Russian Civil War: November 1918–February 1920. Princeton University Press, 1968.

Barros, James. Betrayal from Within: Joseph Avenol, Secretary-General of the League of Nations, 1933–1940. New Haven, Conn.: Yale University Press, 1969.

Black, Cyril E., and Richard A. Falk, eds. Trends and Patterns. The Future of the International Legal Order, vol. 1. Princeton University Press, 1969.

Gurr, Ted Robert. Why Men Rebel. Princeton University Press, 1969.

Hermann, Charles. Crises in Foreign Policy: A Simulation Analysis. Indianapolis: Bobbs-Merrill, 1969.

Knorr, Klaus, and James N. Rosenau, eds. Contending Approaches to International Politics. Princeton University Press, 1969.

McAlister, John T., Jr. Viet Nam: The Origins of Revolution. New York: Alfred A. Knopf, 1969.

Rosenau, James N., ed. Linkage Politics: Essays on the Convergence of National and International Systems. New York: Free Press, 1969.

Smith, Jean Edward. Germany beyond the Wall: People, Politics and Prosperity. New York: Little, Brown, 1969.

Tucker, Robert C. The Marxian Revolutionary Idea: Essays on Marxist Thought and Its Impact on Radical Movements. New York: W. W. Norton, 1969.

Waterman, Harvey. Political Change in Contemporary France: The Politics of an Industrial Democracy. Columbus, Ohio: Charles E. Merrill, 1969.

Young, Oran R. The Politics of Force: Bargaining during International Crises. Princeton University Press, 1969.

Black, Cyril E., and Richard A. Falk, eds. Wealth and Resources. The Future of the International Legal Order, vol. 2. Princeton University Press, 1970.

Falk, Richard A. The Status of Law in International Society. Princeton University Press, 1970.

Knorr, Klaus. Military Power and Potential. Lexington, Mass.: D. C. Heath, 1970.

Whitaker, C. Sylvester. The Politics of Tradition: Continuity and Change in Northern Nigeria 1946-1960. Princeton University Press, 1970.

Black, Cyril E., and Richard A. Falk, eds. Conflict Management. The Future of the International Legal Order, vol. 3. Princeton University Press, 1971.

Frankel, Francine R. India's Green Revolution: Political Costs of Economic Growth. Princeton University Press, 1971.

Gordenker, Leon, ed. The United Nations in International Politics. Princeton University Press, 1971.

Sprout, Harold, and Margaret Sprout. Toward a Politics of the Planet Earth. New York: Van Nostrand Reinhold, 1971.

Black, Cyril E., and Richard A. Falk, eds. The Structure of the International Environment. The Future of the International Legal Order, vol. 4. Princeton University Press, 1972.

Garvey, Gerald. Energy, Ecology, Economy. New York: W. W. Norton, 1972.

Bebler, Anton. Military Role in Africa: Dahomey, Ghana, Sierra Leone, and Mali. New York: Praeger, 1973.

Knorr, Klaus. Power and Wealth: The Political Economy of International Power. New York: Basic, 1973.

Morse, Edward L. Foreign Policy and Interdependence in Gaullist France. Princeton University Press, 1973.

Tucker, Robert C. Stalin as Revolutionary 1879–1929: A Study in History and Personality. New York: W. W. Norton, 1973.

Ullman, Richard. The Anglo-Soviet Accord. Princeton University Press, 1973.

Bienen, Henry. Kenya: The Politics of Participation and Control. Princeton University Press, 1974.

Laszlo, Ervin. A Strategy for the Future: The Systems Approach to World Order. New York: George Braziller, 1974.

Massell, Gregory J. The Surrogate Proletariat: Moslem Women and Revolutionary Strategies in Soviet Central Asia, 1919–1929. Princeton University Press, 1974.

Rosenau, James N. Citizenship between Elections: An Inquiry into the Mobilizable American. New York: Free Press, 1974.

Black, Cyril E., Marius B. Jansen, Herbert S. Levine, Marion J. Levy, Jr., Henry Rosovsky, Gilbert Rozman, Henry D. Smith II, and S. Frederick Starr. The Modernization of Japan and Russia. New York: Free Press, 1975.

Eckstein, Harry, and Ted Robert Gurr. Patterns of Authority: A Structural Basis for Political Inquiry. New York: John Wiley & Sons, 1975.

Falk, Richard A. A Global Approach to National Policy. Cambridge, Mass.: Harvard University Press, 1975.

Kalicki, Jan H. The Pattern of Sino-American Crises: Political-Military Interactions in the 1950s. Cambridge: At the University Press, 1975.

Knorr, Klaus. The Power of Nations: The Political Economy of International Relations. New York: Basic, 1975.

Sewell, James P. UNESCO and World Politics: Engaging in International Relations. Princeton University Press, 1975.

Gordenker, Leon. International Aid and National Decisions: Development Programs in Malawi, Tanzania, and Zambia. Princeton University Press, 1976.

Von Clausewitz, Carl. On War. Edited and translated by Michael Howard and Peter Paret. Princeton University Press, 1976.

Bissell, Richard E. Apartheid and International Organizations. Boulder, Colo.: Westview Press, 1977.

Forsythe, David P. Humanitarian Politics: The International Committee of the Red Cross. Baltimore: Johns Hopkins University Press, 1977.

Garvey, Gerald. Nuclear Power and Social Planning: The City of the Second Sun. Lexington, Mass.: Lexington Books, 1977.

Garvey, Gerald, and Lou Ann Garvey, eds. International Resource Flows. Lexington, Mass.: D. C. Heath, Lexington Books, 1977.

Murphy, Walter F., and Joseph Tanenhaus. Comparative Constitutional Law Cases and Commentaries. New York: St. Martin's Press, 1977.

Sigmund, Paul E. The Overthrow of Allende and the Politics of Chile, 1964-1976. Pittsburgh: University of Pittsburgh Press, 1977.

Bienen, Henry S. Armies and Parties in Africa. New York: Holmes and Meier, 1978.

Sprout, Harold, and Margaret Sprout. The Context of Environmental Politics. Lexington: University Press of Kentucky, 1978.

Ahmed, S. Basheer. Nuclear Fuel and Energy Policy. Lexington, Mass.: D. C. Heath, Lexington Books, 1979.

Kim, Samuel S. China, the United Nations, and World Order. Princeton University Press, 1979.

Billington, James H. Fire in the Minds of Men: Origins of the Revolutionary Faith. New York: Basic, 1980.

Falk, Richard A., and Samuel S. Kim, eds. The War System: An Interdisciplinary Approach. Boulder, Colo.: Westview Press, 1980.

Hsiung, James C., and Samuel S. Kim, eds. China in the Global Community. New York: Praeger, 1980.

Johansen, Robert C. The National Interest and the Human Interest: An Analysis of U.S. Foreign Policy. Princeton University Press, 1980.

Kinnard, Douglas. The Secretary of Defense. Lexington: University Press of Kentucky, 1980.

Kruglak, Gregory T. The Politics of United States Decision-Making in United Nations Specialized Agencies: The Case of the International Labor Organization. Washington, D.C.: University Press of America, 1980.

Ramberg, Bennett. Destruction of Nuclear Energy Facilities in War: The Problem and the Implications. Lexington, Mass.: Lexington Books, 1980.

Onuf, Nicholas G., ed. Law-Making in the Global Community. Durham, N.C.: Carolina Academic Press, 1981.